John Warwick Montgomery

Christ Our Advocate

edition pro mundis

Band 8

im Auftrag des Vorstandes von
Pro Mundis e. V. (Bonn)
herausgegeben von
Dr. Thomas Schirrmacher und Dr. Susanne Lux

Band 1
Inka und Torsten Marold
Immanuel:
Die Geschichte der Geburt eines anenzephalen Kindes

Band 2
Thomas Zimmermanns
Grundriß der politischen Ethik

Band 3
Thomas Schirrmacher
Marxismus - Opium für das Volk?

Band 4
Thomas Schirrmacher, Walter Schrader, Hartmut Steeb (Hg.)
The Right to Life for Every Person
Lebensrecht für jeden Menschen

Band 5
Wilhelm Faix
Die christliche Familie heute

Band 6
Meego Remmel
The Role of Christian Ethics in Postmarxist and Postmodern Estonia

Band 7
Thomas Schirrmacher
Säkulare Religionen
Aufzusätze zum religiösen Charakter von Nationalsozialismus und Kommunismus

Band 8
John Warwick Montgomery
Christ Our Advocate
Studies in Polemical Theology, Jurisprudence, and Canon Law

John Warwick Montgomery

Christ Our Advocate

Studies in Polemical Theology,
Jurisprudence, and
Canon Law

edition pro mundis 8

WIPF & STOCK · Eugene, Oregon

CHRIST OUR ADVOCATE
Studies in Polemical Theology, Jurisprudence, and Canon Law

Copyright © 2016 Verlag fur Kultur und Wissenschaft. All rights reserved. Except for brief quotations in critical publications or reviews, no part of this book may be reproduced in any manner without prior written permission from the publisher. Write: Permissions, Wipf and Stock Publishers, 199 W. 8th Ave., Suite 3, Eugene, OR 97401.

This edition published by Wipf and Stock Publishers in cooperation with Verlag für Kultur und Wissenschaft.

Wipf & Stock
An Imprint of Wipf and Stock Publishers
199 W. 8th Ave., Suite 3
Eugene, OR 97401

www.wipfandstock.com

PAPERBACK ISBN: 978-1-4982-9196-5
HARDCOVER ISBN: 978-1-4982-9197-2

Manufactured in the U.S.A.

For
Dr Edward Hogg
and
Dr Thomas Rodgers
of
Trinity College & Theological Seminary

Patrons et amis

*"... we have an Advocate with the Father,
Jesus Christ the righteous: and he is the
propitiation for our sins; and not for ours only,
but also for the sins of the whole world."*
1 John 2:1-2

CONTENTS

Introduction	9
Acknowledgments	11
Modern Theology and Contemporary Legal Theory: A Tale of Ideological Collapse	13
Canon Law as the Juridic Reflection of Theological Norms?	35
Addendum: *A Comment on the Thinking of Professor J.W. Montgomery*	49
Luther and Canon Law	55
Subsidiarity As a Jurisprudential and Canonical Theory	71
Justice Denied: Church Property Disputes Under Current American Law	81
Addendum: *Attorney-General* v. *Shore (1833)*	94
Christian Education and Worship in State Schools: the American Perspective	105
Church Remarriage After Divorce: A Third Way	117
Addendum: *Marriage in Church After Divorce*	129
Can Blasphemy Law Be Justified?	133
Human Dignity in Birth and Death: A Question of Values	153
Whose Life Anyway? A Re-examination of Suicide and Assisted Suicide	169
Addendum: *Euthanasia Laws Bill 1996 (Australia) Presented*	193

The Embryo Cloning Danger in European Context	197
Addendum: *Human Cloning Regulation in Europe*	210
The Alleged Myth of the Mafia	219
Greek Opposition To Evangelism	237
Prophecy, Eschatology and Apologetics	255
Advocacy, Classical Rhetoric, and Legal Ethics: Must The Good Advocate Also Be A Good Person?	267
Appendix: Four Reviews — and a Defence of the Trial of Christ	283
Duncan Forrester's *Christian Justice and Public Policy*	284
Alister McGrath's *Iustitia Dei*	292
Brian Tierney's *Rights, Laws and Infallibility in Medieval Thought*	302
Norman Geisler's *Baker Encyclopedia of Christian Apologetics*	305
The Trial of Christ Defended: Jean Imbert's *Le Procès de Jèsus*	309
Index of Names	313

INTRODUCTION

A little-known work by L. Frank Baum, author of the celebrated *Oz* series of children's books, is a literary biography entitled, *The Life and Adventures of Santa Claus*. In this delightful volume, Santa is given a fourfold creed:

> *Vivre, c'est penser,*
> *c'est lutter,*
> *c'est chercher,*
> *c'est aimer.*

Since this Introduction is being prepared during the Advent season, it does not seem inappropriate to commandeer the sentiment to describe the contents of this volume of essays covering religion and law, social ethics, and the defence of Christian faith.

Penser: Readers will not be able to avoid serious reflection on such issues as: the parallel decline in systematic theology and jurisprudence (chap. 1); the very nature of ecclesiastical law (chap. 2); whether the major architect of the Protestant Reformation was an antinomian (chap. 3); the theological aspects of the almost universally praised European legal doctrine of subsidiarity (chap. 4); whether church property should remain in the hands of a denomination when the church body no longer holds to its original beliefs (chap. 5); whether worship and prayer should be allowed in state schools (chap. 6); whether divorced persons should be able to remarry in the church (chap. 7); whether laws against blasphemy are hopelessly outmoded (chap. 8); whether abortion, euthanasia, assisted suicide, and embryo cloning can be regarded as consonant with Christian faith (chaps. 9, 10, and 11); whether both God and international criminal conspiracies are unverifiable and therefore analytically meaningless concepts (chap. 12); whether restrictions on evangelism should be permitted under international human rights law (chap. 13); what kind of prophetic evidence can be marshalled in defence of Christian truth claims (chap. 14); and, finally, what constitutes genuinely moral advocacy (chap. 15).

Lutter: The theological orientation of the author is unashamedly *confessional,* that is to say, he holds to the validity of the Ecumenical Creeds of Christendom (Apostles', Nicene, and Athanasian); *Reformation,* i.e., he believes that the Holy Scriptures, as originally given, are correct, reliable, and sufficient to provide the church and the world with perspicuous revelational truth; and *evangelical,* in that he sees the central answer to human need to be a personal, living relationship with Jesus Christ. Every essay in this book is a direct, subtle, or not-so-subtle endeavour to present these perspectives over against opposing viewpoints.

Chercher: If, as reader, you disagree with the author: fine. But you will hardly be able to do so in a responsible way without having to reformulate your reasons for disagreement—or agreement. As Socrates put it, "The unexamined life is not worth living." This book will assuredly assist any reader engaged in the serious investigation of the subjects treated to think more deeply about them.

Aimer: Are love and scholarship (legal or otherwise) inherently antithetical? The Psalmist did not think so when he declared, "O how I love thy law!" This book has been a labour of love—as was the presentation of the essays comprising it in locales as diverse as University College, London; Cardiff, Wales; Philadelphia, Pennsylvania; and Beijing, China. It is fervently hoped that readers will move from its arguments to a greater appreciation of the One who said, "If you love me, keep my commandments."

Strasbourg, France
The Feast of St Nicholas
6 December A.D. 2001

ACKNOWLEDGMENTS

Some (but by no means all) of the essays contained in this book have appeared previously in English, American, German, Dutch, Polish, and Chinese publications. The production of the present volume has given opportunity for slight revisions. Bibliographical data on earlier appearances of essays and reviews follows:

- "Canon Law As the Juridic Reflection of Theological Norms": *Law & Justice: The Christian Law Review* [England], Trinity/Michaelmas 1999. (Bishop Jukes' critique of this essay and the author's rejoinder appeared in the Trinity/Michaelmas 2000 issue.)

- "Luther and Canon Law": *Bibliotheca Sacra* [U.S.], April-June 2001.

- "Christian Education and Worship in State Schools": *Law & Justice*, Hilary/Easter 2000.

- "Can Blasphemy Law Be Justified?": *Law & Justice*, Trinity/Michaelmas 2000.

- "Human Dignity in Birth and Death: A Question of Values": *Christian Legal Journal* [Canada], Spring 1993; *International Journal of Value-Based Management* [Netherlands], 7: 147-58 (1994); *Law & Justice*, Hilary/Easter 1999; *Godnosc ...*, ed. K. Complak (Wroclaw, 2001) [in Polish].

- "Whose Life Anyway? A Re-examination of Suicide and Assisted Suicide": *Nexus: Chapman University School of Law Journal* [U.S.], Fall 1996); *Christian Perspectives on Law Reform*, ed. Paul R. Beaumont (Paternoster Press, England, 1998).

- "The Alleged Myth of the Mafia": *Proceedings of the Seventh International Anticorruption Conference*, 2 vols. (Beijing, China, 1996) [in Chinese and in English]; *Law & Justice*, Trinity/Michaelmas 1996.

- "Greek Opposition to Evangelism": *Religion – Staat – Gesellschaft: Zeitschrift für Glaubensformen und Weltanschauungen* [Germany], I/2 (2000).

- "Prophecy, Eschatology and Apologetics": *Looking Into the Future*, ed. David W. Baker (Grand Rapids, Michigan, 2001).

- "Advocacy, Classical Rhetoric, and Legal Ethics: Must the Good Advocate Also Be a Good Person?": *Law & Justice,* Trinity/Michaelmas 1998.

- Review of *Christian Justice and Public Policy* by Forrester: *Global Journal of Classical Theology* [online journal: www.trinitysem.edu], Vol 2, No. 2 (2000).

- Review of *Justitia Dei* by McGrath: *Modern Reformation* [U.S.], March-April 2000.

- Review of *Rights, Laws and Infallibility in Medieval Thought* by Tierney: *Fides et Historia: Journal of the Conference on Faith and History,* Winter-Spring 1999.

- Review of the *Baker Encyclopedia of Christian Apologetics* by Geisler: *Global Journal of Classical Theology,* Vol. 1, No. 3 (1999).

- The Trial of Christ Defended: *Christianity Today,* 9 April 1982 (under the title: "Jesus Takes the Stand: An Argument to Support the Gospel Accounts").

* * *

A special word of thanks is in order to Dr Thomas Schirrmacher, whose faith in the value of the author's work was the efficient cause of this book's seeing the light of day.

CHAPTER I

MODERN THEOLOGY AND CONTEMPORARY LEGAL THEORY: A TALE OF IDEOLOGICAL COLLAPSE*

Summary: This paper bridges an intellectual chasm often regarded as impassable, that between modern jurisprudence (philosophy of law) and contemporary theology. Our thesis is that remarkably similar developmental patterns exist in these two areas of the history of ideas and that lessons learned in the one are of the greatest potential value to the other. It will be shown that the fivefold movement in the history of modern theology (classical liberalism, neo-orthodoxy, Bultmannian existentialism, Tillichian ontology, and secular/death-of-God viewpoints) has been remarkably paralled in legal theory (realism/positivism, the jurisprudence of H.L.A. Hart, the philosophy of Ronald Dworkin, the neo-Kantian political theorists, and Critical Legal Studies' deconstructionism). From this comparative analysis the theologian and the legal theorist can learn vitally important lessons for their own professional endeavours.

I. INTRODUCTION

Our *fin de siècle* — and, in this case, *fin de millénium* — is characterised by hyperspecialisation run riot. The computer nerd has no idea what is going on outside his software and the rest of us have no clue as to what he is up to. In academia, subject specialities operate like medieval fiefdoms, with little understanding or appreciation of what is occurring elsewhere.

In this paper an attempt will be made to bridge an intellectual chasm often regarded as uncrossable: the chasm between law and religion, or, more specifically for our purpose, that between modern jurisprudence (philosophy of law) and modern theology. It is

---

* This essay was presented by invitation at the symposium "Mere Theism: Liberating Theistic Scholarship," sponsored by Biola University, La Mirada, California, 3-6 December 1998.

the conviction of this essayist that remarkable parallels exist between these two areas in the history of ideas and that lessons learned in the one are of the greatest potential value in the other.

II. A CENTURY OF DETERIORATING THEOLOGY

In my now historic debate with the late Resigned Bishop James Pike at McMaster University, I argued that modern theology was engaging in a systematic process of self-destruction. My remarks on that occasion were captioned, "The Suicide of Christian Theology," and later comprised the first chapter of my book of that title. I there developed an analogy, "The Parable of the Engineers," to make my point: Christian theology was like a great cathedral, constructed according to the design and plan of its Architect or Intelligent Designer; but in our time the engineers, representing modern theological schools of thought, have lost confidence in the original plans and have insisted on going their own way, resulting ultimately in the collapse of the structure.

> Thus did the great cathedral eventually crumble and fall, killing not only the people who had loved it but also the engineers responsible for its loss. Pathetically, there were a few engineers who, right up to the moment of final destruction, still pleaded that the only hope lay in following rigorously the original plans, that the engineers must bring their stylistic ideas into conformity with the architect's, and that deviations from their notions of style did not constitute genuine errors or contradictions in the plans. But their voices were scarcely heard amid the din of engineering teams working at cross-purposes to each other, and the deafening roar of falling masonry.
>
> And the rain descended, and the floods came, and the winds blew, and beat upon that cathedral; and it fell: and great was the fall of it.[1]

My sad tale began with the rise of destructive biblical criticism in the 18th century (Jean Astruc *et al.*) and the development of documentary theories in the 19th (Graf, Kuenen, and Wellhausen on the

---

[1] John Warwick Montgomery, *The Suicide of Christian Theology* (6th printing; Newburgh, Indiana: Trinity Press, 1996), pp. 26-27.

"true" sources of Old Testament writings—a subjective literary approach later to be applied to the New Testament by the advocates of *formgeschichtliche Methode*). Grounded in evolutionary self-confidence as to inevitable human progress, such dehistoricisings of biblical revelation evacuated the text of *de facto* binding force, opening the possibility (nay, the inevitability) of theologies representing little more than human opinion. In our century, the consequential development has been:

> 1. *Theological liberalism or modernism:* Evolving mankind is able to save itself through imitating Jesus and engaging in "social gospel" amelioration of the structures of life.
>
> 2. *Barthian neo-orthodoxy:* Barth recognised modernism's naïvety in discounting human depravity—a fact brought home by the World Wars—but continued to accept biblical criticism, thereby of necessity relegating the miraculous scriptural gospel to the undemonstrable realm of "suprahistory." (A vain but heroic attempt to retain the biblical gospel without the historicity of the biblical text: a classic case of wanting one's cake and eating it too.)
>
> 3. *Bultmannian existentialism:* Owing to the inherent instability of neo-orthodoxy, the theologian now seeks to ground theology in personal experience alone. Biblical revelation is "demythologised" and the *Heilsgeschichte* is reduced to existential, subjective, personal encounter.
>
> 4. *Tillich's ontological theology:* A recognition that existential experience in fact offers no solid ground for theologising, combined with a thoroughly unsuccessful attempt to substitute for it Schelling's idealistic philosophical category of "Being itself."
>
> 5. *Secular and death-of-God theologies:* In the face of the preceding vain and unworkable endeavours to provide non-revelational foundations for theology, together with dogmatic acceptance of the unreliability of the biblical texts, the secular theologians and death-of-Goders deconstruct theology, transforming it into little more than a new humanism.

Now we are going to argue that, in the ostensibly independent area of jurisprudence, a remarkably parallel history of ideological development (or regression, if you will) can be observed—and for precisely the same underlying reasons. Concretely, since the underpinnings of scriptural revelation were removed from natural-law theory in the 18th and early 19th centuries, jurisprudence has developed along the following lines,[2] paralleling in many fundamental ways the theological history of ideas just set forth:

1. Classical positivism / Scandinavian and American legal realism

2. The jurisprudence of H.L.A. Hart

3. The jurisprudence of Ronald Dworkin

4. The neo-Kantian political theorists

5. Critical Legal Studies and jurisprudential deconstructionism

We shall now proceed to chart this history in detail, and, having done so, draw an important lesson from it.

III. THE UNNATURAL SHIFT IN NATURAL-LAW THEORY

Until the latter half of the 19th century, the prevailing philosophy of law in the Western world was so-called "natural-law" theory. Originating with the Greeks in classical times (Aristotle; the Stoics), it profoundly influenced the Roman world (Cicero; Seneca) and was baptised by the great theologians of medieval Christendom (Augustine; Thomas Aquinas). The essence of the Greco-Roman position was that the human race benefits from natural, built-in standards of justice and human laws need to conform to them. To be sure, the Christian theologians, while fully agreeing on the basis of biblical revelation that man is created in God's image (Gen. 1) and has God's law implanted in his heart (Rom. 1), nonetheless recognised the inadequacy of building *simpliciter* a legal system from the conscience of mankind. Thus the Apostle Paul's proclamation to the Stoic philosophers at Athens that a natural knowledge of God

---

[2.] It will be noted that we concentrate here primarily on the history of modern jurisprudence in the common-law world rather than dealing with continental European civil-law jurisprudence (e.g., the influential position of Jürgen Habermas). In point of fact, our basic thesis could also have been illustrated from continental sources, but the symposium's time constraints made this impossible. For insights into European philosophy of law today, readers may wish to consult James E. Herget, *Contemporary German Legal Philosophy* (Philadelphia: University of Pennsylvania Press, 1996).

and of morality is not enough: the unknown god of natural revelation is utterly inadequate without Jesus Christ (Acts 17). Man, after all, is a *fallen* creature and his conscience has been corrupted along with all other aspects of his relationship with his Creator. It follows that mankind, individually and collectively, needs a *special* revelation to clarify and correct misinterpretations of the general revelation of which conscience is one aspect. That special revelation has been provided by grace alone through the Word—the living Word (Christ) and the written word (the Holy Scriptures). The Bible—as Luther would later put it, the cradle in which Christ is offered to us—thus becomes an essential source of knowledge for understanding the true content of natural law and a permanent corrective for conceptions of it based on conscience alone. Scripture corrects and perfects the knowledge of ideal law a fallen race derives from nature and conscience.

It is worthwhile for us to hear two primary-source statements of this Christian approach to natural law; they will serve as an essential point of reference for what follows. The first comes from *Doctor and Student* (full title: *A Dialogue between a Doctor of Divinity and a Student of the Laws of England*), first published in Latin *circa* 1523; prior to Blackstone's *Commentaries*, it served as the leading introduction to the law for fledgling students. The author, probably Christopher St Germain of the Inner Temple, discusses "the law of reason, the which by doctors is called the law of nature of reasonable creatures," and then proceeds to its correction and extension by way of "the law of God":

The law of nature specially considered, which is also called the *law of reason*, pertaineth only to creatures reasonable, that is, man, which is created to the image of God.

And this law ought to be kept as well among Jews and Gentiles, as among christian men: and this law is alway good and righteous, stirring and inclining a man to good, and abhorring evil. And... it is written in the heart of every man, teaching him what is to be done, and what is to be fled; and because it is written in the heart, therefore it may not be put away, ne it is never changeable by no diversity of place, ne time: and therefore against this law, prescription, statute nor custom may not prevail: and if any be brought in against it, they be not prescriptions, statutes nor customs, but things void and against justice. ...

Though the law of reason may not be changed, nor wholly put away; nevertheless, before the law written, it was greatly lett and blinded by evil customs, and by many sins of the people, beside our original sin; insomuch that it might hardly be discerned what was righteous, and what was unrighteous, and what was good, and what was evil. Wherefore it was necessary, for the good order of the people, to have many things added to the law of reason....

The *law of God* is a certain law given by revelation to a reasonable creature, shewing him the will of God, willing that creatures reasonable be bound to do a thing, or not to do it, for obtaining of the felicity eternal ...; as been the laws of the Old Testament, that been called *morals*, and the laws of the evangelists, the which were shewed in much more excellent manner than the law of the Old Testament was: for that was shewed by the mediation of an angel; but the law of the evangelists was shewed by the mediation of our Lord Jesus Christ, God and man. And the law of God is always righteous and just, for it is made and given after the will of God. And therefore all acts and deeds of man be called righteous and just, when they be done according to the law of God, and be conformable to it.[3]

Sir William Blackstone, who in his Vinerian lectures of 1758 at Oxford provided students of the common law in England and America with the first comprehensive textbook on the subject worthy of the name, develops precisely the same argument in discussing "the nature of laws in general":

[3.] *The Doctor and Student*, ed. William Muchall (Cincinnati: Robert Clarke, 1874), pp. 5-7. Cf. John Warwick Montgomery (ed.), *Jurisprudence: A Book of Readings* (4th printing; Strasbourg, France: International Scholarly Publishers, 1992), pp. 3, 7-22.

Th[e] law of nature, being coeval with mankind and dictated by God Himself, is of course superior in obligation to any other. It is binding over all the globe in all countries, and at all times: no human laws are of any validity, if contrary to this; and such of them as are valid derive all their force, and all their authority, mediately or immediately, from this original.

But in order to apply this to the particular exigencies of each individual, it is still necessary to have recourse to reason: whose office it is to discover, as was before observed, what the law of nature directs in every circumstance of life; by considering, what method will tend the most effectually to our own substantial happiness. And if our reason were always, as in our first ancestor before his transgression, clear and perfect, unruffled by passions, unclouded by prejudice, unimpaired by disease or intemperance, the task would be pleasant and easy; we should need no other guide but this. But every man now finds the contrary in his own experience; that his reason is corrupt, and his understanding full of ignorance and error.

This has given manifold occasion for the benign interposition of divine providence; which, in compassion to the frailty, the imperfection, and the blindness of human reason hath been pleased, at sundry times and in divers manners, to discover and enforce its laws by an immediate and direct revelation. The doctrines thus delivered we call the revealed or divine law, and they are to be found only in the Holy Scriptures. These precepts, when revealed, are found upon comparison to be really a part of the original law of nature, as they tend in all their consequences to man's felicity. But we are not from thence to conclude that the knowledge of these truths was attainable by reason, in its present corrupted state; since we find that, until they were revealed, they were hid from the wisdom of ages. As then the moral precepts of this law are indeed of the same original with those of the law of nature, so their intrinsic obligation is of equal strength and perpetuity. Yet undoubtedly the

> revealed law is of infinitely more authenticity than that moral system, which is framed by ethical writers, and denominated the natural law. Because one is the law of nature, expressly declared so to be by God Himself; the other is only what, by the assistance of human reason, we imagine to be that law. If we could be as certain of the latter as we are of the former, both would have an equal authority; but, till then, they can never be put in any competition together.
>
> Upon these two foundations, the law of nature and the law of revelation, depend all human laws; that is to say, no human laws should be suffered to contradict these.[4]

But, by Blackstone's time, Deistic scepticism toward revealed religion had already begun to erode the foundations of his natural-law theory. The Deists and their continental counterparts (the *"philosophes"* of the French Revolution and the so-called Enlightenment) had no problem with a natural law embedded in human conscience, but they firmly rejected the historic Christian claim to a controlling special revelation in Scripture. Characteristically, Thomas Paine's tract, *The Age of Reason,* not only sets the "Book of Nature" over against the "Book of Scripture" but devotes its entire second half to listing alleged errors and contradictions in the Bible, in an effort to destroy its credibility. The American "Founding Fathers" were deeply influenced by such thinking and based their concept of natural rights, as did the authors of the French Declaration of the Rights of Man, on general and not special revelation: "Nature and Nature's God"—not the God of Scripture, the God who in Christ reconciles the world unto Himself.[5] Result: a Deistic natural-law theory, divorced from biblical controls.

Then, by the end of the 19th century, owing to Darwinian "naturalism" taking the ideological stage-centre, even the Deistic creator-god was dropped from the scenario, and natural-law theory became entirely anthropocentric. Mankind was supposed to manifest, on an entirely naturalistic basis, the required ethical principles—or

---

[4.] Sir William Blackstone, *Commentaries on the Laws of England,* I, 41-42.

[5.] See John Warwick Montgomery, *The Shaping of America* (Minneapolis: Bethany, 1976), especially pp. 47 ff. Thomas Jefferson, for example, could not stand the influence Blackstone (as an orthodox Christian and a political Tory) had on American students of the law: see Edward Dumbauld, *Thomas Jefferson and the Law* (Norman: University of Oklahoma Press, 1978), especially pp. 9-10.

the ability to arrive at such—which could serve as an adequate criterion for judging positive law and existing legal systems.

Needless to say, this emasculated form of jusnaturalism was entirely incapable of delivering what was expected of it. Nineteenth-century anthropologists were already pointing out the tremendous diversity of standards, ethical norms, and moral practices in the world's cultures; how was it possible, then, to sustain the idea of a common human "conscience" adequate to judge positive legislation? Moreover, even supposing that such a common standard could be demonstrated, would that make it right? In 1903, English philosopher G.E. Moore identified as the "naturalistic fallacy" the assumption that an "is" (here, common ethical beliefs) can be regarded *ipso facto* as the equivalent of an "ought" (here, proper natural law). And the hopeless generality and lack of specificity of the humanistic natural-law principles made the viewpoint of little practical utility in the legal field. What assistance could secular natural-law theory offer to the day-to-day work of the legislator or judge when it defined true law as "the art of what is good and equitable" (Celsus) or "the abstract expression of the general will existing in and for itself" (Hegel) or "the organic whole of the external conditions of the intellectual life" (Krause)?[6]

IV. CLASSICAL LEGAL POSITIVISM OR REALISM[7]

Just as social-gospel modernism, based on an unjustifiable confidence in human nature, overwhelmed traditional, orthodox theology once the latter's biblical foundations had been eroded, so in the Victorian era a new jurisprudence easily replaced a natural-law theory which no longer relied upon Holy Scripture for its ultimate justification. This jurisprudence came to be known on the European continent as legal positivism, having obvious affinities with the sci-

---

[6]. Cf. John Chipman Gray, *The Nature and Sources of the Law*, ed. Roland Gray (2d ed.; Boston: Beacon Press, 1963), pp. 88-89, 96-99.

[7]. For an introduction to the modern schools of legal thought discussed in this paper, the reader without training in law or jurisprudence may wish to consult Part II of Dennis Patterson (ed.), *A Companion to Philosophy of Law and Legal Theory* (Oxford: Blackwell, 1996).

entific or sociological positivism of Auguste Comte; in the common-law world (England and America) it was generally called legal realism.

The most important influence in the rise of this new movement was utilitarian philosopher and social reformer Jeremy Bentham, who in turn provided the oft-regarded "father of legal positivism," John Austin, with many of his ideas. Bentham wrote a lengthy critique of Blackstone's *Commentaries* in which he declared that Blackstone's "natural and imprescriptable rights" were but "nonsense on stilts." "From the law of nature," cried Bentham, "come imaginary rights—a bastard brood of monsters."[8] Law is not some absolute, eternal set of principles established in the heavens and known to all men through conscience; it is, in Austin's words, simply "a creature of the Sovereign or State."[9] Law, then, is the commands of the sovereign—no more, no less.

On the European continent, the Scandinavian legal realists of the 20th century (Hägerström, Olivecrona, Ross) unfurled the Bentham-Austin banner. Alf Ross, the most influential of the three, asserted in the preface to his work *On Law and Justice* that "the fundamental legal notions must be interpreted as conceptions of social reality, the behaviour of man in society, and as nothing else." He went on to "reject the idea of a specific *a priori* 'validity' which raises the law above the world of facts" and to embrace a "relativistic spirit" in jurisprudence. He believed that he was casting aside "*ought*-propositions" in favour of simple, empirical "*is*-propositions." Law for Ross could be analogised to a game of chess—indeed, reductionistically understood merely in terms of such social game-playing:

[8.] Jeremy Bentham, *Anarchical Fallacies*, in his *Works*, ed. John Bowring (Edinburgh, 1838-1843), II, 501-502. Cf. John Warwick Montgomery, *Human Rights and Human Dignity* (3rd printing; Edmonton, Alberta, Canada: Canadian Institute for Law, Theology, and Public Policy, 1995), pp. 82 ff.

[9.] John Austin, *Lectures on Jurisprudence: or, The Philosophy of Positive Law*, ed. Robert Campbell (4th ed., 2 vols.; London, 1873), II, 550-51. Cf. R.A. Eastwood and G.W. Keeton, *The Austinian Theories of Law and Sovereignty* (London: Methuen, 1929); and Wilfrid E. Rumble, *The Thought of John Austin* (London: Athlone Press, 1985).

> This analysis of a simple model is calculated to raise doubts as to the necessity of metaphysical explanations of the concept of law. Who would ever think of tracing the valid norms of chess back to an *a priori* validity, a pure idea of chess, bestowed upon man by God or deduced by man's eternal reason? The thought is ridiculous, because we do not take chess as seriously as law—because stronger emotions are bound up with the concepts of law. But this is no reason for believing that logical analysis should adopt a fundamentally different attitude in each of the two cases.[10]

The most famous of the continental legal positivists and the one who most fully took that philosophy to its logical conclusion was the Austrian jurisprudent Hans Kelsen. He maintained that each legal system is unique and logically uncriticisable from the outside or from the standpoint of any other legal system. A legal system (*Stufenbau*) will necessarily have a fundamental root principle grounding it (the *Grundnorm*) and one cannot subject that basic norm to any higher standard. In Kelsen's own words: "The search for the reason of a norm's validity cannot go on indefinitely like the search for the cause of an effect. It must end with a norm which, as the last and highest, is presupposed."[11] Law thus constitutes a "coercive order" and is—literally—a law unto itself. The "first cause" is not a transcendent God but rather a necessitarian ultimate norm of the human legal system.

American legal realism put (as might be expected) a practical twist to the notion that law is entirely comprehensible humanistically and sociologically. Philosophical utilitarians and pragmatists William James and John Dewey indirectly assisted the development of the jurisprudential realism of Oliver Wendell Holmes, Jr., and Karl Llewellyn. Holmes coined the famous adage that the law is nothing more pretentious than "the prophecies of what the courts will do in fact."[12] For Llewellyn, law is always "in flux" and a "means to social ends," and since the society changes faster than the law, the law must constantly be reexamined to determine how far

---

[10] Alf Ross, *On Law and Justice* (London: Stevens, 1958), pp. ix-x, 18.

[11] Hans Kelsen, *The Pure Theory of Law*, trans. Max Knight (Berkeley: University of California Press, 1970), p. 194. Cf. John Warwick Montgomery, *The Law Above the Law* (Minneapolis: Bethany, 1975), pp. 32 ff.

[12] Oliver Wendell Holmes, Jr., "The Path of the Law," 10 *Harvard L. Rev.* 460-61 (1897).

24   Chapter 1

and how effectively it is in fact fitting the society. The formal literature of the law (the opinions of the higher courts, the law reports) are, in his view, after-the-fact "rationalisations," for legal decisions in reality are made by the weighing of social needs.[13]

What have been the consequences of legal positivism or realism as a philosophy of law? It has contributed mightily to unprincipled court decisions such as *Roe v Wade* which are little more than attempts to identify the social forces in the contemporary society and pander to them: Pilate pragmatically releasing Barabbas and giving over our Lord to be crucified because of the pressure of the crowd.[14]

Even more appalling is the fact that without a higher standard to judge legal systems from the outside, legal positivism can do nothing in the face of the atrocities brought about by legal systems such as the Stalinist or the Nazi whose *Grundnorm* and total social fabric are fundamentally flawed. Indeed, just as the two World Wars of our century dealt the deathblow to the old religious modernism, so those same evidences of institutionalised human depravity cut the ground from under positivistic jurisprudence. As the great Belgian philosopher of law Ch. Perelman succinctly put it:

[13.] Karl Llewellyn, *Jurisprudence* (Chicago: University of Chicago Press, 1962), pp. 55 ff.; *The Common Law Tradition: Deciding Appeals* (Boston: Little, Brown, 1960), pp. 35-45.

[14.] See John Warwick Montgomery, *Slaughter of the Innocents* (Westchester, Ill.: Crossway Books, 1981); "The Rights of Unborn Children," 5 *Simon Greenleaf L. Rev.* 23-72 (1985-86), and reprinted in Montgomery et al., *Christians in the Public Square: Law, Gospel and Public Policy* (Edmonton, Alberta: Canadian Institute for Law, Theology and Public Policy, 1996), pp. 175-212.

This conception of juridical positivism collapses before the abuses of Hitlerism, like any scientific theory irreconcilable with the facts. The universal reaction to the Nazi crimes forced the Allied chiefs of state to institute the Nuremberg trials and to interpret the adage *nullum crimen sine lege* in a non-positivistic sense because the law violated in the case did not derive from a system of positive law but from the conscience of all civilized men. The conviction that it was impossible to leave these horrible crimes unpunished, although they fell outside a system of positive law, has prevailed over the positivistic conception of the grounding of the law.[15]

V. HART AND DWORKIN

The weaknesses of classical legal positivism have understandably led to energetic efforts at refining or redoing that jurisprudence to make it less problematic and vulnerable to criticism. In many respects, the work of H.L.A. Hart, Ronald Dworkin, and the neo-Kantian political philosophers such as John Rawls and Alan Gewirth remind us of the endeavours of Barth, Bultmann, and Tillich to create a meaningful theology after the collapse of the old modernism while still maintaining its position that the Bible is incapable of serving as a trustworthy historical revelation.

H.L.A. Hart, late professor of jurisprudence at Oxford, recognised that the Austinian-Benthamite command theory of law was inadequate. He therefore saw the need to talk about a "minimum content of natural law": on semi-sociological premises, he argues that all law must take into account five basic facts about human nature: human vulnerability, approximate equality of strength and intellect, limited altruism, limited resources (e.g., food, shelter), and limited understanding and strength of will.[16]

It will be observed, however, that these five considerations are purely descriptive, not normative, and thus are not the equivalent

---

[15.] Ch. Perelman, "Can the Rights of Man Be Founded?," in *The Philosophy of Human Rights: International Perspectives*, ed. Alan S. Rosenbaum (Westport, Conn.: Greenwood Press, 1980), p. 47. See also John Warwick Montgomery, "Law and Justice," in *God and Caesar*, ed. Michael Bauman and David Hall (Camp Hill, Pa.: Christian Publications, 1994), pp. 319-41, and reprinted in Montgomery *et al.*, *Christians in the Public Square* (*op. cit.*), pp. 133-50.

[16.] H.L.A. Hart, *The Concept of Law* (Oxford: Oxford University Press, 1961), chap. 9.

functionally of traditional natural-law theory. What happens, for example, when one of the facts (say, human vulnerability) *conflicts* with another (say, limited resources)? Which *ought* to prevail? Without genuine, extrinsic norms, Hart cannot tell us.

Hart correctly sees that the Austinian notion of all law being direct commands is in fact hopelessly simplistic. Many genuine laws do not function that way at all (e.g., in the realms of constitutional and procedural law). He therefore stressed that not only is there a direct application of law by way of what he calls "primary rules," but also there are "secondary rules" which determine ultimately what goes into the system and whether and how the system can be changed. Hart identified three kinds of "secondary rules": the rule of change; the rule of adjudication; and—most important—the rule of recognition, by which decisions are made as to what is and what is not a true part of the legal system.

But though Hart was a practical English thinker, lacking Kelsen's Germanic, metaphysical temperament, he remained a positivist to the end: his rule of recognition has the same ultimate limitation as Kelsen's *Grundnorm*. The rule of recognition at the root of a given legal system stands above and beyond extrinsic criticism. One can criticise the lesser rules in the system for their lack of conformity with that rule, but since each legal system exists *sui generis*, there is no way to question the system's rule of recognition itself. To use Hart's own analogy, it is like the standard metre bar in Paris, by which all metre sticks are measured: there is no sense in asking if *it itself* is of the right length.[17]

And so Hart's rehabilitation of classical command-theory remains hobbled by its fundamental notion that no eternal principles exist to judge legal systems, making them of necessity relativistic and their foundations arbitrary. One thinks of Karl Barth— desperately trying to restore the essential themes of sin and grace to a denuded modernistic theology, but unable to succeed in prin-

---

[17] *Ibid.*, pp. 105-106.

ciple because he could not bring himself to reject modernism's higher criticism of the Bible.[18]

The most recent attempt to refine, and indeed go beyond, classical positivism has been offered by Ronald Dworkin, an American who is H.L.A. Hart's successor as professor of jurisprudence at Oxford. Dworkin takes Hart's positivism a step further. He says: to understand a legal system, you cannot even stop with *rules*; you must go on from rules, primary and secondary, to *principles*. What does he mean by "principles"? Rules, he notes, are all-or-nothing, whereas the principles behind the rules "incline" toward particular legal results. Illustration: the legal *principle* that no-one must profit from his or her own wrong. That is *not* all-or-nothing. Why? Because of the *rule* of adverse possession (often wryly called "legal theft")—the rule that says that if you can occupy in an open, uninterrupted, and hostile manner for a sufficient length of time a particular piece of land under the conditions the common law sets forth, you may obtain the legal title or interest to it. In such an instance, you *will* profit from your own wrong. So, behind the rules there lie general principles, inclining to but not forcing particular legal consequences.

And where, pray tell, do these fundamental principles come from? Here, Dworkin introduces the ideal judge—a kind of Platonic philosopher-king in judicial garb. Judge Hercules develops the needed principles in the course of his judicial activity. Writes Dworkin:

> You will now see why I call our judge Hercules. He must construct a scheme of abstract and concrete principles that provides a coherent justification for all common law precedents and, so far as these are to be justified on principle, constitutional and statutory provisions as well.[19]

How does the godlike Hercules find these essential principles? Dworkin offers the following (may we say: hopelessly inadequate) account:

[18.] John Warwick Montgomery, "Karl Barth and Contemporary Theology of History," in his *Where Is History Going?* (Minneapolis: Bethany, 1972), pp. 100-117.

[19.] Ronald Dworkin, *Taking Rights Seriously* (London: Duckworth, 1977), pp. 116-17.

28   Chapter 1

We could not devise any formula for testing how much and what kind of institutional support is necessary to make a principle a legal principle, still less to fix its weight at a particular order of magnitude. We argue for a particular principle by grappling with a whole set of shifting, developing and interacting standards (themselves principles rather than rules) about institutional responsibility, statutory interpretation, the persuasive force of various sorts of precedent, the relation of all these to contemporary moral practices, and hosts of other such standards.[20]

The net, to put it mildly, is thrown very widely here—with no more assurance that true principles will be preserved from the sociological *vox populi* than we found in American legal realism.

Dworkin argues for "law as integrity," and by this he means even-handedness and consistency of application. He points out that we would never stand for "checkerboard" legal approaches such as resolving the pro-life, pro-choice conflict by making abortion criminal for pregnant women born in even years but not for those born in odd years.[21] Agreed: but Dworkin gives us no adequate, principled answer as to whether abortion *per se* is right or wrong.[22] And one can have even-handedness and consistency in the most damnable legal systems. Nazi law was quite even-handed and consistent: *all* Jews were to wear the yellow star and *none* of them could, for example, hold a position of public trust.[23]

Dworkin's philosophy of law, in spite of its merit in providing insights well beyond those of the positivists and realists who preceded him, still leaves us without the substantive criteria needed to judge the adequacy of any given expression of positive law. He sees

---

[20] *Ibid.*, pp. 40-41.

[21] Ronald Dworkin, *Law's Empire* (London: Fontana, 1986), chap. 6. A further collection of Dworkin's essays is published under the title *Freedom's Law* (Oxford: Oxford University Press, 1996).

[22] See Dworkin's treatment of the abortion issue in his book, *Life's Dominion* (New York: Knopf, 1993). I have critiqued his non-solution in my article "New Light on the Abortion Controversy?," 60/7 *New Oxford Rev.* 24-26 (September 1993).

[23] See, *inter alia*: *Le droit national-socialiste*, préface de Pierre Cot (Paris: Marcel Rivière, 1936); Edith Roper and Clara Leiser, *Skeleton of Justice* (New York: E.P. Dutton,1941); *Les lois de Vichy*, ed. Dominique Rémy (Paris: Editions Romillat, 1992); Ingo Müller, *Hitler's Justice: The Courts of the Third Reich*, trans. D.L. Schneider (Cambridge, Mass.: Harvard University Press, 1991); Richard H. Weisberg, *Vichy Law and the Holocaust in France* (New York: New York University Press, 1996).

that traditional positivism fails in that respect, and he clearly longs for more solid, principled grounds for legal decision-making. His amorphous principles, however, and the mystical functioning of his ideal judge, Hercules, remind us a bit of Rudolf Bultmann, whose reaction to Barthian inadequacies was to turn what should have been a theology of objective, revelatory truth (Luther's "the entire gospel is *extra nos*") into a confused mess of existential, subjective pottage.[24]

VI. THE NEO-KANTIANS, CLS, AND JURIS-PRUDENCE DECONSTRUCTED

In the face of existential theology's inability to arrive at any objective principles, Paul Tillich went back to Schelling and rationalistic ontology in his vain search for extrabiblical theological foundations. Similarly, the most influential political philosophers and rights analysts of our time (John Rawls, Alan Gewirth) have attempted to develop along neo-Kantian lines a substitute for discredited natural-law theories and inadequate positivisms.

> Both Rawls and Gewirth have given expression to treating persons as equals in terms of variant interpretations of Kantian universalizability. Gewirth has followed Kant more literally: he has argued that ethical reasoning, as such, is marked by a certain phenomenology—namely, in reasoning ethically, an agent abstracts from her or his particular ends, and thinks in terms of what general requirements for rational autonomy the agent would demand for the self (so idealized) on the condition that the requirements be consistently extended to all other agents alike. Rawls's argument is more abstract but to similar effect: we start not from the particular agent, but from the concept of rational persons who must unanimously agree upon, while under a veil of ignorance as to who they are, the general critical standards in terms of which their personal relations will be governed. For Rawls, the veil of ignorance performs the same function as Gewirth's abstraction of the agent from her or his ends (in thinking ethically, one respects higher-order capacities of personhood, not lower-ends which happen to be pursued); and, the contractual agreement is the functional equiva-

---

[24.] Cf. John Warwick Montgomery, "Luther's Hermeneutic vs. the New Hermeneutic," in his *In Defense of Martin Luther* (Milwaukee: Northwestern Publishing House, 1970), pp. 40-85.

lent of Gewirth's universalization (what all persons would agree to comes to the same thing as what any person, suitably idealized, would demand for one's self on the condition that it be extended to all alike). Now, importantly, both these theories appeal to consequences in arguing that certain substantive principles would be universalized (Gewirth) or agreed to (Rawls). Thus, Gewirth has argued that the universalizing agent would assess the necessary substantive or material conditions for rational autonomy and would universalize those conditions; the consequences of universalization thus importantly determine what would be universalized. Correspondingly, Rawls's contractors consider the consequences of agreeing to certain standards of conduct as part of their deliberations.[25]

For Rawls, human beings placed under the "veil of ignorance" as to their special advantages will, by rationalistic necessity, arrive at his two fundamental Principles of Justice (embracing civil and social rights) and thus establish a rationally-sound political and legal order.[26] In Gewirth's case, this same result is supposedly achieved by a modern argument paralleling Kant's assertion of his Categorical Imperative ("act only on that maxim which you can will to be a universal law"): human beings, as purposive agents, require freedom and well-being to function, so they must rationally concede such freedom and well-being (i.e., fundamental civil and social rights) to others as well. Result: a just legal and political order.[27]

Robert Paul Wolff, author of one of the most penetrating examinations of Rawls's philosophy, identifies the central fallacy in all such rationalisms.

---

[25] David A.J. Richards, "Human Rights and the Moral Foundations of the Substantive Criminal Law," 13/4 *Georgia L. Rev.* 1411-12 (Summer 1979).

[26] John Rawls, *A Theory of Justice* (Oxford: Oxford University Press, 1972); *Political Liberalism* (New York: Columbia University Press, 1993); "Reply to Habermas," 92/3 *J. Philosophy* 132-80 (March 1995).

[27] Alan Gewirth, *The Community of Rights* (Chicago: University of Chicago Press, 1996), especially pp. 16-20.

Even if Rawls's theorem can be established, the self-interested moral skeptic may still decline to make a once-and-for-all commitment, even to a principle chosen from self-interest. Fidelity to principle is not, after all, deducible from bare formal rationality.[28]

This strikes equally at Rawls and at Gewirth—and likewise at Robert Nozick[29] and at all others relying on neo-Kantian rationalistic assumptions. People simply do not have to act rationally; they do not have to exercise "fidelity to principle" even when the principle can be shown to be formally logical.

Why is this? Because of original sin: the radical selfcentredness which fallen mankind displays. Unregenerate people generally refuse to function under a "veil of ignorance" or on the basis of a rational principle of universalisation or "generic consistency" when the result would be to their own selfish disadvantage. Like the secular natural-law thinkers of the 18th century upon whom Rawls and Gewirth try to improve (note, for example, Rawls's use of Enlightenment contract-theory as a model), the modern neo-Kantians blissfully disregard the fact of human depravity. Their political and ideological structures thus lack the very necessitarian character for which they were built. As jurisprudential towers of Babel, they not only do not reach to heaven; they produce confusion of thought.[30]

And when in an intellectual discipline even the most ambitious efforts to reach solid ground fail—what then? The history of contemporary theology offers a pregnant illustration. When Tillich's "Being itself" collapsed into either pantheism or analytical meaninglessness (your choice!), the direct consequences were "secular theology" and the death-of-God movement.[31] And in philosophy of

---

[28] Robert Paul Wolff, *Understanding Rawls: A Reconstruction and Critique of "A Theory of Justice"* (Princeton, N.J.: Princeton University Press, 1977), p. 20.

[29] Cf. Robert Nozick, *The Nature of Rationality* (Princeton, N.J.: Princeton University Press, 1993).

[30] For a more detailed critique, see Montgomery, *Human Rights and Human Dignity* (*op. cit.*), pp. 92-98, 182-84. Deryck Beyleveld's herculean effort to vindicate Gewirth's principle of generic consistency is, sad to say, a failure, for it ignores the impact of human depravity on all rationalistic moral systems: *The Dialectical Necessity of Morality* (Chicago: University of Chicago Press, 1991).

[31] John Warwick Montgomery, "A Philosophical-Theological Critique of the Death of God Movement," in Bernard Murchland (ed.), *The Meaning of the Death of God* (New York: Random House, 1967), pp. 25-69.

law, the conspicuous lack of success of the neo-Kantian thinkers to provide an adequate foundation for jurisprudence—against the background of the failures of secular natural-law thinking and the amorality of legal positivism—has produced the deconstructivist Critical Legal Studies movement.

CLS, as it is popularly known, appeared on the American law-school scene in the 1970s; it has since become an important influence in British legal education as well. The two most noteworthy advocates of the position are Roberto Unger and Duncan Kennedy, whose emphases and concerns, while differing in certain respects, are fundamentally the same.[32] These thinkers build upon the pragmatic, social orientation of American legal realism, and carry to a far greater extreme Llewellyn's view that formal legal judgments are little more than rationalisations of social practice. For CLS, the law is to be viewed from the standpoint of radical scepticism: all legal judgment is a matter of choosing one set of values over another. That being so, the purpose of legal activity is not a search for principles of justice embedded in and developed by the legal tradition, but the conscious advancement of a political vision. The law is inherently indeterminate; its literature has no single and objective meaning, being capable of virtually any interpretation; legal principles are contradictory; indeed, the law, in the final analysis, is but a tool generally serving the interests of the powerful and the maintenance of the status quo. So convinced advocates of CLS will follow the approach of critical neo-Marxist Antonio Gramsci[33] and endeavour to destabilise the liberal legal culture in favour of those it sees as oppressed. Indeed, even the Rule of Law itself and civil or human rights are suspect and must not be accepted uncritically—

[32.] On CLS, see Roberto M. Unger, *The Critical Legal Studies Movement* (Cambridge, Mass.: Harvard University Press, 1986); Mark Kelman, *A Guide to Critical Legal Studies* (Cambridge, Mass.: Harvard University Press, 1987); Peter Fitzpatrick and Alan Hunt (eds.), *Critical Legal Studies* (Oxford: Basil Blackwell, 1987); Tibor R. Machan, "How Critical Is Critical Legal Studies?," 1/4 *Academic Questions* 54-64 (Fall 1988); Ian Grigg-Spall and Paddy Ireland (eds.), *The Critical Lawyers' Handbook* (London: Pluto Press, 1992); Anthony Carty (ed.), *Post-Modern Law: Enlightenment, Revolution and the Death of Man* (Edinburgh: Edinburgh University Press, 1990).

[33.] For a careful treatment of Gramsci's life and ideas, see Alastair Davidson, *Antonio Gramsci: Towards an Intellectual Biography* (London: Merlin Press, 1977).

for these ideals encourage the fiction that people are in fact treated equally under the law, whereas in our modern "liberal" societies the law actually functions as a lid on the garbage can of an inequitable social system favouring those who control it.

The affinities of CLS with radical Marxism are obvious; less apparent is its dependence on Herbert Marcuse's "critique of pure tolerance," an important theoretical source of the student revolutionary movements of the 1960s.[34] One could, of course, engage in systematic critique of CLS's self-defeating deconstructivism, pointing out, as has legal philosopher J.W. Harris, that "the thought of vanguard lawyers armed with real destabilisation power conjures up nightmare visions of re-education camps."[35] But all we wish to do here is to emphasise that CLS in the realm of jurisprudence functions precisely as do "secular theology" and the death-of-God movement in the theological sphere: it constitutes an intellectual and spiritual dead-end. Beyond it there be not even dragons, only silence. For the theory has cannibalistically eaten up the very subject-matter which it was supposed to explain and justify.

* * *

Is there a common cause for these parallel deteriorations in modern jurisprudence and contemporary theology? To me it seems quite evident that the two spheres share at least one common feature. Both theology and law purport to deal with values: theology, with a transcendent God, the same yesterday, today, and forever, whose eternal will mankind needs to know and obey for everlasting felicity; law, with genuine and inalienable standards of justice. But in neither case can the relativistic human situation give rise to the absolute values sought. Out of flux, nothing but flux. Theology, therefore, necessarily engages in a process of self-destruction when

---

[34.] John Warwick Montgomery, "Marcuse", in *The Suicide of Christian Theology* (op. cit.), pp. 209-212. See also John Warwick Montgomery, "The Marxist Approach to Human Rights: Analysis & Critique," 3 *Simon Greenleaf L. Rev.* (1983-1984).

[35.] J.W. Harris, "Legal Doctrine and Interests in Land," in John Eekelaar and John Bell (eds.), *Oxford Essays in Jurisprudence: Third Series* (Oxford: Clarendon Press, 1987), p. 197.

it leaves aside the only verifiable revelation God has ever provided to a sinful race, the Holy Scriptures. To build a theology on any other foundation than that of God's Word is to build on sand.

And legal philosophy has an equal need for the God of the universe to declare, once for all and uncontaminated by human sin and fallibility, the true principles for the ordering of human society — so that law can be conformed to justice and righteousness. By setting biblical revelation aside, natural-law theories destroyed themselves, and no amount of human speculation since has been able to rectify the loss.[36] A fallen race will not find or be able to sustain intelligent jurisprudential design without listening to the Intelligent Designer. But listening how? and where?

> God, who at sundry times and in divers manners spake in time past unto the fathers by the prophets, hath in these last days spoken unto us by his Son, whom he hath appointed heir of all things, by whom also he made the worlds; who being the brightness of his glory, and the express image of his person, and upholding all things by the word of his power, when he had by himself purged our sins, sat down on the right hand of the Majesty on high.... Unto the Son he saith, Thy throne, O God, is for ever and ever: a sceptre of righteousness is the sceptre of thy kingdom.[37]

[36.] This applies also, sadly, to John Finnis's original rethinking of natural-law theory: *Natural Law and Natural Rights* (Oxford: Oxford University Press, 1980) and *The Fundamentals of Ethics* (Oxford: Oxford University Press, 1983). Although a Roman Catholic Christian, Finnis's reconstruction of natural-law theory takes place within the secular, humanistic frame of reference: special revelation is not appealed to and Finnis declares that his work "offers a rather elaborate sketch of a theory of natural law without needing to advert to the question of God's existence or nature or will" (*Natural Law and Natural Rights*, p. 49; see also the whole of chap. 13 on "Nature, Reason, God," pp. 371-410).

[37.] Hebrews 1:1-3, 8. Cf. John Warwick Montgomery, "Law and Christian Theology: Some Foundational Principles," 2/3 *Christian Legal J.* [Canada] 24-31 (Spring 1993), reprinted in Montgomery *et al., Christians in the Public Square* (*op cit.*), pp. 117-32; and *Law and Morality: Friends or Foes? An Inaugural Lecture* (Luton, England: University of Luton, 1994).

CHAPTER 2

CANON LAW AS THE JURIDIC REFLECTION OF THEOLOGICAL NORMS?

It has frequently been asserted, particularly by conservative churchmen, that the fields of theology and canon law relate to each other in a simple and straightforward way: theology derives and systemises revealed truth from revelational sources (Scripture and Tradition: Romanism, Eastern Orthodoxy, Anglo-Catholicism; *sola Scriptura*: Reformation Protestantism), whilst canon law presents these theological truths juridically.[1] It follows from such a viewpoint that juridic norms are validated if and only insofar as they do in fact conform to the revelational data to which they endeavour to give juridical expression. How satisfactory is this conceptualisation?

We shall briefly examine the two most often expressed contemporary arguments against this traditional interrelating of canon law and theology and proceed to what is hoped to be a more fruitful critique of that viewpoint.

I. CAN SCRIPTURE EVER YIELD A SINGLE, CONSISTENT THEOLOGY?

If common law norms are to be justified by testing them against revelational sources, the latter must provide a coherent, dependable body of theological data. But it is exactly this understanding of

[1] Cf. the great Lutheran canon-law scholar J.H. Boehmer's *Jus Ecclesiasticum Protestantium* (6 vols., 1714) and his classic edition of the *Corpus Juris Canonici* (2 vols., 1747). The critics who succeeded in repressing John Selden's *Historie of Tithes* (1618) did so on this theory; they were appalled that Selden appeared to justify the payment of tithes by way of ecclesiastical law even though he found their justification inadequate theologically (by the "divine moral law").

Scripture which has been brought into question since the rise of modern biblical criticism. The modern advocates of Old Testament documentary criticism, developed largely from the work of Graf, Kuenen, and Wellhausen ("J-E-P-D" theory), and of New Testament *formgeschichtliche Methode* and its many variants (Dibelius, Bultmann, the post-Bultmannians) argue that the traditional, "static" interrelating of canon law with revelational theology is no longer possible owing to our new understanding of the biblical sources.

We are told that, as a result of "the assured results of the higher criticism," the Bible cannot today be seen as it was during most of Christian history: as a propositional revelation yielding a unified theology. The Bible is fundamentally a human product, reflecting the varied cultural settings in which the many writers of Scripture operated. Moreover, later editing of original materials has produced multiple layers of meaning which militate against any notion of a single biblical theology.

In the case of the New Testament, the Gospels and their underlying strands of tradition do exactly what is even more evident in the Epistles: they reflect a wide variety of theologies which are the natural products of the multifarious "faith communities" which made up the early Christian Church. To think that one can derive a single dogmatics from these biblical materials is no longer possible.

And if there is no single, static theology to be found in Scripture, there is no single, consistent theological standard against which the norms of canon law can be tested. Canon law must, in consequence, be rethought as fully as systematic theology: it must be reconceived in dynamic, pluralistic, and relativistic terms—as the juridical reflection of current faith experience in today's varied and ecumenical church environment.[2]

[2.] Cf. George A. Lindbeck, "Papacy and *Ius divinum:* A Lutheran View," in *Papal Primacy and the Universal Church* (Minneapolis: Augsburg, 1974), pp. 193-208. Of his view, Avery Dulles writes: "Lindbeck's own position, therefore, is that the *ius divinum* terminology is today unserviceable. Thanks to modern biblical criticism and the development of historical consciousness, we can no longer think of divine ordinances as distinct from human initiatives" (Dulles, "*Ius divinum* As an Ecumenical Problem," 38 *Theological Studies* 698 [1977]). Lindbeck, incidentally, was one of my teachers at doctoral level.

Canon Law as the Juridic Reflection of Theological Norms? 37

What can be said of this approach to the biblical sources of canon law? It should be fairly clear that if the critics are correct, not only does one lose the possibility of employing Scripture as an objective criterion for the soundness of canon law norms, but one also loses, equally and at the same time, the possibility of arriving at any single coherent theology. Both dogmatics and canon law inevitably become chameleonic: they take on the changing existential and cultural situation of the moment. Canon law becomes a reflection of the length of the canonist's (or biblical critic's) foot.

In point of fact, the "assured results of higher criticism" are by no means assured, and one is not at all compelled to go down the critics' path. A generation ago, G. Ernest Wright *(The Old Testament Against Its Environment)* and Floyd V. Filson *(The New Testament Against Its Environment)* offered overwhelming evidence of the uniqueness and coherence of scriptural teaching over against the worldviews of the societies with which the biblical authors had immediate and tangential contact. The mere fact that the so-called Ecumenical Creeds (Apostolic, Nicene, Athanasian), summarising the central biblical message, came to be accepted by Christendom in general is a powerful argument for the objective clarity and unity of scriptural teaching.

As to the higher critical methodology, four points are worth making: (1) Documentary theories are not based on objective textual evidence; unlike the "lower" or "textual" critics who work with actual manuscript sources, the higher critics limit themselves to literary judgments which, by their very nature, involve a high degree of personal subjectivity. The earliest copies of all our Bible books (including the Dead Sea scroll Isaiah) do not present the assumed fragments or supposed sources alleged by the critics; they display the same holistic texts we have today. The documentalist thus ironically builds his theories without documents, and the resultant hypotheses of one critic often differ wildly from those of another—a clear sign that something very unscientific is going on. Critics cannot agree where one "source" begins and another leaves off, and (to take one example) there are Pentateuchal theorists such as Morgenstern who have divided the Mosaic writings to the point of K and

38   Chapter 2

K_1 documents. One ignores at one's peril the results of such a survey as H.F. Hahn's:

> This review of activity in the field of Old Testament criticism during the last quarter century has revealed a chaos of conflicting trends, ending in contradictory results, which create an impression of ineffectiveness in this type of research. The conclusion seems to be unavoidable that the higher criticism has long since passed the age of constructive achievement.[3]

(2) The use of parallel critical methods in other academic fields has proven so unfruitful that these techniques have been largely discredited outside of biblical scholarship. Today it is held that (as one of my Cornell classics professors put it), "If the *Iliad* and *Odyssey* were not written by Homer, they were written by someone of the same name about the same time!" H.J. Rose waxes eloquent on the Homeric authorship issue: "The chief weapon of the separatists has always been literary criticism, and of this it is not too much to say that such niggling word-baiting, such microscopic hunting of minute inconsistencies and flaws in logic, has hardly been seen, outside of the Homeric field, since Rymar and John Dennis died."[4] As to the continued presence of "such niggling word-baiting" in biblical criticism, Professor Yamauchi has stated at the close of a lecture which was later expanded into an exceedingly important monograph: "If we applied the criterion of 'Divine Names' [the *Elohim* vs *Jehovah* argument as concerns Genesis 1 and 2] to Ugaritic, Egyptian, or Arabic texts, we should see that the principle was not valid. I could multiply examples for all other criteria of the documentary hypothesis."[5]

[3.] Herbert F. Hahn, *The Old Testament in Modern Research* (rev. ed.; Philadelphia: Fortress Press, 1966), p. 41.

[4.] H.J. Rose, *Handbook of Greek Literature from Homer to the Age of Lucian* (London: Methuen, 1934), pp. 42-43.

[5.] Edwin Yamauchi, *Composition and Corroboration in Classical and Biblical Studies* ("International Library of Philosophy and Theology. Biblical and Theological Studies"; Philadelphia: Presbyterian and Reformed Publishing Co., 1966); the lecture which formed the basis of this monograph was read at the 20th Annual Convention of the American Scientific Affiliation on August 24, 1965. For a lucid overview of the scholarly fallacies in the documentary method, see Gleason L. Archer, Jr., *A Survey of Old Testament Introduction* (Chicago, 1964), pp. 73-165 (especially pp. 96-100).

(3) The rationalism involved in post-dating such biblical prophecies as Isaiah's so as to make them follow the events predicted is foreign to all legitimate scholarship. Such presumptive judgments of what God can or cannot do is not incidental to higher criticism and to its views of biblical authorship, as one can see from the use of the same method in postdating Gospel material: it is widely held that Matthew, Mark and Luke must have been written or edited after the destruction of Jerusalem in A.D. 70, for otherwise Jesus' "predictions" of the fall of the city (Matt 24; Mark 13; Luke 21) would be inexplicable! And sheer rationalism is likewise the basis of the view that the early Church painted a variegated New Testament picture of Jesus in accord with the "variety of theological viewpoints" reflected in its own diverse faith-experience; in point of fact, the New Testament writers claim primary source contact with Jesus and precise accuracy and consistency in describing what He objectively said and did (Luke 1:1-4). The Gospel writers tell us that it was *Jesus* who determined *their* message—in diametric contrast to the view so often heard today that the early Church was responsible for freely shaping our picture of Jesus.

(4) Worth noting also are the bizarre results when the direct affirmations of Pauline authorship in the New Testament are disregarded in favour of gratuitous ascriptions of multiple authorship. Macgregor and Morton employed the "literary style" of Romans and Galatians as a computer criterion for testing the authorship of the other New Testament letters claiming to be Pauline, and concluded that none of the latter were actually written by Paul. Subsequently, Macgregor and Morton's book on the subject was itself subjected to computer-analysis using parallel criteria, and it was likewise "proven" that their work was actually the product of multiple authorship![6]

In sum, there is neither necessity nor value in arguing against the traditional relationship between theology and canon law on the ground of the alleged unreliability of biblical source material. And

---

[6.] See 9 *Christianity Today* 588 (February 26, 1965); and cf. Cameron Dimwoodie, "Notes on the Use of Computing Machines in New Testament Literary Research," 1/2 *New College Bulletin* [University of Edinburgh]. 18-25 (1964).

the canonist chops off the limb on which he sits when he attempts to do so.[7]

II. IF TRADITION IS A SOURCE OF REVEALED TRUTH, MUST WE NOT RECOGNISE THAT REVELATION IS ALWAYS IN FLUX?

A second attack on the conservative view that canon law norms should be straightforward juridic reflections of objective revelational truth is frequently made today in those theological circles (Roman Catholic, Eastern Orthodox, Anglo-Catholic) where Tradition as well as Scripture is regarded as a valid revelational source. The argument proceeds somewhat along the lines of Karl Adam's "organic" analogy in his immensely influential *Wesen des Katholizismus:* the Church and its doctrine grow like a tree from a seed, and though Scripture is that seed, the subsequent development at any stage cannot be predicted or justified by analysing the scriptural seed *per se,* since the Spirit, working in the Church, continually sanctifies Tradition for the proper interpretation of Scripture and for the right guidance of theological development.

Here are two typical expressions of this approach, the first from Roman Catholic theologian George Tavard, the second from Eastern Orthodox John Mayendorff:

> The scientific reading of a text may well determine the notional sense conveyed by its words, but it cannot approach the real sense. After science has done its necessary work, the letter still remains to be personally understood and assimilated as spirit.... The question of how much of Revelation may be known with certainty through Scripture alone raises a false problem: it assumes that Scripture has a noetic purpose as a source of knowledge, rather than a kerygmatic purpose as the proclamation of a Word from God.... If scientific exegesis cannot arrive at some of the Church's docirines. we should remember that scientific study cannot by itself discern the sense of the Spirit. We should therefore continue this scientific study, with faith and in the light of the analogy of faith, until the Spirit, witnes-

---

[7.] For a sobering illustration in the area of Anglican canon law discussions of divorce, see Montgomery, "Marriage in Church After Divorce," Addendum to Chapter 7, *infra.*

Canon Law as the Juridic Reflection of Theological Norms? 41

sing interiorly to the heart of the Church, graciously opens new insights into His mystery.[8]

> The authenticity of Scriptural texts is not necessarily a formal or verbal authenticity. The Word of Life is not a theological encyclopedia which has only to be opened at the right page for the desired information to be found, exhaustively treated. Modern exegesis discovers more and more—as for instance the works of Oscar Cullmann, or Joachim Jeremias, have shown—that essential Christian truths, such as the doctrine of the Sacraments, not treated directly by the inspired authors, are considered by them as self-evident.... This makes it quite clear that Scripture, while complete in itself, presupposes Tradition, not as an addition, but as a *milieu* in which it becomes understandable and meaningful.... Revelation, in fact, is not a formal dictation of certain formally defined truths to the human mind: Revelation in Jesus Christ is a new fellowship between God and man, established once and for all, a participation of man in divine life.[9]

So, reasons the critic of the conservative approach to deriving canon law from objective theology, if tradition is a constitutive factor in the makeup of theological truth, and if that tradition is never constant but is always engaged in organic growth, then canon law norms can never be fixed either. Conformity of canon law to revelational standards can never be more than an *ad hoc* conformity: a temporary fix in relation to the status of revealed truth at the moment, subject to instantaneous change as Tradition alters our understanding of what Scripture in fact means and how we should for the present apply it corporately and individually.

How sound is this argumentation? At first glance, it would appear incontrovertible if Tradition is in fact a genuine source of revealed truth, since tradition is *ex hypothesi* never complete but always processing. In the Roman Church, the classic response has always been that the Church itself, by way of its Magisterium, distinguishes Tradition from mere tradition—determining what constitutes true tradition at any given point in ecclesiastical history and thereby establishing a firm revelational ground (even though, ad-

---

[8] George Tavard, "The Meaning of Scripture," in *Scripture and Ecumenism: Protestant, Catholic, Orthodox and Jewish*, ed. Leonard J. Swidler ("Duquesne Studies. Theological Series," 3; Pittsburgh: Duquesne University Press, 1965), pp. 70, 72-73.

[9] John Meyendorff, "The Meaning of Tradition," *ibid.*, pp. 45-46.

mittedly, that ground continually shifts as the Church receives more light as to the content and meaning of the Faith). Canon law may thus still be judged by its conformity or lack of conformity to revelation at any given point in the Church's ongoing history.

The epistemological problem here, however, lies in justifying the Church's magisterial authority in the first place. If one simply assumes that authority as an *a priori* starting-point, one confuses what the analytic philosophers call a synthetic (factual) assertion with an analytic (purely formal) claim: in a contingent universe factual claims such as the authority of a given church body cannot logically be regarded as self-evident; they must be supported by factual evidence.

And if the Romanist appeals for factual support to scriptural texts (the Petrine theory passage, Matt. 16:13-19, etc.), he must agree that the biblical text has an objective meaning *apart* from any interpretation the Church or its Tradition places upon it: otherwise, his reasoning becomes perfectly circular. Moreover, it can readily be shown on the basis of the Greek text of the Matthean passage (our only source for what Jesus said in Aramaic) that there is no necessary one-to-one identification of Peter with the "rock" on which the church is founded ("Thou art *petros*—a little stone—and upon this *petra*—a solid, rock-like foundation—I will build my church").[10]

Sophisticated modern Roman theologians are thus reduced to such exceedingly weak formulations as "if the New Testament presents a chief apostle, a principal spokesman and confessor of the faith, would not a presumption that his function continued in others be at least entertainable as a position Christians might take as believers?"[11] But this "presumption" is surely a rebuttable one, and the issue is clearly not whether such a view is "entertainable" but whether it is demanded by scriptural revelation! The burden of

---

[10.] See Montgomery, "The Petrine Theory Evaluated by Philology and Logic," in his *The Shape of the Past: An Introduction to Philosophical Historiography* (2d ed.; Minneapolis: Bethany, 1975), pp. 351-57.

[11.] Carl J. Peter, "Dimensions of Jus Divinum in Roman Catholic Theology," 34 *Theological Studies* 247 (1973).

showing that it is has hardly been discharged by argumentation of this kind.

A further problem with the assertion of Tradition as a source of revealed truth is the uneasy and unclear relationship between Tradition and Scripture. It is held that all genuine divine law set forth by the *Traditio* must have its roots in Scripture itself, i.e., that Scripture is the fount of all true Tradition. But, as Roman scholars themselves admit, the connections between many vitally important dogmas of the Roman Catholic Church and biblical *fontes* are virtually, if not entirely, absent. Consider, as obvious examples, the assumption of the blessed Virgin or the Tridentine decree of March 1547 (to be believed on pain of excommunication) that "Christ Our Lord had instituted all the [i.e., all seven] Sacraments of the New Law."[12] And if the Tradition must be derived or justified in any degree at all from scriptural sources, the Scripture must have an objective, determinable meaning apart from the Tradition and from church authority, or (as we have noted earlier) there results a complete *petitio principii*.

One of the most serious repercussions of the "organic" approach to theological formulations is that nothing can be stated with finality as to divine law and thus no pronouncements of canon law can have apodictic certainty. If, along the lines of Jürgen Moltmann's "theology of hope," "the ultimate validation of truth claims for Christian faith is in the future, when the substance of things hoped for in the present will be seen face to face,"[13] then Christian theology and canon law fall into the same unverifiable abyss as the Hegelian dialectic philosophy of history and the Marxian worldview

---

[12.] *DS* 1601; see Piet F. Fransen, "Criticism of Some Basic Theological Notions in Matters of Church Authority," 19/2 *J. Ecumenical Studies* 60 ff. (1982). It is argued by not a few Roman Catholic theologians (Rahner, Peter, *et al.*) that tenuous biblical bases for church doctrine and law should pose no insuperable barrier as long as the resulting Church teaching is "irreversible." Dulles *(op. cit.,* p. 695) points out, however, that "these authors are reluctant to specify exactly what in the later development was in fact irreversible." More important is the fairly obvious consideration that evil and error can also become institutionally irreversible. *Ecclesia semper reformanda est!*

[13.] Peter, *op. cit.,* pp. 246-47.

whose truth can only be revealed in a futuristic, millennial classless society.[14]

Moreover, the placing of any extrinsic interpretive authority over scriptural revelation puts Scripture at the mercy of that interpreter. The Roman Magisterium is by no means the only claimant to that authoritative role. Muslims argue that the Koran must provide the true interpretation of any and all biblical passages. Mormons regard the Book of Mormon as the only definitive interpreter of the meaning of the Bible. Christian Scientists read Scripture through the eyes of Mrs Eddy's *Science and Health, with Key to the Scriptures.* New-Agers and Charismatics find the "true" significance of biblical material by way of their inner, subjective, spiritual experiences. Whose extrabiblical interpretive criterion is to be preferred to the others? How can any one or all these criteria be justified as genuinely revelational? We suggest that no such justifications are sustainable and that these positions mutually cancel each other out.[15]

But if a dynamic, progressive Tradition is not to be employed alongside biblical revelation, does it follow that Scripture is indeed capable of interpreting itself? In terms of contemporary "hermeneutical circle" reasoning, must we not say that the Church invariably and necessarily impacts the understanding of Scripture even as Scripture impacts the Church's life and beliefs?

Our response is the same as must be given to those (e.g., advocates of Critical Legal Studies) who oppose Dworkin's "one right answer" thesis: to be sure, we bring our own background and prejudices to the interpretation of a statute, a judicial opinion, a work of literature, or a sacred text; but we must be willing maturely to identify our biases and subordinate them to what the text is in fact saying. Diverse and contradictory interpretations of a text need to be arbitrated and judged by the text itself. Objectivity of interpreta-

---

[14.] See Montgomery, *Where Is History Going? A Christian Response to Secular Philosophies of History* (Minneapolis: Bethany, 1969); and his "The Marxist Approach to Human Rights: Analysis & Critique," 3 *Simon Greenleaf Law R.* (1983-84).

[15.] Cf. Walter R. Martin, *The Kingdom of the Cults* (rev. ed.; Minneapolis: Bethany, 1985), *passim*.

tion may not be perfectly attainable, but it can be approximated if we see the hermeneutical circle as merely descriptive of what often constitutes bad exegesis, never as a normative approach to be encouraged.

If texts (including but not by any means limited to the Bible) were not capable of self-interpretation, we would enter upon an infinite regress: how could one know that the coloured glasses one uses to understand the text are the right ones? And what does one's *own* interpretation of the text *really mean?* Any deconstruction gratuitously assumes the objective comprehensibility of the deconstructor's analysis, but logically that interpretation should possess no greater objectivity of meaning than the text which is the subject of the interpretation. In short, do we really know what Derrida means? If the scriptural texts cannot be relied on to mean what they say, how can one rely on the interpreters or the Tradition to mean what they appear to be saying?[16]

III. SO IS CANON LAW BUT THE JURIDICAL MIRROR-IMAGE OF DIVINE, REVEALED LAW?

We have discovered the inadequacy of the two most common contemporary objections to the notion of canon law norms as justified merely by their conformity to divine law objectively revealed: that the Scriptures provide no single, consistent theology able to serve as a canonical standard, and that Tradition, as interpreter of Scripture, never provides a final revelational understanding upon which theology or canon law can base its pronouncements. Does it therefore follow that the conservative view is correct that the validity of juridic norms in canon law depends solely on their conformity to revelational standards? We do not think so.

Canon law is a *relational endeavour:* it does not merely translate dogmatic formulations into juridical categories; it provides a legal bridge between Scripture and the needs of the contemporary

---

[16] See Montgomery, "Legal Hermeneutics and the Interpretation of Scripture," in *Evangelical Hermeneutics,* ed. Michael Bowman and David Hall (Pennsylvania: Christian Publications, 1995), pp. 15-29.

church. A parallel is offered by the field of apologetics. Unlike the dogmatician, who endeavours straightforwardly to systematise revelational truth in the most consistent manner, the apologist takes the truths of dogmatics and provides arguments for them which best fit the mindset of the apologist's own time. Thus Augustine of Hippo and the Renaissance defenders of Christian faith used Platonic categories; Thomas Aquinas employed Aristotelian thought-forms; John Locke and William Paley used empirical arguments; Kierkegaard and Gabriel Marcel defended the faith existentially. The test of a good apologetic is twofold: not just conformity with revelational truth (though this, of course, is essential—otherwise one isn't really defending "the faith once delivered to the saints"), but *also* relevance to the thought-patterns of the contemporary unbeliever.

Canon law operates analogously. It must take its substantive content from revelational standards: otherwise it is providing juridical formulations not of divine truth but of human opinion, and is simply another human legal system on a par with the Roman-law, Civil-law, or Common-law traditions. But the correct abstract formulation of divine truth in juridical form is not enough: that constitutes a necessary but not a sufficient test of the quality of the canon lawyer's work. Also vital is the sound juridical application of divine truth to the conditions of the church of the day.

Concretely, scriptural standards on marriage, divorce, and homosexuality remain the same today as they always were, since the biblical revelation remains the same. But at the end of the 20th century the Western Church faces societal changes in which, for example, many young people live together without a legally or ecclesiastically sanctioned marriage and children are born to such unions; and homosexuals often regard themselves as unjustly discriminated against by the Church. Today's canon lawyers have the opportunity, whilst not in any way compromising biblical teaching as to the permanence of marital commitment and unqualified biblical opposition to homosexual practices, to formulate juridical principles which would, *inter alia,* assimilate permanent unions (even without the benefit of civil or ecclesiastical formalities) to the biblical phenomenon of "betrothed spouses" (think of Mary and Joseph)—and to distinguish juridically between homosexual temperaments (cf. congenital alcoholics) which are by no means sinful *per se*, and homosexual lifestyles, which the church must not tolerate because Scripture will not tolerate them.

To use Dworkin's pregnant illustration of the "serial novel" of the law: the ideal canon lawyer will be a Judge Hercules (better, in this case, Judge Solomon?) who shapes the future chapters of canon law to fit as fully as possible the revelationally-sound preceding chapters, while making sure that his formulations meet the genuine needs of the Church of the present. By insisting always on conformity to biblical standards, he will avoid Dworkin's error of leaving the source of legal principles vague and imprecise.[17] By insisting on relevance in his formulations, he will avoid positivistic, Pharisaic legalism.

In sum, the standard critiques of the classic view that canon law norms are simply a reflection of divinely revealed law assume that biblical revelation is not a reliable constant (but it is!). If canon law is *relational*—relating divine truth to a human community of believers in real time—then the *de facto* non-constant element is that community of believers, not the revelational source of the Church's theology. For canon law to be static, *both* relational factors would have to be constant and unvarying. Since that is not the case, we cannot properly say that the validity of juridic norms in canon law is dependent *solely* on their conformity to revelational truth. The Scriptures "cannot be broken" and Jesus Christ is indeed "the same yesterday, today, and forever": but the Church is frequently broken and never remains the same—at least until the Church Militant be-

---

[17.] "We could not devise any formula for testing how much and what kind of institutional support is necessary to make a principle a legal principle, still less to fix its weight at a particular order of magnitude. We argue for a particular principle by grappling with a whole set of shifting, developing and interacting standards (themselves principles rather than rules) about institutional responsibility, statutory interpretation, the persuasive force of various sorts of precedent, the relation of all these to contemporary moral practices, and hosts of other such standards"—Ronald Dworkin, *Taking Rights Seriously* (London: Duckworth, 1977), pp. 40-41. Cf. Montgomery, *Law and Morality: Friends or Foes? An Inaugural Lecture* (Luton: University of Luton, 1994).

comes the Church Triumphant. And at that point canon lawyers will presumably become redundant.

Addendum

A COMMENT ON THE THINKING OF PROFESSOR J.W. MONTGOMERY IN HIS ARTICLE, "CANON LAW AS THE JURIDIC REFLECTION OF THEOLOGICAL NORMS?"

Professor Montgomery summarises the thinking of certain individuals concerning the relationship of theology and Canon Law by stating that these disciplines can be understood as in the sense of theology deriving and systematising revealed truth from revelational sources. Then Canon Law presents these theological truths juridically. He notes how some contemporary arguments are opposed to these formulations and suggests that they have no valid base. He does not agree with such statements and proceeds in this article to examine, and to some extent, refute these statements.

He firstly asks the question as to whether scripture can ever yield a single consistent theology. He reviews the opinions of those who feel that the rise of modern biblical criticism has destroyed for ever the possibility of such a consequence being drawn out of scripture. Professor Montgomery is by no means impressed or convinced of what are called the assured results of higher criticism which have had the effect of reducing the certainty which Christians tended to place in scripture as their norm of belief from which one could derive a theology and eventually perhaps Canon Law. Professor Montgomery then continues to examine the attack launched on the conservative view that Canon Law norm should be straightforward juridic reflections of objective revelational truth. He presents what he feels is the Roman Catholic teaching on *Tradition* noting how it is to be distinguished from mere tradition. For him this understanding of tradition is one which establishes a source of revelation which would be in constant flux and therefore it is not possible to establish a secure base from which to understand any juridical developments or pronouncements on the part of the church. While Professor Montgomery claims to have discovered the inadequacy of the two most common contemporary objections to the notion of Canon Law norms as justified merely by their conformity to divine law objectively revealed, yet he also holds that the validity of juridic norms in Canon Law does not depend solely on their conformity to revelational standards.

For Montgomery Canon Law is a revelational endeavour. It provides a legal bridge between scripture and the needs of the contemporary church. He holds that its substantive content must derive from revelational standards. Canon Law must also have a sound application of divine truth in the traditions of the church today. He holds therefore that if Canon Law is held to be *relational*, that is to say, relating divine truth to human community believers in real time, then the de facto non-constant element is that community of believers, not the revelational source of the church's theology. I can to some extent agree with this position. However, Catholic ecclesiology assists in arriving at a more precise understanding of the relation between law and theology.

Professor Montgomery uses language and terminology which is not familiar to those who are students and practitioners of the Canon Law of the Catholic Church, whether it be for the Latin code or the Oriental code. It may be that I have not fully understood the point he is making and therefore I do not want particularly to offer detailed criticism of the statements he makes in this relatively short article. I find that it proceeds from a basis of what I would regard as a very undeveloped ecclesiology, and a very under-developed concept of the nature of revelation. The teaching of the Second Vatican Council on Revelation in the Constitution "Dei Verbum" set out with great clarity the way in which the church understands how she has received from the Father in Heaven the good news of salvation who is Jesus Christ. In that great document we are reminded how Jesus Himself came on earth to teach. We are also reminded how, in the context of that teaching, it was the response of those who were selected by Jesus Himself to receive His person and His teaching who had the responsibility to pass on to succeeding generations the truth that comes from the Father in Heaven. In the transmission of the good news who is Jesus Christ and His works and teaching it is clear from the actions of Christ and His teaching that He wished to establish in His church an enduring instrument of teaching the truth and securing the development of that same truth. That instrument is the divinely established hierarchy based in the college of Bishops who have succeeded to the Apostles. The transmission of revelation is the duty of the whole body of those who are signed with the Blessed Trinity in baptism and confirmed in the Sacrament of Confirmation. Yet in that transmission of truth the church is endowed with the organ of securing that truth and promoting it in the shape of the sacred magisterium.

In the transmission of the truth it is for the whole church under the guidance of the sacred magisterium, to work at reflection and exploration on God's intervention in human history. Tradition is a term which aptly includes part of this work of exploration. However, since one is dealing with truth and with the essential and necessary person of Jesus Christ, the teaching of the church can never be in contradiction to that which was received in the beginning and which is to endure to the end of time. Exploration of the truth does not mean invention of new proposals for eternal salvation. It does mean being able to handle the interaction between the truth which is Jesus and His teaching and the developing experience of the human race in the extraordinary manifestations of interaction between the human race and the universe given it by God to use and to adorn to God's glory.

It is very interesting contrasting the efforts of Professor Montgomery to explore the relationship between Canon Law and its basis in scripture and theological norms with the vision given us by Pope John Paul II in the Apostolic Constitution *Sacrae Disciplinae Leges* by which the Pope presented to the church the Latin code: "And in fact a Code of Canon Law is absolutely necessary for the church. Since the church is established in the fall of a social and visible unit, it needs rules, so that its hierarchical and organic structure may be visible; that its exercise of the functions divinely entrusted to it, particularly of sacred power and of the administration of the sacraments, is properly ordered; that the mutual relationships of Christ's faithful are reconciled in justice based on charity, with the rights of each safeguarded and defined; and lastly, that the common initiatives which are undertaken so that the Christian life may be ever more perfectly carried out, are supported, strengthened and promoted by Canonical laws."

Professor Montgomery has done us a service in this article by pointing out the consequence of trying to understand the Canon Law without reference to a secure basis in ecclesiology. Law of its very nature is directed towards the good of a community. It is the understanding of the community established and founded by Jesus Christ which gives validity for the proper devising of law to serve that community. It is quite true that Jesus Christ Himself was born into a community which was very conscious of living under the law, which came from God in origin. But at the same time He Himself was to proclaim that the law was the servant of the community not its master. We well remember the Lord's pronouncement that the Sabbath was made for man not man for the Sabbath. The first Christians who were Jews had to learn how to build upon that law which Jesus Himself said He had come to fulfil. They had to do this in the context of a community which was initially struggling to proclaim the good news that Jesus had been put to death but had risen again and He was truly the Son of God. As the centuries go by that proclamation continues in all its force and validity but its consequences as lived out by the community of the faithful followers of Jesus have required over the years further developments of law in order that the charity inspiring the followers of Christ may flourish yet more. As the Pope says in *Sacrae Disciplinae Leges*, "The purpose of the Code is not in any way to replace faith, grace and charisms and above all charity in the life of the church of Christ's faithful. On the contrary, the Code rather looks towards the achievement of order in the ecclesial society, such like while attributing a primacy to love, grace and the charisms, it facilitates at the same time an orderly development in the life both of the ecclesial society and of the individual persons who belong to it." It will be seen that this approach to law, coupled with the insights given in the nature of revelation itself and the process of exploration but not new invention of that revelation, the Code of Canon Law must itself expect to develop and to be subjected to change but not any change which would in any way be a contradiction of the truth of the gospel and the values established therein.

It is to be hoped that the work of Professor Montgomery will contribute to a further exploration on the part of students and users of the Code of Canon Law, in both the Latin and the Eastern churches, of the great gift that has been given to us in these years following the Second Vatican Council and its foundation in the revelation of Jesus Christ.

Bishop John Jukes OFM Conv.
Bishop of Strathearn
7 April 2000

A BRIEF REPLY TO BISHOP JUKES

I much appreciate the bishop's comments on my article. Bishop Jukes well understands the thrust of my essay and provides a very helpful summary of the approach to canon law commonly held in post-Vatican II Roman Catholicism.

The bishop holds that I suffer from "a very undeveloped ecclesiology and a very under-developed concept of the nature of revelation." This is, essentially, because I do not agree with him that "the teaching of the church can never be in contradiction to that which was received in the beginning [from Christ and His Apostles] and which is to endure to the end of time." For the bishop, ecclesiology embraces and subsumes revelational theology (as well as epistemology); for me it does not.

The problem here is quite straightforward: Is revelation inseparable from and a function of the ecclesiastical community, or is it an independent, objective given by which the community must continually be judged to determine its conformity to Christ? The bishop maintains the former; I, the latter. My problem with his understanding is twofold: First, the history of the empirical church has been a history both of wondrous activity in carrying out our

Lord's mission to "preach the gospel to every creature" and of horrendous departures from the original teachings of Christ and of the Apostles (the Great Schism, the Babylonian Captivity of the Church, the Renaissance papacy, the Inquisition, canonical legalism, etc., etc.). Secondly, if one starts, as does the bishop, with the *a priori* that one's own community simply *is* the true revelational community, one entirely short-circuits the fundamental epistemological problem of identifying which ecclesiastical community among the competing denominational claims does in fact best represent—or represent at all—Christ's church.

The bishop surely agrees that *"ecclesia semper reformanda est."* But reformation is possible only on a most limited basis when the source of the problem (a sinning church) is the only standard for correcting it. As the maxim of natural justice expresses it (12 Coke Rep. 13), no-one can be a judge in his own cause. I must, therefore, for my part, rest with the sage words of the 16th century *Formula of Concord* (Solid Declaration, Summary Formulation, 9): "God's Word alone is and should remain the only standard and norm of all teachings, and no human being's writings dare be put on a par with it, but everything must be subjected to it." Here arises a genuine opportunity to base theology, ecclesiology, and canon law on more than shifting sand.

Professor John Warwick Montgomery

CHAPTER 3

LUTHER AND CANON LAW

On the Eve of All Saints' Day, October 31, 1517, Martin Luther posted his 95 Theses on the Castle Church door in Wittenberg, thereby launching what would become the Protestant Reformation and a major turning point in the history of the Western world. Less well known is a similarly dramatic event at Wittenberg's Elster Gate three years later, on December 10, 1520, when Luther, in response to the burning of his writings by Roman officialdom, publicly consigned to flame the bull of excommunication against him[1]—and the corpus of medieval canon law.[2]

Critics of Luther such as Roman Catholic apologist-historian Grisar have argued that his symbolic burning of the canon law reflected a deep-seated antinomianism on the Reformer's part: Luther was allegedly jettisoning law in favor of personal, individual spiritual experience. Yet other critics of the Lutheran Reformation, in particular Ernst Troeltsch, have held that the Reformer's theology—especially his doctrine of the two kingdoms—justified a quietism vis-à-vis the activities of the state which encouraged institutitional legalism and political statism.[3] The extensive develop-

---

[1.] With an earned doctorate of the Sacred Scriptures and a lifelong concern with public education and scholarship, Luther was in no sense a censorious "book-burner"; the Elster Gate event was purely symbolic. See John Warwick Montgomery, "Luther, Libraries, and Learning," 32/2 *Library Quarterly* [University of Chicago] (April 1962), reprinted in John Warwick Montgomery, *In Defense of Martin Luther* (Milwaukee, WI: Northwestern, 1970), pp. 114-39.

[2.] "'Canon law' refers to the body of ecclesiastical rules or laws imposed by [church] authority in matters of faith, morals, and discipline" ("Canon Law," *Oxford Dictionary of the Christian Church*, ed. F.L. Cross [New York: Oxford University Press, 1957]).

[3.] See Duncan B. Forrester, *Christian Justice and Public Policy* (Cambridge: Cambridge University Press, 1997), pp. 210–14, and my critical review of this book in the Appendix section of the present work.

ment of *Kirchenordnungen* (*KOO*)—Protestant compendia of church law in the lands that went over to the Reformation—have been used to support this view.

However, one cannot have it both ways: Luther cannot be both antinomian and the fomenter of legalism! A reevaluation of Luther's approach to canon law is called for. Two questions in particular need to be answered: Why precisely did Luther burn the corpus of canon law? and What was his theological judgment on church law in general?

I. THE ELSTER GATE INCIDENT

Luther's own narrative of the ceremony appears in his *Briefswechsel*,[4] but we shall reproduce a synoptic account as given by one of the greatest historians of the Lutheran Reformation, E.G. Schwiebert.

> Early in the morning of December 10, 1520, Philip Melanchthon nailed a significant document on the *Schwarze Brett*, the university bulletin board, announcing the long-awaited reaction on the part of Luther to the burning of his books all over Germany. The announcement invited the doctors and masters of the University and the student body to assemble at Holy Cross Chapel at 9 A.M. just outside the east gate of the city. A pile of wood had been gathered at the spot near the Elbe where the town burned the clothing of those infected with pest and where cattle were butchered. The occasion was the burning of certain books by means of which the Papacy and the Roman hierarchy were particularly entrenched.
>
> After the gathering had assembled, one of the masters, probably Agricola, started the fire. From one of Luther's letters, written around 10 A.M. that morning to Spalatin, it is clear that the *Decretum* of Gratian, the papal decretals, *Sextus Clementinae Extravagantes*, the *Summa Angelica*, and some of Eck's and of Emser's books were included in the list. But the principal collection of writings which Luther wished to destroy was the *corpus iuris canonici*, that body of Canon Law which gave the Pope all the extravagant powers which Eck, Emser, and others tried to defend. One after the other the various tomes were consigned to the flames. Finally, Luther

---

[4.] *Weimarer Ausgabe* (the standard, critical edition of Luther's writings in German and Latin), *Briefswechsel*, 2, 234.

unexpectedly drew a printed copy of the bull *Exsurge, Domine* from his gown and threw it into the flames with the remark: "Because thou hast destroyed the truth of God, may the Lord consume thee in these flames." Since historical research has proved that he did not utter the oft-repeated traditional phrase: "Because thou hast offended the Holy One of God," the criticism directed against him by those critics who claimed he was referring to himself falls by the wayside. Luther may have talked before about burning the bull *Exsurge, Domine*, yet Boehmer maintains that all 16th-century evidence points to the idea that burning Pope Leo's bull was just sudden impulse of the moment. Luther, therefore, on this occasion impulsively burned the papal bull which threatened him with excommunication, but he intentionally destroyed the whole basic framework upon which the Roman Church had been built. After the burning of these books and the bull the audience sang the *Te Deum* and the *De profundis*, whereupon the faculty returned to the college.[5]

From that time on, the teaching of canon law was discontinued at the University of Wittenberg[6]—as it would later be prohibited in the English universities following Henry VIII's split with Rome.

The motive behind Luther's act is suggested by his words, "Because thou hast destroyed the truth of God, may the Lord consume thee in these flames." But to understand what Luther meant requires a close examination of his thinking.

II. LUTHER'S VIEW OF CANON LAW

In the years immediately preceding and following his burning of the *corpus juris canonici*, Luther made a number of specific statements concerning the canon law of his day.

His *Commentary on Galatians* of 1519 includes this passage: "The fewer the laws by which a state is governed, the more fortunate the state is. But our church polity, which had only the one law of love so that it might be the most fortunate of all, must now, because of the wrath of omnipotent God, instead of this one now extinct law [of love], bear clouds and forests and oceans of laws, so that you are

---

[5.] E.G. Schwiebert, *Luther and His Times* (St. Louis: Concordia, 1950), pp. 490–91.
[6.] *Ibid.*, p. 20.

hardly able to learn even their names."[7] Here, Luther shows his antipathy to the needless proliferation of church legislation.

Luther's criticism, it should be noted, was not that of the uninformed person who in every age complains about "too much law." Luther had spent a year at the University of Erfurt studying canon law under Professor Henning Goede before entering the Augustinian cloister, and he personally owned a copy of the *corpus juris canonici*. His detailed knowledge of the canon law is evident from his extensive use of it in preparing for his celebrated Leipzig debate with renowned Roman Catholic theologian Johann Eck in 1519.

Luther's opposition to the canon law of the Roman Church went far deeper than objecting to its prolixity. In his *Exposition of Psalm 1:2* of that same year (1519), Luther distinguished the Roman canon law as a human product from the genuine, revealed Law of God as set forth in the Scriptures. For Luther no mistake could be greater than confusing the two. "See to it that you separate very far and very widely the Law of the Lord from the laws of any human beings whatsoever; and be extremely careful that you do not mix these two classes of laws into one chaotic body and perish miserably for so doing. This is what pestilential teachers are now doing when they either turn the Law of God into mere human traditions or turn human traditions into the Law of God."[8]

A year later, in his immensely influential *Letter to the Christian Nobility of the German Nation* (1520), Luther again and again castigated the canon law of the Church of Rome. "The medical men I leave to reform their own faculties; the jurists and theologians I shall take in hand. And I say, to begin with, that it would be well if the canon law, from the first letter to the last—and especially the decretals—were utterly blotted out."[9] He continues:

> Today canon law is not what is in the books but what is in the sweet will of the pope and his flatterers. Your cause may be thoroughly established in the canon law, still the pope has his *scrinium pectoris* [chamber of his heart], and all law and the whole world

[7.] *Weimarer Ausgabe*, 2, 217.
[8.] Ibid., 5, 32.
[9.] Ibid., 6, 459.

must be guided by it. Now this *scrinium* is frequently ruled by a knave, even by the devil himself. But they boast that it is ruled by the Holy Spirit. Thus they deal with Christ's poor people. They give them many laws, but they themselves keep none of them. Others, however, they compel either to keep them or else to buy a release from them.... In the Bible more than enough directions have been penned for our guidance in life. The study of the canon law only stands in the way of the study of Holy Scripture.[10]

In these passages Luther returns to the theme that there is too much church law and reiterates his fundamental point that the Roman canon law is no more than a human product. Unlike the divinely revealed Scriptures, the *corpus juris canonici* is a bureaucratic tool by which the church authority of the day manifests itself, oppressing the consciences and spiritual lives of the faithful. The papacy employs that law arbitrarily (*scrinium pectoris*), claiming its legislation and judgments to be the Holy Spirit's. But the penitential system thereby upheld, with its indulgences and dispensations for purchase, is the very opposite of the biblical way of salvation. Such a canon law must be blotted out so that the true message of Scripture can again be appreciated.

Following his heroic stand before Emperor Charles V at the Diet of Worms and the Emperor's decree that placed him under the ban of the Empire, Luther went into exile at the Wartburg Castle in the Thuringian forest above Eisenach. There he translated the New Testament into the vernacular, incidentally stabilising, almost single-handedly, the High German language. From the Wartburg he wrote a letter in 1521 to his fellow Augustinians back at Wittenberg. In it he declared: "The pope's rule is the canon law. In it he ordains, establishes, and earnestly commands—charging the disobedient with mortal sin and threatening them with eternal damnation—rules and regulations concerning food, drink, clothing, persons, churches, altars, chalices, corporals, books, incense, wax, banners, holy water, reading, singing, fasting, prepends, tribute—and who can tell the story of the devil of Romish sanctity?"[11]

[10.] *Ibid.*
[11.] *Ibid.*, 8, 540–41.

Was Luther correct in these criticisms, or are they the rantings of a disturbed mind suffering from a profound authority problem?[12] Confirmation that Luther's evaluation of the content and functioning of late medieval canon law was not far off the mark comes from eminent Roman Catholic canonists of the present day. Kuttner writes of "the transformation from 'sacramental' law into the legal techniques of the twelfth century":

> It would be superficial to condemn this as "unchristian." But the new jurisprudence created problems and tensions from which the canon law of the later Middle Ages was to suffer. With the juridical refinement of canonical thought there came an evergrowing complication of the judicial and administrative process; with the enhancing of the pope's function as guardian and reformer of the law, there came the evergrowing need for trained personnel in the Roman Curia, and with it, all the fiscalism and other ills that commonly bedevil a vast governmental machinery everywhere in the world. ... There was also ... the petty reality of legalism: all too often the technical machinery of the law would become an end in itself and clatter along for its own sake. An unhealthy *imitatio imperii* crept over the conduct of the papal office; an often callous routine turned the delicate instrument of dispensations into a marketable tool for flouting just law. Canon law was ripe for reform on all levels; but the answer of the Church to the challenge of the Reformation remained fragmentary.[13]

Peter Shannon, evaluating the Roman Catholic Code of Canon Law in force from 1918 to 1967, characterises even this modern formulation as suffering from four great evils: "a seeming unawareness of basic theology," "a regrettable ignorance of ecclesiology," "an emphasis on centralization rather than subsidiarity," and "an unevangelical over-emphasis on the letter of the law."[14] Except for his use of modern terminology, Shannon seems to be saying pre-

---

[12.] The latter was the psychoanalytical diagnosis of Harvard University's Erik Erikson (*Young Man Luther*), made famous in John Osborne's dramatic hit "Luther." This portrait of the Reformer has been thoroughly exploded; see Montgomery, *In Defense of Martin Luther*, pp. 14–15.

[13.] Stephan Kuttner, "Reflections on Gospel and Law in the History of the Church," in *Studies in the History of Medieval Canon Law*, ed. Stephan Kuttner (Aldershot, U.K.: Variorum, 1990), 9:207–8.

[14.] Peter Shannon, "The Code of Canon Law, 1918–1967," 8/3 *Concilium* 26–30 (1967). See also Rudolf Pesch, "The New Testament Foundations of a Democratic Form of Life in the Church," 3/7 *Concilium* 48–59 (1971).

cisely what Luther put more colorfully early in the sixteenth century.

III. LUTHER PROPERLY UNDERSTOOD

As the great Luther scholar Roland Bainton insisted, to comprehend the Reformer one must comprehend his *theology*—since Luther's actions were always consciously or unconsciously orientated in reference to his central beliefs.

The fallacy of attributing Luther's burning of the *corpus juris canonici* to antinomianism should now be clear. But Kuttner, whom we have just cited approvingly on the deterioration of the pre-Reformation canon law, unfortunately throws Luther into this very antinomian pot. Kuttner speaks of Tertullian's "church of Love vs. the church of Law" (*ecclesia spiritus* vs. *ecclesia episcoporum*); the medieval sect of the Cathari/Albigensians; and mystical Joachim of Fiore who believed in an imminent "Third Age of the Spirit," wherein hierarchy, church authority, and all canon law would wither away— much as Marxists believe that state and law will disappear following apocalyptic class-war, and the dictatorship of the proletariat transmute itself into a millennial classless society. "This," declares Kuttner, "leads up to the symbolic burning of 'all the pope's books' of canon law by Martin Luther in 1520."[15]

Hardly! Luther was anything but a sixteenth-century charismatic mystic opposing his inner spiritual vision to the ordered structure of corporate Christianity. What led Luther to desire that the existing canon law be "utterly blotted out" was his studied conviction that the canon law of his day functioned chiefly to support a theologically corrupt church authority: one operating at cross-purposes to the gospel itself.

Schwiebert puts it this way: "In a letter to Spalatin at this time, Luther clearly shows the trend of his thinking leading to the conclusion that the Papacy and the whole Roman system were entrenched

---

[15.] Kuttner, "Reflections on Gospel and Law in the History of the Church," p. 201.

in Canon Law.... By this act Luther symbolized the destruction of the very system that gave the Roman hierarchy its power."[16]

Erasmus was more perceptive than Kuttner. When that great Renaissance humanist was waiting at Cologne with Luther's prince, Frederick the Wise, elector of Saxony, for Emperor Charles V to arrive from Aachen, he declared: "Luther sinned in two respects, namely, that he knocked off the crown of the pope and attacked the bellies of the monks."

Luther's central theology is thus the key to understanding his opposition to the Roman canon law. Four essential elements in his theology relate to this issue.

A. Justification by Grace through Faith

What Luther scholar Philip Watson called Luther's "Copernican revolution in theology" occurred when Luther discovered—principally through his study of the Psalms and Paul's Epistle to the Romans—that there is no way to earn God's forgiveness. Forgiveness, he learned, has already been provided as a free gift through Christ's death on the cross. Luther succinctly expressed this point in his Explanation of the Third Article of the Apostle's Creed (*Shorter Catechism*): "I believe that I cannot by my own reason or strength believe in Jesus Christ, my Lord, or come to Him; but the Holy Ghost has called me by the Gospel, enlightened me with His gifts, sanctified and kept me in the true faith; even as He calls, gathers, enlightens, and sanctifies the whole Christian Church on earth."

From this truth followed—like the night succeeds the day—the conclusion that a canonical system legitimising and indeed encouraging the earning of merit (from the papal Treasury of Merit) for the alleged amelioration of the spiritual condition of the faithful was antithetical to the very heart of the Christian message. Commenting on Galatians 5:2 in the year 1531, Luther fulminated: "All (be they papists, Jews, Turks, or heretics) who teach that anything is neces-

---

[16.] Schwiebert, *Luther and His Times*, p. 20.

sary for salvation besides faith in Christ or who institute any work or cult or observe any rule, tradition, or ceremony of any sort with the opinion that by these they would obtain forgiveness of sins, righteousness, and life everlasting—such persons hear the sentence of the Holy Spirit here pronounced against them by the apostle that Christ is of no benefit whatever to them."[17]

Justification by grace alone, through faith alone in Christ's saving work on the cross, became for Luther and his followers the *articulus stantis et cadentis ecclesiae* ("the article by which the church stands or falls"). Anything inconsistent with it, even though longstanding in the church, had to be rooted out for the sake of the salvation of God's people. R. Scott Clark well summarizes this basic theological teaching:

> In the years 1513–19, as he lectured through the Psalms, Romans, and Galatians, and as he was driven to work out his theology in controversy with Eck and his other critics, Martin Luther (1483–1546) fundamentally rejected the medieval scheme of progressive justification. He came to see that the Good News is that Christ is the righteousness of God (*iustitia Dei*) and that this righteousness is *outside* of us. Sinners are not justified because they are sanctified, but rather, they are justified because Christ fulfilled all righteousness, and his righteousness has been imputed to us. Luther's doctrine of justification was judicial (*actus forensis*). For Luther, justification was a legal matter, a declaration and accounting by God. No longer are we to think that God says we are just only because we really are *intrinsically* just. Rather, we are just because Christ was and his justice is credited or *imputed* to us.[18]
>
> With this recovery of the forensic doctrine of justification came the correlate doctrine of faith. From 1518, Luther began to speak of faith no longer as an infused virtue, a disposition toward obedience, but rather as a divinely wrought gift, the instrument which looks away from one's self and lays hold of Christ and his righteousness. For Luther and the Protestants, it is not faith *per se*, but Christ, the object of faith who justifies and saves. Faith does not look within (to sanctification), but without: to Christ. The corollary to the Protestant definition of faith was a revised definition of grace. It was no

---

[17] *Weimarer Ausgabe*, 40, II, 10.

[18] It is this doctrine of justification that is enshrined in the *Augsburg Confession* (1530), Art. 4; *Belgic Confession* (1561), Articles 22–23; *Heidelberg Catechism* (1563), Ques. 60; and *Westminster Confession of Faith* (1647), Chap. II. [Clark's text.]

longer considered to be a medicinal substance with which we are infused for transformation and eventual justification, but a way of describing God's unmerited favor (*favor Dei*) toward sinners. It is these truths that we uphold in the slogan: by grace alone, through faith alone, in Christ alone.[19]

B. The Proper Distinction Between Law and Gospel

Justification by grace through faith means that no works-based or law-based understanding of salvation can be tolerated. From this follows, in Luther's theology, a clear distinction between the functions of the saving gospel and those of law (including canon law). In his great New Year's sermon of 1532, on Galatians 3:24–25, Luther declared:

> The difference between the Law and the Gospel is the height of knowledge in Christendom. Every person and all persons who assume or glory in the name of Christ should know and be able to state this difference....
>
> To be sure, both are God's Word: the Law, or the Ten Commandments, and the Gospel; the latter first given by God in Paradise, the former on Mount Sinai. But everything depends on the proper differentiation of these two messages and on not mixing them together....
>
> Therefore place the man who is able nicely to distinguish the Law from the Gospel at the head of the list and call him a Doctor of Holy Scripture, for without the Holy Spirit the attainment of this ability to differentiate is impossible....
>
> By "Law" we should understand nothing but God's Word and command by which He tells us what we are to do and not to do and demands our obedience or work....
>
> The Gospel is such a doctrine or Word of God as does not demand our works or command us to do anything but bids us simply receive the offered grace of the forgiveness of sins and eternal salvation and be satisfied to have it given to us as a free gift.[20]

[19.] R. Scott Clark, "Regensburg and Regensburg II: Trying to Reconcile Irreconcilable Differences on Justification," 7/5 *Modern Reformation* 6 (September–October 1998) (italics his).

[20.] *Weimarer Ausgabe*, 36, 25, 29–31.

In what has been regarded as the most important Lutheran theological treatise ever produced in America, C.F.W. Walther's *The Proper Distinction between Law and Gospel*, the implications of this doctrine are set forth in a series of twenty-five theses. Here are seven of them:

> The first manner of confounding Law and Gospel is the one most easily recognized—and the grossest. It is adopted, for instance, by Papists, Socinians, and Rationalists and consists in this, that Christ is represented as a new Moses, or Lawgiver, and the Gospel turned into a doctrine of meritorious works. ...
>
> The Word of God is not rightly divided when sinners who have been struck down and terrified by the Law are directed, not to the Word and the Sacraments, but to their own prayers and wrestlings with God in order that they may win their way into a state of grace; in other words, when they are told to keep on praying and struggling until they feel that God has received them into grace.
>
> The Word of God is not rightly divided when the preacher represents contrition alongside of faith as a cause of the forgiveness of sin.
>
> The Word of God is not rightly divided when faith is required as a condition of justification and salvation, as if a person were righteous in the sight of God and saved, not only by faith, but also on account of his faith, for the sake of his faith, and in view of his faith.
>
> The Word of God is not rightly divided when the preacher tries to make people believe that they are truly converted as soon as they have become rid of certain vices and engage in certain works of piety and virtuous practises.
>
> The Word of God is not rightly divided when a person's salvation is made to depend on his association with the visible orthodox Church and when salvation is denied to every person who errs in any article of faith.
>
> The Word of God is not rightly divided when the person teaching it does not allow the Gospel to have a general predominance in his teaching.[21]

[21.] C. F. W. Walther, *The Proper Distinction between Law and Gospel*, ed. and trans. W. H. T. Dau (St. Louis: Concordia, 1928), Theses 5, 9, 12, 14, 16, 20, 25.

Luther's opposition to the corpus of canon law stemmed in large part from the fact that it "turned the gospel into a doctrine of meritorious works"; encouraged the faithful to "win their way into a state of grace" by following the penitential system; focused attention on "contrition" as a work satisfying to God; redefined biblical faith as another kind of good work; substituted "works of piety and virtuous practices" for trust in the unmerited work of Christ; made conformity with church rules the test of true Christian belief; and, in general, moved the gospel to the wings while placing legal requirements at stage center.[22]

C. The Three "Uses" of the Law

The medieval theologians had distinguished three uses or functions of the Law, and the Protestant Reformers and dogmaticians retained the classification. As Stump writes,

> The Law has three uses, the Political, the Elenchtico-pedagogical, and the Didactic. By the Political use is meant the use of the Law as a curb to hold in check wicked men, and to protect society against their aggressions. By the Elenchtico-pedagogical use is meant its use to convict men of sin and thus indirectly to lead them to Christ (Gal. 3:24). This use of the Law refers primarily to the unconverted. But there is an Elenchtico-pedagogical use of the Law even for the regenerate, inasmuch as the Christian's life should be a daily repentance, and the law enables him to see his daily shortcomings and his need of Christ more and more clearly. The Didactic use of the Law is its use as a guide for the Christian mind and conduct.[23]

But Luther and his followers insisted that in none of its functions could the Law save (*lex semper accusat*, "law always condemns"), and that the most important of the three uses is the pedagogical, in which the Law serves as a *paidagogos* to lead us to Christ. The Law shows how far short people fall in relation to God's perfect standards, thus driving them to the cross and Christ's mercy, much as the

---

[22.] Cf. Timothy J. Wengert, *Law and Gospel: Philip Melanchthon's Debate with John Agricola of Eisleben over "Poenitentia"* (Carlisle, U.K.: Paternoster, 1997).

[23.] Joseph Stump, *The Christian Faith* (Philadelphia: Muhlenberg, 1942), pp. 309–10. See also John Warwick Montgomery, *Law and Gospel: A Study Integrating Faith and Practice*, 2d ed. (Edmonton: Canadian Institute for Law, Theology and Public Policy, 1994), chapters 1–4.

Greek *paidagogos*/slave took the child to his teacher (Gal. 3).[24] The Law cannot itself impart salvation; it can only bring a sinner to the One who alone saves. For Luther, the *corpus juris canonici* was doing anything but that, and so it had to be removed from the ongoing life of the church.

D. The Two Kingdoms

Luther dramatically expressed this doctrine in his image of the two hands of God. The earthly kingdom, or God's left hand, refers to the creative structures *(Schöpfungsordnungen)* operative in political, economic, familial, cultural, and religious institutions.[25] These structures are God's work, to keep fallen mankind from anarchical and sinful self-destruction. But they do not save. At best, while preserving society and making life more livable, they can (in terms of the pedagogical use of the Law) reveal one's shortcomings and point one to Christ. Only God's right hand, the heavenly kingdom, is the true sphere of salvation, and it functions by grace and not by law. For Luther, the papal church of his day had lost its bearings, and the *corpus juris canonici* had allowed and encouraged the heavenly dimension of the visible church to be swallowed up by earthly considerations.

The two-kingdoms doctrine—note well—insists that the church is itself an "order" and thus functions, like the state or the family, as an element in the earthly kingdom; it thus cannot avoid having some kind of organizational structure and legal framework. Luther was by no means a Rudolf Sohm, arguing that the Law and the Church are fundamentally incompatible.[26] The work of

---

[24.] For John Calvin, the third use of the Law was the most important—a reflection, doubtless, of his particular stress on Old Testament Law and God's sovereignty. See John Warwick Montgomery, *Crisis in Lutheran Theology*, rev. ed. (Minneapolis: Bethany, 1973), 1:124–27.

[25.] Cf. Emil Brunner, *The Divine Imperative*, trans. Olive Wyon (Philadelphia: Westminster, 1947), Book 3; John Warwick Montgomery, *The Shape of the Past*, rev. ed. (Minneapolis: Bethany, 1975), pp. 358–74; and idem, *Human Rights and Human Dignity*, rev. ed. (Edmonton: Canadian Institute for Law, Theology and Public Policy, 1995), pp. 198 ff.

[26.] Rudolf Sohm, *Kirchenrecht*, 2 vols. (Munich: Duncker and Humbolt, 1892); and idem, *Das altkatholische Kirchenrecht und das Dekret Gratians* (Leipzig: Duncker and Humbolt, 1918).

68   Chapter 3

Luther's associates—Bugenhagen in northern Germany and Scandinavia, and Melanchthon in central and southern Germany—to establish extensive legal structures for the fledgling territorial churches that went over to the Reformation is sufficient proof of that.[27] But what Luther would not tolerate was a transformation of the church from a biblically centered agency for the proclamation of free grace and unmerited salvation in Christ into a legal structure functioning largely for its own benefit[28] and operating from top to bottom by entrenched mechanisms of works and merit. Luther was not against law in general or canon law in particular, but he was diametrically opposed to the *misuse* of law—most especially where human souls were at stake.

IV. CONCLUDING OBSERVATIONS

How Luther approached canon law is anything but an antiquarian matter. Here are three, among many, wider ecclesiastical and legal areas touched upon by the foregoing discussion.

A. The Nature of Anglican Theology and Canon Law

Traditionally, Anglicanism is seen through the prism of the Elizabethan settlement (a national church characterised by theological "comprehension") and the conflict between Calvinist low-churchmanship and Anglo-Catholic, Oxford-movement high-churchmanship—the broad, low, high spectrum. But Jacobs and Tjernagel have decisively shown that the earliest theological influence on the Anglican Church of the Reformation came directly from Witten-

---

[27] See A.L. Richter, ed., *Die evangelischen Kirchenordnungen des sechszehnten Jahrhunderts*, 2 vols. (Weimar: Verlag des Landes-Industriecomptoirs, 1846). Cf. also W. Maurer, "Reste des kanonischen Rechtes im Frühprotestantismus," *Zeitschrift der Savigny-Stiftung*, Kan. Abt. 51 (1965), pp. 190–253; and Jaroslav Pelikan, "Verius servamus canones," 11 *Studia Gratiana* 367–87 (1967).

[28] Cf. The famous statement of Pope Leo X (whose indulgence sales in collusion with Albrecht of Brandenburg precipitated the posting of the 95 Theses and who issued the bull of excommunication against Luther): "God has given us the papacy: let us enjoy it while we live."

berg.[29] That being so, might Anglicans not benefit from a closer study of the distinctive approach to law and gospel characteristic of Luther's theology, together with a careful examination of the great sixteenth- and seventeenth-century Lutheran productions in the area of Protestant church law?[30]

B. The Conjunction/Disjunction of Medieval and Post-Reformation English Canon Law

Over against the classic Stubbs-Maitland debate, Richard Helmholz has argued for an essential continuity of pre- and post-Reformation English canon law, claiming that the conflicts are more apparent than real and can be satisfactorily explained by permissible regional and local variations within the canonical rules and practices themselves.[31] Without denying that such variations did in fact exist, early Lutheran theology, which heavily impacted the English scene in the first half of the sixteenth century, delivered a crushing blow to the medieval canonical synthesis. Might it not be the case that, whereas in relatively routine and minor matters, regional differences did indeed allow for conservatism and continuity, the Reformation perspective could not simply rely on the canonical past where critical, central, salvific issues were at stake? Here, genuine discontinuity was inevitable.

[29.] Henry E. Jacobs, *The Lutheran Movement in England during the Reigns of Henry VIII and Edward VI* (Philadelphia: G. W. Frederick, 1890); and N.S. Tjernagel, *Henry VIII and the Lutherans* (St. Louis: Concordia, 1965).

[30.] For example, J.H. Boehmer, *Jus ecclesiasticum Protestantium*, 6 vols. (1714). It is sad to read in the autobiography of F.R. Barry, Bishop of Southwell during World War II, the consequences of his ordaining two refugee German Lutheran pastors to fill gaps in his diocese because of the war service of his clergy: though they preached the "pure word" of God, it was "totally incomprehensible to a middlebrow English congregation and no parish could stand it for very long at a time" (F. R. Barry, *Period of My Life* [London: Hodder and Stoughton, 1970], p. 151).

[31.] Richard H. Helmholz, *Roman Canon Law in Reformation England* (Cambridge: Cambridge University Press, 1990); and idem, *The Spirit of the Classical Canon Law* (Athens, GA: University of Georgia Press, 1997).

C. The "Formal Principle" of All Theology

Help at this point may come from Hart's insistence that a true revolution in legal thought occurs only when the system's fundamental "rule of recognition" changes: the rule by which one judges what should and what should not be part of the system itself.[32] Many "primary" (i.e., ordinary, substantive) canonical rules in Hart's sense of the term may not have changed much after the Reformation, but, for Reformers in Luther's wake, the "secondary" rule of recognition had certainly changed: canon law was no longer justified because of its approval by pope or council. In England, legitimation now had to come from the sovereign in Parliament.

As for Luther himself, taking his historic stand before Charles V at Worms—and for evangelical Protestantism in general from that day to this—the matter of authority could be stated very simply: "Unless I am convinced by the testimonies of the Holy Scriptures or evident reason (for I believe in neither the Pope nor councils alone, since it has been established that they have often erred and contradicted themselves), I am bound by the Scriptures that I have adduced, and my conscience has been taken captive by the Word of God; and I am neither able nor willing to recant, since it is neither safe nor right to act against conscience. God help me. Amen."[33]

---

[32] H. L. A. Hart, *The Concept of Law* (Oxford: Clarendon, 1961), chapters 5–6. Cf. John Warwick Montgomery, "Why a Christian Philosophy of Law?" in *Christian Perspectives on Human Rights and Legal Philosophy*, ed. Paul R. Beaumont (Carlisle, U.K.: Paternoster, 1998), p. 80.

[33] *Weimarer Ausgabe*, 7, 836–38. See Gordon Rupp's excellent treatment of this event in his *Luther's Progress to the Diet of Worms*, 2d ed. (New York: Harper Torchbooks, 1964), pp. 96–99.

CHAPTER 4

SUBSIDIARITY AS A JURISPRUDENTIAL AND CANONICAL THEORY

> La subsidiarité ressemble singulièrement *au sabre de Monsieur Prud'homme* qui, on le sait, devait servir "à défendre les Institutions et, au besoin, à les combattre."
> — J.-J. Kasel, *Luxemburger Wort*, 6 Mai 1999

The interaction of religion and law in Western society has been much neglected in modern secular and positivistic jurisprudence.[1] A striking contemporary illustration of that interaction is the doctrine of subsidiarity, enshrined in European Community law by Article 3b EC and "originat[ing] in Catholic social doctrine, having been authoratively laid down in the Papal Encyclicals *Quadragesimo Anno* in 1931 and *Pacem in Terris* in 1963."[2]

Subsidiarity theory is of particular interest because of its controversial nature. In both theology and law it has elicited strong reactions, to say the least. In a 1986 *Concilium* article, Peter Huizing took to task the final report (1985) of the Extraordinary Synod of Bishops questioning the proper applicability of the principle to Roman Catholic church life; according to Huizing the Bishops' position was "in complete contradiction to the text of Pius XII to which it refers."[3] At the New Europe Forum in Brussels in June of 1998, I was amused

---

[1] Montgomery, *Law & Morality: Friends or Foes? An Inaugural Lecture* (Luton: University of Luton, 1994). Cf. Troplong, *De l'influence du Christianisme sur le droit civil des Romains* (Paris: Charles Hingray, 1843).

[2] Kapteyn and VerLoren van Themaat, *Introduction to the Law of the European Communities from Maastricht to Amsterdam*, ed. Gormley (3d ed., incorporating the 5th Dutch ed.; The Hague: Kluwer, 1998), p. 135.

[3] Huizing, "Subsidiarity," 188 *Concilium* (1986), 118. Huizing italicises the quoted judgment for emphasis.

to hear a Christian civil servant in the office of the European Commission speak of subsidiarity in almost the reverential terms one is accustomed to use in citing Holy Scripture. On the other hand, fellow barrister friends at Lincoln's Inn, including serious Christian believers, have had nothing good whatever to say about the impact of the doctrine on European Community relationships.

It would appear, therefore, that no justification is required to examine closely the subsidiarity concept with a view to evaluating its inherent value (or dysvalue).[4] We shall begin with an attempt to determine precisely what subsidiarity means, legally and theologically, and then proceed to a critique of it.

I. WHAT IS SUBSIDIARITY?

As defined by Pope Pius XI in *Quadragesimo Anno* (15 May 1931), subsidiarity means that "all the activity of the community is by virtue of its being and conception subsidiary. It has the task of supporting the members of the community, but should not annihilate or swallow it up." More explicitly: "Let the public authority leave to the lower groupings the care of lesser matters where it would expend an inordinate effort. It will thus be able to carry out more freely and more effectively those functions which belong only to it because it alone can perform them."

[4.] The literature of the subject is very extensive. On the *legal* side, the following publications are highly recommended: Wilke and Wallace, *Subsidiarity: Approaches to Power Sharing in the European Community* ("Discussion Paper No. 27"; London: Chatham House, 1990); Adonis and Tyrie, *Subsidiarity* (London: IEA, 1990); *Proceedings of the Jacques Delors Colloquium, 1991: Subsidiarity* (Maastricht, 1991); Emiliou, "Subsidiarity: An Effective Barrier Against 'the Enterprises of Ambition'?," 17/5 *European L. Rev.* (1992), 383-407; Duff (ed.), *Subsidiarity Within the European Community* (London: Federal Trust, 1993); Begg et al., *Making Sense of Subsidiarity: How Much Centralisation for Europe?* (London: CEPR, 1993); Pescatore, in Due et al. (eds.), *Festschrift für Ulrich Everling* (Baden-Baden, 1995), II, 1071. Important *theological* references include: Bertrams, "De principio subsidiarietatis in iure canonico," 46 *Periodica de re morali* (1957), 13-65; Kaiser, "Das Prinzip der Subsidiarität in der Verfassung der Kirche," 133 *Archiv für Katholisches Kirchenrecht* (1964), 3-13; "De principio subsidiarietatis in iure canonico," *Acta conventus internationalis Canonistarum Romae diebus 20-25 maii 1968 celebrati* (Vatican, 1970), pp. 297-306; Metz, "La subsidiarité, principe régulateur des tensions dans l'Eglise," 22 *Revue de droit canonique* (1972), 155-76.

Following the Second Vatican Council, the First Universal Assembly of the Synod of Bishops was convened (1967) and considered the principle of subsidiarity in conjunction with the establishing of basic principles for the revision of the Code of Canon Law. The practical effect of subsidiarity is seen, *inter alia*, in the fact that diocesan bishops "obtained the authority to exempt believers for whom they had direct care in exceptional cases from having to observe the universal law of the Church, if they regarded that as something that was in the interest of their spiritual well-being."[5] Principle 5 allowed universal norms to be "adapted to local needs by local procedures."[6] In the revised Code of Canon Law of 1983, owing to the employment of the subsidiarity principle, "local churches, dioceses, parishes and religious communities are no longer seen as administrative parts of one single world Church, but rather as independent subjects of the Church's life and law and as communities in which and from which the one Church exists."[7]

European Community law (Art. 3b EC) understands the subsidiarity concept in the following terms: "In areas which do not fall within its exclusive competence, the Community shall take action, in accordance with the principle of subsidiarity, only if and in so far as the objectives of the proposed action cannot be sufficiently achieved by the Member States and can therefore, by reason of the scale or effects of the proposed action, be better achieved by the Community."[8] The principle has been reinforced by way of the Interinstitutional Declaration of 25 October 1993 on democracy, transparency, and subsidiarity,[9] and the annexed Interinstitutional Agreement on procedures for implementing the principle of sub-

---

[5] Huizing, *op. cit.*, p. 119.
[6] *Ibid.*, p. 120.
[7] *Ibid.*
[8] Subsidiarity is specifically reflected in such provisions of the EC Treaty as Arts. 118a, 126-129b, 130, and 130g. An excellent legal commentary on Art. 3b EC is provided in Hunnings (ed.), *Encyclopedia of European Law* (London: Sweet & Maxwell, 1998), I, Const. Texts R.3: August 1996, sec. 12.0120A - 12.0132A.
[9] Bull. EU 10-1993, point 2.2.1: approved by the European Parliament, *Official Journal* (1993), C329/132, draft C 329/133.

sidiarity.[10] Community agricultural law provides a concrete illustration of the potential impact of subsidiarity in practice:

> Community agricultural law contributes, albeit negatively, to the possible or impossible operationalization of the principle of subsidiarity. It may be recalled that a policy of price intervention leads by its very nature to a far-reaching centralization of legislation at the highest level.... Seen in this light, the 'U-turn' from price intervention to direct income support is of major importance, given that the unity of the common market in the long term cannot be maintained by price intervention alone. The CAP thus demonstrates that the centralization of legislation is a result of the chosen model of market intervention, which in its turn finds its essential justification in the need to maintain the free movement of goods. A policy of direct income support and structural policy instruments, based on regional differences, involves far greater possibilities for the Member States to apply Community legislation, within certain limits, and supplement it having regard to their own specific circumstances.[11]

From the foregoing discussion, it should be evident that both in theological and in legal contexts subsidiarity entails in principle (whatever may be the case in practice) the notion that in any organisation or communal structure higher levels are to concede to lower levels, and that "the decision-making process be carried out as close to the citizen as is viable."[12] Ideally, subsidiarity should work in behalf of greater democratisation and a greater sensitivity on the part of central authority to the needs and competences of those at grassroots level.

II. SUBSIDIARITY CRITIQUED JURISPRUDENTIALLY

But does the subsidiarity concept really carry the legal weight attributed to it by its advocates? Specialists in European Community law have been deeply troubled by the deficiencies and the inherent ambiguities seemingly built into the very notion of subsidiarity.

[10.] Bull. EU 10-1993, point 2.2.2: approved by the European Parliament, *Official Journal* (1993), C331/132, draft C 329/133.
[11.] Kapteyn and VerLoren van Themaat, *op. cit.*, pp. 1168-69.
[12.] Hunnings, *op. cit.*, sec. 12.0120A.

Legal historians have observed that before World War II the principle of subsidiarity was employed in corporatist State structures (Italy and Portugal, for example) to strengthen and justify the actions of the central authority vis-à-vis the society at large; and that "experience in Germany and in the United States shows that it [subsidiarity] does not hinder the gradual strengthening of central authority."[13] Subsidiarity, in other words, is no insurance policy against the growth of centralised authority, since it does not define what specific functions of a society are in fact best carried out at lower, rather than higher, levels.

Weatherill regards subsidiarity as "a question rather than an answer" and sees its value as having "stimulated a more intense, thoughtful examination of how the evolving European market should be regulated."[14] The problem is that the principle does not appear to provide the needed answer to the vital question of how to interrelate the levels of a hierarchical structure.

The Encyclopedia of European Law opines that

> It is unlikely to be in the judicial application of nebulous tests of efficiency and necessity that the principle of subsidiarity will prove its worth. In the political sphere it may make the Commission more restrained in the measures it proposes and the Council more cautious in the measures it adopts. Subsidiarity depends for its political effectiveness on its acceptance into the "institutional culture" of the Community.[15]

Kapteyn and VerLoren van Themaat make the point even more strongly: "It must be concluded that the principle of subsidiarity as such is neither a useful new legal guarantee against an unreasoned expansion of Community competences, nor an acceptable point of departure, with all the possible practical consequences, for all politicians."[16]

[13.] Kapteyn and VerLoren van Themaat, *op. cit.*, p. 135. See also Kapteyn, in Hellingman (ed.), *Europa in de steigers: van Gemeenschap tot Unie* (Deventer, 1993), pp. 41-44.

[14.] Weatherill, *Law and Integration in the European Union* (Oxford, 1995), pp. 172-73.

[15.] Hunnings, *op. cit.*, sec. 12.0120N. See also Beaumont and Moir, *The European Communities (Amendment) Act 1993* (London: Sweet & Maxwell, 1994), p. 45.

[16.] Kapteyn and VerLoren van Themaat, *op. cit.*, p. 136.

As is well known, the inclusion of subsidiarity in European Community law was "particularly championed by the U.K. which tends to perceive it as a means of renationalising, and reclaiming competences currently exercised by the Community."[17] Less well known is the fact that the public-relations use of the concept was an important factor in the very narrow "yes" vote in the second Danish plebiscite on that country's ratification of the Maastricht Treaty.[18] Ironically, however, the principle does not guarantee any particular division of powers between Member States and the Community: "it can be invoked as a justification of Community action, but also in opposition to it."[19]

Some analysts of subsidiarity have gone much further in their negative evaluation of the theory. Lord Mackenzie Stuart has referred to the definition of subsidiarity in the EC Treaty as a "rich and prime example of gobbledygook."[20] In his classic and frequently cited scholarly analysis of subsidiarity, Mackenzie Stuart likens it to a "busted flush" in poker and concludes that even at best it is little more than "a prophylactic against the contagion of Brussels"—a "political maxim, not a legal one."[21]

III. SUBSIDIARITY AS A THEOLOGICAL CONCEPT

If, as is the case, the politico-legal employment of subsidiarity was preceded by and took its cue from the theological development of the concept, its true value or lack of it should be identifiable by theological analysis. Let us now turn to this fundamental aspect of the question.

---

[17] Hunnings, *op. cit.*, sec. 12.0120B.
[18] Cass, "The Word That Saves Maastricht? The Principle of Subsidiarity and the Division of Powers Within the European Community," 29 *Common Market L. Rev.* (1992), 1107.
[19] Kapteyn and VerLoren van Themaat, *op. cit.*, p. 139.
[20] Letter-to-the-Editor, *The Independent*, 15 June 1992.
[21] Mackenzie Stuart, "Subsidiarity: A Busted Flush?," in *Constitutional Adjudication in European Community and National Law*, ed. Curtin and O'Keeffe (Dublin, 1992), pp. 19-23.

When Pope Pius XII spoke of subsidiarity to the new members of the College of Cardinals in conjunction with the College's internationalisation (20 February 1946), he based his justification of subsidiarity squarely on the Pauline teaching of the "diversity of gifts" in Ephesians 4:11-16 and I Corinthians 12. But do these passages in fact set forth the principle that "the decision-making process be carried out as close to the citizen as is viable"?[22]

The problem here is not that posed by Roman Catholic traditionalist Jean Hamer, who argues that the Universal Church must not be reduced theologically to a subsidiary position.[23] The difficulty is much more basic than that, for it stems from inadequate exegesis of the key biblical texts.

One must be particularly careful in interpreting the Pauline "diversity of gifts" passages. Poor exegesis of these texts has led to some of the gross theological errors of the contemporary charismatic movement (the so-called "Toronto blessing," etc.). What precisely is the Apostle teaching in Ephesians 4 and I Corinthians 12? Not the necessity of a charismatic "second blessing" or the requirement to experience miraculous "gifts of the Spirit" such as "speaking in tongues"—nor the modern doctrine of subsidiarity.

These texts present the analogy of the church as a "body," with her members performing their particular God-given functions and not insisting that they instead carry out functions more appropriate to other members of the same body. ("The eye cannot say unto the hand, I have no need of thee: nor again the head to the feet, I have no need of you....") But nowhere is a hierarchy of levels set forth or a summons given to subordinate higher-level functions to lower-level activity. The purpose of these New Testament passages is not to advocate or encourage democracy in the church (or, for that matter, to discourage it): it is to exhort believers to discover their particular gifts so as to maximise the effective preaching of the gospel

---

[22.] See above, our text at note 12.

[23.] Huizing, *op. cit.*, pp. 121-22. Huizing is quite right, in the context of the centralist, hierarchical, authoritarian Roman Catholic Church, to criticise Hamer and the conservative Bishops for not seeing how very much their church body needs the democratisation suggested by the Papal use of the concept of subsidiarity.

and thus to carry out the prime purpose of the Church Militant (Matthew 28: 18-20 and parallel passages).[24] No mandatory church order (democratic or hierarchical) is taught in the "diversity of gifts" passages, and thus no subsidiarity doctrine in the modern sense can be found there.

The problem with subsidiarity is that it *does* in a sense establish a mandatory structural order: one in which centralised or higher authority always has the burden of proof in justifying its actions. If that burden is not discharged, action automatically devolves upon the lower levels of the system.

But, logically (and Scripture is evidently aware of this in that it refuses to baptise an "episcopal," "presbyterian," "congregational," or any other particular form of church order),[25] decisions should be made on *whatever* level they can be made most efficiently, without any built-in preference for "lower" or "higher." The issue is not which hierarchical level is more fundamental and therefore preferable as a locus for decision-making, but the achieving of maximum efficiency in carrying out the overarching purpose of the organisation or society.

In the church, it simply is not the case that decisions should be taken centrally only if they cannot be taken locally. In the 19th century, missions to China were left largely to the personal "calling" of individual missionaries (Hudson Taylor, the "Cambridge Seven"), rather than taken on as a central task of the church. Result: sporadic and mediocre impact on the most populous country in the world, which today is controlled by Marxist ideologues, unopposed, for the most part, by a docile, non-Christian population.[26] Efficient missionary work *can* be performed by individuals, but, in order to "preach the gospel to every creature," centralised organisation,

---

[24.] Cf. Montgomery, *Damned Through the Church* (Minneapolis: Bethany, 1970).

[25.] Cf. *Augsburg Confession*, Art. VII: "It is not necessary that the ceremonies or other human observances should be everywhere alike." See also Cranfield, Kilgour, and Montgomery, *Christians in the Public Square: Law, Gospel & Public Policy* (Edmonton, Alberta, Canada: Canadian Institute for Law, Theology & Public Policy, 1996).

[26.] Montgomery, *Giant in Chains: China Today and Tomorrow* (Milton Keynes, England: Nelson Word, 1994).

planning, and direction are vital—and such "centralism" does not need to justify itself by subsidiarity reasoning.

The same point applies in the secular realm. (Here, likewise, Scripture does not mandate a particular political form for the state—monarchial, oligarchic, democratic, etc.) *Can* railways be operated privately and locally? Certainly: this was the case in most countries during the first century of their existence. *Ought* railways not be centralised, owing to a subsidiarity belief that they should be kept close to the grassroots level? A comparison of the efficient, well-funded, well-managed SNCF in France over against today's miserable British rail "system" of private ownership should answer that. Jacksonian democracy, in which everything needs to be decided by referendum at grassroots level, is almost as bad politically as dictatorial centralism in which (as in certain former Marxist countries of the Eastern bloc) toothpaste was overproduced by bureaucratic fiat while toothbrushes were in short supply. Neither centralisation nor decentralisation is a positive value in itself: the choice will depend in each individual instance on the purpose of the decision in relation to the overall goals of the society.

The influential economist Tinbergen saw this clearly, and offers a far more realistic approach than does subsidiarity doctrine. Tinbergen argues that "the fundamental problem of qualitative economic policy is to find the 'optimum order,' that is, a set of institutions which maximises national or social well-being."[27] This will mean ideally that when social decision-making affects third parties or has external effects in general, these decisions will be taken at a sufficiently high level that the external effects outside the sphere of legal competence of the decision-makers can be neglected. Decision-making will not automatically be set at a low level or at a high level: it will be at the level of "optimum order" in terms of "social well-being."

The Papal development of subsidiarity is the product of a theological failing by no means limited to Roman Catholics: that of

---

[27.] Tinbergen, *International Economic Integration* (2d ed.; Amsterdam, 1965), p. 58. See also Tinbergen, *et al., Reshaping the International Order: A Report to the Club of Rome* (New York, 1976), especially p. 86.

basing a teaching on single passages of Scripture taken out of context and without regard to the totality of biblical teaching ("the whole counsel of God").[28] The Bible informs us, from cover to cover, that "all have sinned and come short of the glory of God" (Romans 3:23): sin cannot be restricted to any subgroup of the human race or to any one party or level of human society. Neither central government nor local government, neither corporate nor individual activity, is exempted from the radical self-centredness afflicting a fallen race. It follows that to require central authority to justify its decisions—to carry the burden of proof in decision-making—and to exempt the grassroots from that same obligation is grossly to misunderstand the human condition.

Subsidiarity tacitly assumes that the centrist, higher levels are more tainted with original sin than the democratic, lower levels. Not so. Every societal level must equally justify its actions in terms of the greater societal good, and none is in a pre-set subsidiarity relationship vis-à-vis the other. No societal level is holier than another, but, *Deo gratias*, the Holy Spirit of God still "moves where He will," convicting the world "of sin and of righteousness and of judgment"; and "where sin abounds, grace doth much more abound: that as sin hath reigned unto death, even so might grace reign through righteousness unto eternal life by Jesus Christ our Lord."[29]

---

[28] Acts 20:27; cf. Matthew 4:4 (parallel: Luke 4:4) and the Reformation hermeneutic principle of the "Analogy of Faith."
[29] John 3:8, 16:7-11; Romans 5:20-21.

CHAPTER 5

JUSTICE DENIED: CHURCH PROPERTY DISPUTES UNDER CURRENT AMERICAN LAW

Summary: This essay deals with a particular kind of ecclesiastical property dispute: that in which one party claims that those now in control of the property have deviated from the original theological principles of the church or religious organisation and that in consequence title to the property should now vest in those who do in fact represent that original position. It is the author's contention, based on both personal experience and jurisprudential analysis, that current American law makes virtually impossible successful legal recourse in such cases.

I. THE ENGLISH POSITION

As background for understanding today's American law in this area, it is important to compare and contrast the English approach to church property disputes involving questions of theological deviation.

In *Attorney-General v Pearson* (1817 and 1835), a Presbyterian meeting house had come under the control of Unitarians, whereupon a bill was brought by those still believing in the Holy Trinity to quiet title and appoint new trustees. The Court of Chancery ultimately concluded that the original founders of the Presbyterian charity "never could have meant that that particular doctrine [the denial of the Trinity] should be taught in this chapel as part of the worship and service of God" and declared that the decree "ought to be so framed as to exclude those particular doctrines which the information complains of from being preached in the chapel," the

Unitarian believers being prohibited from serving as trustees.[1] The Chancellor's rationale is worth quoting:

> If any persons seeking the benefit of a trust for charitable purposes should incline to the adoption of a different system from that which was intended by the original donors and founders; and if others of those who are interested think proper to adhere to the original system, the leaning of the Court must be to support those adhering to the original system, and not to sacrifice the original system to any change of sentiment in the persons seeking alteration, however commendable that proposed alteration may be.[2]

Pearson served as precedent in a closely related case, that of *Attorney-General v Shore* (1836). Here, Lady Hewley, a Presbyterian, founded a charity for the benefit of "poor and godly preachers of Christ's Holy Gospel." The charity came under Unitarian influence, and the Chancellor ruled that Lady Hewley "never intended that her bounty should be applied for the purpose of promoting or encouraging the preaching of Unitarian doctrines." In consequence, the Unitarian trustees were removed—so as "to give effect to the intent of the founder."[3]

The leading case to establish what would come to be known as the "implied trust" doctrine in English church property disputes is *Craigdallie v Aikman* (1820). A Scottish dissenting group (the "Associate Synod of Burgher Seceders") bought land and built a chapel thereon, but later split in a doctrinal dispute; the issue before the Court was the proper ownership of the property. After prolonged litigation, the Court of Session refused to turn the chapel over to the splinter group, since the judges could not find any discernible difference between the views of the protagonists (a not uncommon phenomenon among the "Wee Frees," perhaps?). The House of Lords affirmed in these words:

> When this matter was formerly before the House, we acted upon this principle, that if we could find out what were the religious principles of those who originally attended the chapel, we

---

[1] 58 Eng. Rep. 848, 855 (V.C. 1835); *cf.* 36 Eng. Rep. 135 (Ch. 1817).
[2] 36 Eng. Rep. at 157.
[3] 58 Eng. Rep. 855-58 (Ch. 1836). For the appeal to the House of Lords, see *Shore v Wilson*, 8 Eng. Rep. 450 (H.L. 1842).

should hold the building appropriated to the use of persons who adhere to the same religious principles.... And supposing that there is a division of religious opinions in the persons at present wishing to enjoy this building, the question then would be, which of them adhered to the opinions of those who had built the place of worship, and which of them differed from those opinions? Those who still adhered to those religious principles being more properly to be considered as the *cestui que* trusts of those who held this place of worship in trust, than those who have departed altogether from the religious principles of those who founded this place, if I may so express it.[4]

The essence of the English approach, as set forth in these classic cases and in the modern cases following them, is that when a religious organisation obtains property an "implied trust" is created that the property shall be used for the purposes represented by that organisation. If a dispute arises between those holding to the original purpose and those no longer doing so, the Court will declare that title rests with those still maintaining the original position. Any other decision would vitiate the trust implied in the obtention of the property in the first place. The Court's function is not to establish "true" or "proper" religious doctrine; it merely determines factually and by the construction of the religious body's own affirmations of belief what constitutes its teaching. Having done that, it compares the original teaching with the positions of the protagonists and rules for that party consistently upholding the beliefs of the founders.

II. THE AMERICAN APPROACH

1. *A Personal Illustration.* My special interest in this topic arises from my experience as an expert theological witness in an American trial dealing with precisely the stated issue. On 9 January 1969, in the Court of Common Pleas of McKean County, Pennsylvania, began the trial of *Eire Conference Central Office, the United Methodist Church v Sawyer Evangelical United Brethren Church*.[5] The Sawyer Church had been a member of the pietistic Evangelical United

[4.] 4 Eng. Rep. 435, 439-40 (H.L. 1820).
[5.] No. 1, December Term 1968 (in Equity).

84   Chapter 5

Brethren denomination which, a few years prior to the trial, had voted itself into the large, hopelessly liberal and broad-church United Methodist denomination. Sawyer objected strenuously to this merger, claiming that it compromised the evangelical character of the United Brethren and violated the commitments of those who founded their local congregation. They then endeavoured to establish themselves as an independent congregation and to retain their church property. The Eire Conference of the United Methodists reacted with a lawsuit to recover the property for the new, merged denomination.

My extended testimony had as its purpose to show that in fact the United Methodists no longer maintained, in theory or in practice, the evangelical beliefs which had been characteristic of the Sawyer Church and that the EUB-Methodist merger had thus constituted for the congregation a fundamental deviation from its original trust purposes. The material I presented was most embarrassing to the United Methodist leadership and received much publicity locally and nationally, but Sawyer lost the case. Why? On two counts: first, the denomination of which it had been a part had in fact voted itself into the United Methodist Church (a fact not to be contested—perhaps analogous to Austria's having entered the Third Reich by referendum?); and secondly—more to the point for our present discussion—because to rule on doctrinal issues would have forced the judge (said he) to violate the First Amendment of the Federal Constitution by entangling the state in purely religious questions.[6]

[6.] After losing its (heavily encumbered) property to the United Methodists, the Sawyer congregation then started from scratch with no debts and built a far larger and nicer church which grew rapidly, owing in large part to the cummunity's disgust with the United Methodist reliance on litigation and sympathy for the Sawyer congregation. In 1994, I was invited to the new facility as guest for the 25th anniversary of the refounding of the church. My remarks on that occasion included the following: "I believed then, and I believe now, that you could not have gone into the Methodist-EUB merger with integrity. You would have broken faith with those who founded the church and who gave their time and talents to your congregation since its origins. Losing physical facilities was trivial in comparison with retention of theological purity. What does it profit a congregation to gain the whole world of real property and lose its own soul? Like Mary (of Mary and Martha), you 'chose that good part which shall not be taken away' (Luke 10:42), and God has honoured your choice. You sought first the Kingdom of God and His righteousness, and all the rest has been added."

2. *The Earlier American Law.* But the judge's reasoning in the Sawyer case is a very recent development. Earlier, American courts followed to a considerable extent the English "implied trust" doctrine. Here are two illustrations from 19th century state court decisions:

> It is the duty of the court to decide in favour of those, whether a minority or majority of the congregation, who are adhering to the doctrine professed by the congregation, and the form of worship in practice, as also in favour of the government of the church in operation, with which it was connected at the time the trust was declared. *App v. Lutheran Congregation*, 6 Pa. 201, 210 (1847).

> The guarantee of religious freedom has nothing to do with the property. It does not guarantee freedom to steal churches. It secures to individuals the right of withdrawing, forming a new society, with such creed and government as they please, raising from their own means another fund and building another house of worship; but it does not confer upon them the right of taking the property consecrated to other uses by those who may now be sleeping in their graves. The law of intellectual and spiritual life is not the higher law, but must yield to the law of the land. *Schnorr's Appeal*, 67 Pa. 138, 147 (1870).

An important refinement of the "implied trust" doctrine was introduced in the U.S. Supreme Court case of *Watson v Jones* (1872).[7] Here the Court recognised that the "trust" could not properly be characterised without first determining the polity of the church in dispute. A distinction (which, in fact, can be found in some earlier state court decisions) was drawn between two major types of church polity: the *hierarchical*—where the local congregation is part of a structured church body with central authority, episcopal or synodical—and the *congregational*—where, as in Baptist churches, the local congregation is autonomous. The Court asserted that church splits in the hierarchical context would generally favour the retention of property by the faction remaining with the denomination (i.e., the denomination's own church law would prevail), whilst in the case of autonomous local congregations their own constitutions would be the determining factor in deciding who had

---

[7.] 13 Wall. 679 (1872).

title to the church property.[8] It has occasionally been argued that *Watson* sounded the death knell to the "implied trust" doctrine in American church property disputes; that this is hardly so is evidenced by *Bouldin v Alexander*—a U.S. Supreme Court case of the very next term—in which the Court expressly declared the legitimacy of enquiring into issues of doctrinal deviation: "In a congregational church, the majority, if they adhere to the organization and to the doctrines, represent the church. An expulsion of the majority by a minority is a void act."[9]

3. *The Law Changes.* It was precisely "implied trust" reasoning which was used by the Georgia Supreme Court in the 1969 case subsequently reversed by the U.S. Supreme Court, thereby creating the current American law on ecclesiastical property disputes.

Increasing theological liberalism in the Southern Presbyterian Church (the "Presbyterian Church in the United States"), which would later merge with the even more liberal Northern Presbyterians, resulted in a significant number of congregations withdrawing from the Southern Presbyterian Church and attempting to retain their church property. In spite of the admittedly hierarchical nature of the denomination—the Presbytery being the controlling unit of government—the Georgia Supreme Court ruled in favour of two dissenting congregations on the ground of the denomination's departure from doctrine and consequent violation of implied trusts. The Court found that the Southern Presbyterian

> General Assembly's declaration that foreordination was no longer necessary for Reformed theology was contrary to one of the basic tenets which has made Presbyterianism significantly different from other denominations. The General Assembly's endorsement of civil disobedience which would allow a citizen to decide whether or not he will obey the law, is a radical venture into civil affairs. It is absolute defiance of law and order, and is the road to anarchy. Also, the General Assembly's recommendation as to what steps should be taken to secure peace in Vietnam is an entry into diplomatic and

---

[8.] The polity issue entered into the Sawyer Church case, discussed above: since the United Methodist Church is a hierarchical (quasi-episcopal) body, the judge—himself a United Methodist!—deferred to the denominational claim to title.

[9.] 15 Wall. 131, 140 (1872).

military matters beyond the church's function as delineated by its Westminster Confession of Faith and Book of Church Order.[10]

This case went to the U.S. Supreme Court as *Presbyterian Church in the United States v Mary Elizabeth Blue Hull Memorial Presbyterian Church* (1969). There the highest tribunal in the land reversed and remanded on the ground that the Georgia decision violated the principle of the separation of church and state enshrined in the First Amendment to the Federal Constitution. The Court declared:

> The First Amendment severely circumscribes the role that civil courts may play in resolving church property disputes.... First Amendment values are plainly jeopardized when church property litigation is made to turn on the resolution by civil courts of controversies over religious doctrine and practice. If civil courts undertake to resolve such controversies in order to adjudicate the property dispute, the hazards are ever present of inhibiting the free development of religious doctrine and of implicating secular interests in matters of purely ecclesiastical concern. Because of these hazards, the First Amendment enjoins the employment of organs of government for essentially religious purposes, *Abington School Dist. v Schempp*, 374 U.S. 203 (1963); the Amendment therefore commands civil courts to decide church property disputes without resolving underlying controversies over religious doctrine.... The departure-from-doctrine element of the Georgia implied trust theory requires the civil court to determine matters at the very core of a religion— the interpretation of particular church doctrines and the importance of those doctrines to the religion. Plainly, the First Amendment forbids civil courts from playing such a role.[11]

Hull thus ended the employment of "implied trust" doctrine in American church property litigation—whatever the particular polity of the church in question.[12]

A later U.S. Supreme Court case, *Jones v Wolf* (1979), made clear that the civil courts could not simply absolve themselves of church property disputes. Such disputes could, and should, still be resolved, but only as long as "neutral principles of law" were em-

---

[10] 224 Ga. 61, 77 (1968).

[11] 393 U.S. 440, 449-50 (1969).

[12] To be sure, *express* religious and charitable trusts continue to be recognised by American courts—the trusts which Leeder discusses in the English context in her *Ecclesiastical Law Handbook* (London: Sweet & Maxwell, 1997), pp. 236-39.

ployed in achieving this. If, however, "in such a case the interpretation of the instruments of ownership would require the civil court to resolve a religious controversy, then the court must defer to the resolution of the doctrinal issue by the authoritative ecclesiastical body."[13] What, precisely, is meant by the "neutral principles of law" approach? Professor Oaks set forth three theories of its possible meaning, none of which seems particularly helpful: "nondetermination of religious law or polity"; "neutrality in religious decision making"; and "deference to church decisionmakers." Of one thing, however, he is sure: "After a century of influence in church property controversies, the fictional implied trust doctrine is dead."[14]

III. A CRITIQUE OF THE CURRENT AMERICAN LAW

Among influential American jurisprudents, the demise of the "implied trust" in church property litigation has been welcomed. Thus Professor Paul Kauper of the University of Michigan, in an extended treatment of the *Hull* case, opines:

> The power of a civil court to pass on the question whether a religious body is making substantial departures from the fundamental doctrines necessarily requires the court to identify and appraise both the fundamental doctrines and the substantiality of the alleged departures in order to decide which group in a divided congregation is entitled to control the property. Thus a civil court becomes the judge of religious doctrine. Moreover, by freezing the doctrine and usages on an implied trust basis, the civil courts by their decisions were placed in a position of obstructing further development of doctrinal positions or even of challenging new applications of established doctrine. Obviously, the application of the implied trust rule in connection with the departure-from-doctrine standard constituted a considerable intrusion by an organ of government into ecclesiastical affairs.... Freedom of affiliation is particularly important in this day of the ecumenical movement. The Supreme Court by its recent decision has facilitated the freedom of the churches to further this movement. Parishioners and ministers dissatisfied with

---

[13.] 443 U.S. 595, 604 (1979).
[14.] Dallin H. Oaks, *Trust Doctrines in Church Controversies* (Macon, Georgia: Mercer University Press, 1984), pp. 117-25.

the policies adopted and actions taken by churches at the national level and congregations at the local level, where such actions are taken in accordance with the organization's own internal law, may of course withdraw, but in doing so they forfeit their claim to use of the church's property.[15]

Two points deserve critical comment here. First, there is an unstated philosophical/theological bias in favour of ecumenical change at the expense of fidelity to an existing organisational commitment. Why should the labours and contributions of members of a religious organisation over the years—perhaps over generations—be diverted to other purposes in the interests of contemporary ecumenicity, particularly when the original contributors oppose such modifications of their theology and church practice? Does ecumenicity trump fidelity?

Secondly, Kauper is simply wrong that for a court to decide "departure-from-doctrine" questions it must necessarily place itself in the role of judging religious doctrine. In England, it has long been recognised that a civil court can determine the meaning of ecclesiastical documents—just as it can effectively construe other sorts of documents—without itself substantively creating or establishing the underlying doctrine. In the well-known and influential case of *Gorham v Bishop of Exeter* (1850), the Privy Council made this important distinction with considerable clarity:

> This Court, constituted for the purpose of advising Her Majesty in matters which come within its competency, has no jurisdiction or authority to settle matters of faith, or to determine what ought in any particular to be the doctrine of the Church of England. Its duty extends only to the consideration of that which is by law established to be the doctrine of the Church of England, upon the true and legal construction of her Articles and Formularies.[16]

Interestingly enough, one of the leading authorities on American church law roundly took the Supreme Court to task in this area.

---

[15] Paul G. Kauper, "Church Autonomy and the First Amendment: The Presbyterian Church Case," in *The Supreme Court Review 1969* (Chicago: University of Chicago, 1969), pp. 352, 377.

[16] Moore's Special Report 462 (P.C.). See Edmund F. Moore (ed.), *The Case of the Rev. G.C. Gorham Against the Bishop of Exeter* (London: Stevens and Norton, 1852), p. 472.

Focusing on the Court's judgment in the *Watson* case, to which reference has already been made, Carl Zollman wrote:

> A refusal by the courts in a proper case to construe the constitution, canons or rules of the church and revise its trials and the proceedings of its governing bodies, instead of preserving religious liberty, destroys it *pro tanto*. If a person who connects himself with a religious association is to be placed completely at its mercy irrespective of the agreement which he has made with it, the conception of religious liberty as applied to such a case becomes a farce, a delusion, and a snare. Such a conception opens the doors wide for the most odious form of religious tyranny.[17]

This argument can be made even more strongly. The 14th Amendment to the American Constitution provides a legal guarantee against unjust discrimination. But the moment religious believers wishing to keep church property from falling into the hands of those who have departed from the faith are unable to prevent the violation of their trust, they suffer a discriminatory disenfranchisement. If a rod and gun club is changed into a chess club by its administrators, members can go to court and prove that, according to the original purpose of the organisation, they have the right to recover the funds or property; in making their case, the members must prove that the administrators have violated the original intent of the organisation. But if church members go to court to recover property absorbed into a church union which has altered the doctrinal perspective of the original church body, they are not allowed to offer any theological evidence of the changes—thus being prevented from establishing their case. The upshot is that the members of secular organisations have their interests protected in such situations, but church members are left entirely vulnerable in the face of (for example) ecumenical unions of ecclesiastical bodies. This would appear to be a clear instance of the discriminatory removal of constitutional protection from churches and religious organisations, in defiance of the equal protection clause of the 14th Amendment.

---

[17] Carl Zollmann, *American Church Law* (St Paul, Minnesota: West Publishing, 1933), pp. 237-38.

How has this sad state of affairs come about? Clearly, it is due to the increasing pressure of a secular society. Courts are afraid to deal with religious questions for fear of offending diverse societal interests—even though the law is supposed to protect even minority interests fearlessly. A similar deprivation of protection can be seen in the area of American family law, where, as a result of secularisation and judicial loathing to have to deal with the messy causes of divorce, widespread "no fault" divorce legislation has been passed: in such jurisdictions, particularly in American community-property states, the "innocent" party to a divorce (i.e., the party not causing the breakup) cannot prevent an equal division of assets by showing the fault of the other party.[18]

Indeed, on the American scene, there is a powerful general tendency to "privatise"—to remove legal protections from—socially sensitive problem areas. An especially sad example is Ronald Dworkin's argument that abortion should be left to personal conscience and not legislated, since the abortion controversy represents competing philosophical-religious issues which would be better removed from the courts entirely. (In a public exchange with Dworkin, I pointed out that the same argument would have left slavery to the mercy of states-rights decision-making and prevented any federal legislation to stamp it out.)[19]

If we agree with Kauper that the *Hull* decision allows to American civil courts "only the narrowest kind of review" of religious property disputes, we are compelled to observe that it perforce now provides "only the narrowest kind" of protection for the property of religious organisations.[20] With a parallel increase in secularisation in England, accompanied by a recognisable decrease in doctrinal seriousness on the part of English religious bodies, the courts of England need to be particularly careful not to make the American mistake. To do so would leave religious property holders in a posi-

---

[18.] Cf. Montgomery, "Commentary and Response," 35/1 *The Jurist* 4-5, 81 ff. (1975).

[19.] On Professor Dworkin's position, as set forth in his book, *Life's Dominion*, see Montgomery, "New Light on the Abortion Controversy," 60/7 *New Oxford Rev.* 24-26 (September 1993).

[20.] Kauper, *op. cit.*, p. 374.

tion of particular vunerability when they should be able to rely on the law to protect the trusts which they and their forebears have created. The common law of trusts arose at a time of social ferment to preserve the right of ecclesiastics to benefit from property holdings and to prevent the unjust escheating of landed interests[21]; in our time of even more rapid social change it is particularly important that English courts remain vigilant to preserve the express and implied trusts which inure to the benefit of religious believers.

[21.] Walter Wheeler Cook, "Origin and Nature of Trusts," 6 *American Law and Procedure* 361-71 (1958).

Addendum*

THE
UNITARIANS DEFEATED.

SUBSTANCE
OF
THE JUDGMENT
DELIVERED DEC. 23, 1833,
BY
HIS HONOUR
THE
RIGHT HON. SIR LAUNCELOT SHADWELL,
VICE-CHANCELLOR OF ENGLAND,
IN THE CASE OF THE
ATTORNEY-GENERAL *v.* SHORE,
AS TO
THE CONSTRUCTION OF THE TRUST-DEEDS
OF
DAME SARAH HEWLEY,
DECEASED.

Printed by Permission of the Vice-Chancellor

LONDON:
JAMES FRASER, REGENT STREET.
1834.

[*Reproduced from a copy in the author's rare book collection]

Chapter 5

SUBSTANCE, &C.

His HONOUR, immediately after Sir Edward Sugden's reply, delivered his judgment as follows:

Before stating my opinion upon the trust, I must first of all say, that I should be extremely sorry if any person entertained an opinion that I thought harshly of the Unitarians as a body; because it has happened to me to have had intercourse with various persons, from the earliest part of my life, and whom I have known for many years, who are of that persuasion, and with whom I have lived with great cordiality and friendship; but it does not appear to me that the question in this case to be determined is, whether they were properly called Christians or not; but whether it was consistent with what appeared on the trust-deeds of Lady Hewley, having regard to such evidence as had been produced of what her sentiments were, that the Unitarians could be allowed to participate in the benefit of her charity; she having stated, that the first trust was for "poor and godly preachers, for the time being, of Christ's holy Gospel;" and then repeating phrases which evidently shewed that she alluded to the same sort of persons who might happen to be widows of persons, or exhibitioners, and so on, as would fall under the first denomination.

The will of Sir J. Hewley has been put in, which commenced with the following words:—"This is the last will and testament of Sir J. Hewley, who being, of God's mercy, of perfect memory, and so on, first committing my spirit to God who gave it, hoping to find mercy to me a sinner, and to be saved only by the merits and mediation of Jesus Christ, my alone Saviour and Redeemer." I must here remark the manner in which the will was witnessed—"Witness my hand and seal, 24th of June, in the year of our Lord God 1682;" and therefore I consider that the will testified, from the beginning to the end, his belief in the divinity of the Redeemer.

I must now refer to the words of the will of Mrs. Sarah Hewley:—"I, Dame Sarah Hewley, widow, having first committed my immortal soul into the hands of my Redeemer, to be washed in his blood, and made meet to be partaker with the saints," &c.; she then proceeded to make her will. The natural inference from this will was, that she not only believed in the divinity of the Redeemer, but looked for salvation through his merits, in that sense in which the Church of England understood that he was the Redeemer,—"that he had paid the price," and that for the price which he had paid, God would be pleased to forgive the sins of all that turned unto him.

The next document is the will of Dr. Coulton: he also had used similar phrases:—"I commit my immortal soul into the hands of Almighty God, my Creator, and which I beseech him mercifully to look upon, not as it is in itself, polluted with sin, but as it is redeemed and purged with the precious blood of his only beloved Son, and my most sweet Saviour Jesus Christ, in confidence of whose merits and mediation alone it is that I cast myself upon the mercy of God, for the pardon of my sins and the hope of eternal life." He, it was to be remarked, was one of Lady Hewley's trustees, and was the person that preached at St. Saviour's Chapel, where she attended during her life, and he preached her funeral sermon.

Then, looking at the words of the deed, I am necessarily driven (inasmuch as the rules were directed by the deed to be observed) to a consideration of Bowles's Catechism, which, according to the rules, the poor almspeople were directed to repeat; and for the purpose of determining the question before me, I am bound, not merely to consider the questions and answers, but also the texts in the margin, which are manifestly referred to in support of the answers. One question was—"What was the sin of our first parents?—Eating the forbidden fruit. What was the fruit of that eating?—It filled the world with sin and sorrow. In what condition is the posterity of our first parents born?—In a sinful and miserable condition." That last answer comprehended all the posterity of Adam. "Wast thou born in that condition?—Yea, I was conceived in sin, and am by nature a child of wrath, as well as others. What is Jesus Christ?—The Son of God manifest in the flesh." Now that answer referred to that very singular verse at the end of the third chapter of St. Paul's Epistle to Timothy, which, according to the translation of the Scripture used at that time, could not leave a doubt in the mind of any person as to the divinity of the Redeemer, because, according to the received translation, it was put in this way:—"And without controversy great is the mystery of godliness; God was manifested in the flesh, justified in the spirit, seen of angels, preached unto the Gentiles, believed on in the world, received up into glory." Now, no man could doubt that this text was intended to convey the only conclusion that could be formed, which was, that not merely the office and mission of our Saviour were divine, as stated in the answers of the defendants, but that his person was divine.

It then went on in another part—"In what order doth God work faith by the word ?—First he shews men their sins, and then their Saviour. Why does he observe this order?—That Christ may be the more precious to the soul. How doth faith work love?—It lays hold upon the infinite love of Christ, and works a mutual love in us." Now that expression, "the infinite love of Christ," of necessity conveyed the notion that he was divine, for none but a divine being could have infinite love. Persons might appeal to their own common reading and observations of what passed every day, and I appeal to the testimony given before the committee of the Lords and Commons upon the state of Ireland, for proof of this proposition, that the Presbyterians do hold that the only effectual view of religion, for the purpose of softening the hearts of men, and turning them to God, is the view of the Father's love in sending his Son to appear upon earth and suffer as a man. That was the very view which was taken by a pious Presbyterian minister, who was examined with regard to the *Regium Donum* at Belfast.

Now the first donation in Lady Hewley's trust was to "poor and godly preachers of Christ's holy Gospel." I cannot but suppose, as she was not a Conformist, that she did mean those persons, not being members of the Church of England, who did entertain, among others, the firmest belief in the divinity of our Redeemer's person, in the necessity of the sacrifice he made, because of the universality of sin, commonly called original sin ; and that she would, as Sir Edward Sugden has stated with great propriety, have shaken with horror at the notion of her charity being given to the sustenance of persons who not only disbelieved these two doctrines, but who actually preached against them. It has also been argued (and I must say I do not remember a case which has been argued with more ingenuity and ability by all the members of the bar concerned in it) that the principal object of this lady was to support poor ministers, widows of poor ministers, and the other persons included in her trust-deed, who would themselves be the supporters of what was called the great doctrine of the Presbyterians—that sort of unrestrained method of disseminating the faith which would not submit to be bound by any test or creed, or by any thing except the words of Scripture.

Now, the book mentioned in the Catalogue of Books at the end of the Sixth Report of the Unitarian Society, which was called an Improved Version of the New Testament, afforded a strong inference that persons who would assist the publication of it cannot come under the description of "poor and godly preachers of Christ's holy Gospel," even according to the view which had been taken of those words by the defendants' counsel. Surely it is immaterial whether a creed is expressed in a form of words, or whether a thing called a translation is propounded to mankind which refuses to give the literal sense of words, and in lieu of words expressing the literal sense of the words in the original text, substitutes other words. Where the literal meaning of a word was doubtful, translators might place one word in the text of the translation and another in the margin, in order that a choice might be made; and many cases may be imagined in which the idiom of the English language would not permit the literal rendering of word for word from the Greek or the Hebrew; but where persons had obviously and systematically gone out of the plain way, and had chosen not to give the literal meaning, but to give an assumed and arbitrary meaning, for the purpose of misleading the ignorant reader, those persons must be considered as in effect imposing a creed upon the reader, and not giving him the benefit of judging for himself by means of the pure word of Scripture. I make this observation in consequence of the translation given in that book of the first chapter of the Epistle of Paul to the Hebrews; for it appears most clearly, that the persons who composed the translation did not intend, when they made what they called a translation, to render that first chapter literally, but did intend to infuse a creed. A comparison of the text in Griesbach* with the new version would make this plain. The text began thus: πολυμερῶς καὶ πολυτρόπως πάλαι ὁ Θεὸς. And the translation was—"God, who in several parts and in several manners formerly spake to our fathers by the prophets." Now, I do not mean to say that they have not translated the word πολυμερῶς properly; it might refer to many parts of space, or many parts of time. Our authorised translation was—"God, who at sundry times." These new translators, however, thought proper to give themselves the character of extreme accuracy, by not adopting that which was good enough, but apparently selecting something which they thought better. The translation then proceeds: "In the last of these days hath spoken to us by his Son, whom he hath appointed heir of all things, for whom also he constituted the ages." Now, the words in the original were (according to Griesbach)—δι οὗ καὶ τοὺς αἰῶνας ἐποίησεν. Feeling themselves, therefore, a little pushed hard when they translate δι οὗ "for whom," they have recourse to a note, by which it appeared that two or three persons had fancied that might be the proper translation. Supposing it to be so, it appeared to shew a very great intention to be extremely correct, though it certainly was not the received translation; nor do I think that any Greek scholar, unless he were previously biassed in favour of a particular theory, would dream that such was the proper translation. The original text then proceeds:—ὃς ὢν ἀπαύγασμα τῆς δόξης, καὶ χαρακτὴρ τῆς ὑποστάσεως αὐτοῦ. And what was the pretended accurate translation of these words? "Who being a ray of his brightness, and an image of his perfections"—χαρακτὴρ τῆς ὑποστάσεως αὐτοῦ, an image of his perfections!!! I was perfectly astonished, and could hardly have conceived it possible before I had read it, that any person could have ventured to call this an improved version of the Scriptures which has rendered the word ὑποστάσις "perfections." It was perfectly plain, in that

---

* The edition of Griesbach alluded to was the octavo London edition of 1809; and the edition of the Improved Version alluded to was the duodecimo edition of 1819.

passage, the parties never meant to give a translation, but that they meant to fetter the understanding of the reader by imposing their creed in the shape of a translation. They then said—"and ruling all things by his powerful word,"—φέρων τε τὰ πάντα τῷ ῥήματι τῆς δυνάμεως αὐτοῦ. They might as well have said, "by the word of his power;" but they did not choose to give the literal translation; they chose rather to substitute words of their own, which might express the sense, but which, it was quite clear, did not express the literal meaning. To this they annex a meagre note, in which they first give their view of the meaning of the words, and then add the literal translation from the Greek. The translation then proceeds: "for to which of those messengers spake God at any time, Thou art my Son, this day I have adopted thee?" The passage they meant to translate was, τίνι γὰρ εἶπέ ποτε τῶν ἀγγέλων, Υἱός μου εἶ σύ, ἐγὼ σήμερον γεγέννηκά σε. There was not the slightest pretence to translate the word γεγέννηκα "I have adopted."

The defendants' counsel had read passages from Locke's Essay on the Reasonableness of Christianity, in which he states, that by the terms "Son of God" the Jews understood the Messiah. And so they did: for in the second Psalm it is said, "The rulers take counsel together against Jehovah, and against his Messiah." And shortly afterwards: "I will declare the decree: Jehovah said unto me, Thou (art) my Son; this day have I begotten thee." The word in the Hebrew which thus represents something incomprehensible with regard to the Divine nature, but which of necessity conveys to the human mind the notion of the relation that subsists between Father and Son, is uniformly translated in the Septuagint by the word γεγέννηκα when applied to a father. It is the word which several times occurs in the fifth chapter of Genesis, in which there was a detailed account of the births of all the antediluvian patriarchs given in succession: the very verb used in the second Psalm was the verb used in that chapter, and the word used in the Septuagint was quoted by St. Paul.

The gentlemen who had translated the Unitarian Testament had made it plain on the face of it that they meant to establish a doctrine, that our Saviour was not begotten in that sense in which the term was taken by the Church of England, and by the orthodox Dissenters as they were called, to signify some divine operation, by means of which the nature of the Redeemer was the same as that of the Father. That they meant to oppose. And for the purpose of avoiding the inference which might be made in the mind of an unlearned reader, they wilfully altered the word, and substituted a creed instead of a translation. And it is to be observed, that with respect to these important words, for the first time obtruded on the notice of the world, "an image of his perfections," and "adopted," the translators have not thought it right to add a note, or give the least hint to the unlearned reader that the translation is at all unusual, or in the least degree doubtful; though the notes upon the words "for whom" and "his powerful word," and the singular expression, "in several parts," would induce an unlearned person to think that the new translators were minutely scrupulous and fastidiously accurate, and he would put confidence in them accordingly. The translation then goes on: "And let all the messengers of God pay homage to him; and of these messengers *the Scripture saith.*" Now, it was to be observed, that here the words "the Scripture" were both in *italics*, as they ought to be if they were introduced at all, because there were no words corresponding with them in the original. The word "saith" evidently referred, as it appeared from their own translation, to God; but they chose to vary the phrase by saying first, "*God saith*" and then "the Scripture saith," which seems an alteration not only without any necessity, but totally unjustifiable. Then they said, "And of these messengers the Scripture saith, Who maketh the wind his messengers, and flames of lightning his ministers." It is truly astonishing to find such a translation as "flames of lightning" given to the words πυρὸς φλόγα, which could not admit of that translation. It might be said that was what was intended, but certainly that was not said. They translated, "God is thy throne for ever and ever; a sceptre of rectitude *is* the sceptre of thy kingdom;" and it might perhaps be true that that translation was right, though the commonly received translation is apparently less forced and more natural; but there was this observation to be made upon it—that they had introduced in the mode of printing, as it stood in their version, the first word "is" not in *italics*, and the second word "*is*" in *italics*. The unlearned reader would therefore, of course, consider the first word "is" as the rendering of a word found in the original text, and the second word "is" as a word supplied by the translators, there being no corresponding word in the original text. If in the original, either of the Hebrew or Greek text, there were a word corresponding with "is" between the words corresponding with "God" and "thy throne," it would be difficult to avoid adopting the new translation. But there is not any such word either in the Hebrew or in the Greek. Here, then, is an attempt to support a translation altogether novel by an interpolation totally unauthorised.

There is but one more observation to be made on the translation. The new translators having in the first instance translated the passage, Ὁ ποιῶν τοὺς ἀγγέλους αὐτοῦ πνεύματα, "who maketh the winds his messengers," said at the end "are they not all servants?" by way of translating οὐχὶ πάντες εἰσὶ λειτουργικὰ πνεύματα. Supposing them to be right in the first instance in translating it "winds his messengers," it was clear they ought in the latter part to have said "are they not all ministering winds?" (λειτουργικὰ πνεύματα), to be consistent with themselves: at any rate, if they thought proper to change the phrase, and translate the word πνεύματα "wind" first, and afterwards "spirits," they should have translated it "ministering spirits," which would have the sense of servants; but still it would be a correct translation, which theirs was not. I have taken this as a specimen of the whole; I have looked at a variety of passages, and I do not remember to have seen any translation which could be considered more unsatisfactory, more arbitrary, more fanciful, more foolish, and, I am sorry to say, more false, than this thing called by the Unitarians an improved version; and sure am I, that Lady Hewley would have thought it the worst calamity that could have happened to her, that persons should be considered entitled to participate in her charity, professing to call themselves "godly preachers of Christ's holy Gospel," who would give their sanction to the publication of such a work as that. For the reasons I have assigned, she would, if the matter had been duly explained to her, have seen that it militated against that principle which the defendant's counsel said was the principle on which she desired her charity to be administered—namely, the principle of free discussion, without creed, and by appealing only to the Scriptures as they stood.

There is a vast number of other passages; but it is perfectly useless to go through them. One remark, however, may be made upon the criticism of the new translators. They print in italics the latter part of the first, and the whole of the second chapter of St. Matthew, and the whole of the second chapter, and all the first chapter of St. Luke, except the four first introductory verses ; and this they do, as they tell us in the notes in p. 2, and p. 111, because those chapters and parts of chapters are to be considered as of doubtful authority, though they are to be found in all the manuscripts and versions which are now extant. In the progress of improvement, it may be discovered, that no parts of Scripture are genuine and authentic, except the first verse of Genesis and the last of Revelation; and, according to the argument for the defendants, the preachers upon those two verses only might still be considered, as godly preachers for the time being of Christ's holy Gospel, within the intent and meaning of Lady Hewley's trust-deeds. I find, by the evidence, that Mr. Wellbeloved and Mr. Kenrick, and some third trustee, were subscribers to the institution called the Unitarian Society, which enumerated amongst the books it circulated this improved version of the Scriptures, as it was called; and my opinion is, that the question being, not who should participate, but what given individuals should be excluded, it is satisfactorily made out, that no person who believes as Mr. Wellbeloved has stated in his sermon he believes, or who acts as Mr. Wellbeloved has acted with regard to supporting that Unitarian Society which had published such a book as the improved version, could be considered as entitled to share in the charity of Lady Hewley.

Therefore I think it clear, that no stipend ought to be continued to Mr. Wellbeloved, or to any person preaching the doctrines he does ; and it is also clear, that the charity itself cannot be administered according to the intention of Lady Hewley, at least there is no reasonable security that it can be administered according to her intention, if it is allowed to remain in the hands of persons who thought as he did, and who had acted as he had. I have no evidence whatever to induce me to believe that he had any thing to do with the improved version, more than in assisting by his subscription the publication of it, nor have I ever heard, nor have I the slightest conception, who were the fabricators of the book ; but I am quite certain Lady Hewley never would have thought this book did contain Christ's holy Gospel, or that the persons who disseminated this book were to be considered disseminators of Christ's holy Gospel.

Therefore, my decree must, in substance, declare, that NO PERSONS WHO DENY THE DIVINITY OF OUR SAVIOUR'S PERSON, AND WHO DENY THE DOCTRINE OF ORIGINAL SIN, AS IT IS GENERALLY UNDERSTOOD, ARE ENTITLED TO PARTICIPATE IN LADY HEWLEY'S CHARITY; AND THAT THE FIRST SET OF TRUSTEES MUST BE REMOVED.

It is sufficiently manifest that this lady never intended that there should be trustees of one sort to administer the dealing out of the funds amongst the persons who were named in the first deed, and trustees of a second sort to superintend the hospital which contained the poor almswomen.

I therefor think, that ALL THE TRUSTEES WHO ARE DISSENTERS AND DENY THE DOCTRINE OF OUR SAVIOUR'S DIVINE PERSON, AND THE DOCTRINE OF ORIGINAL SIN, MUST BE REMOVED; AND THOUGH THERE IS NO OBJECTION PERSONALLY TO MR. PALMER, YET AS IT APPEARS THAT HE IS A MEMBER OF THE CHURCH OF ENGLAND, HE OUGHT NOT TO BE CONTINUED A TRUSTEE.

THE END.

CHAPTER 6

CHRISTIAN EDUCATION AND WORSHIP IN STATE SCHOOLS: THE AMERICAN PERSPECTIVE

I. THE ENGLISH SCENE

In an important article surveying the place of religious education and worship in the English school system, John M. Hull, Professor of Religious Education at the University of Birmingham, pointed up the positive features of state support: significant financial assistance; the "immense strength to the subject" provided by making religion a compulsory element in the curriculum; and the value of integrating the "spiritual and moral" into general education through required collective worship.[1]

Though one Education Act seems to follow another almost on an annual basis, the legal position of Christian faith in the English state school system seems quite firmly entrenched. Section 7(1) and (2) of the Education Reform Act 1988 asserts, *inter alia*, that "the collective worship required in the school by section 6 of this Act shall be wholly or mainly of a broadly Christian character"; worship is "of a broadly Christian character if it reflects the broad traditions of Christian belief without being distinctive of any particular Christian denomination." Department for Education Circular 1/94, para. 63, declares that collective worship "must contain some elements which relate specifically to the traditions of Christian belief and which accord a special status to Jesus Christ." A letter (14 July 1994)

[1.] John M. Hull, "Church-Related Schools and Religious Education in the Publicly-Funded Educational System of England," *Proceedings of the European Consortium of Church and State Research* (Milan, 1992), pp. 196-99.

from the then Secretary of State for Education, in response to a communication from the Board of Deputies of British Jews, leaves little room for doubt : "The term 'broadly Christian,' as defined in section 7(2) of the 1988 Act, does not denote elements of worship which are merely consonant with Christianity, but which are distinctive of Christianity.... The element of Christianity which distinguishes it from other faiths is the status accorded to Jesus Christ." Students may opt out of required collective worship in English schools, but if they do attend, they will (assuming that the Act of Parliament is being implemented in letter and in spirit) enter into a distinctively Christian worship experience.

To be sure, as the just mentioned letter from the Board of Deputies of British Jews clearly indicates, England today is a multicultural society in which many religions, not just one, are present. Moreover, as in most Western nations, so in the British Isles, secularism is on the rise. In consequence, opposition to the statutory place of Christian education and worship in the state school system is becoming more and more vocal from a number of quarters.

Thus, in a Templeton London Lecture at the Royal Society of Arts on 12 December 1994, the same Professor Hull whom we cited above called for the repeal of section 7 of the 1988 Education Reform Act and for the substitution of exercises of "collective spirituality" in the schools, thereby avoiding offence to other religions and to the non-religious. Respondents included a Muslim and a Jew — both of whom, amusingly, felt not a little uncomfortable with Professor Hull's promotion of what appeared to be a vague, New Age-like spirituality.[2]

The tension between the existing approach to Christian education and worship in the English state schools and current questionings of that approach suggests that comparison with an entirely different constitutional style might be fruitful. We therefore cross the water to see how the same issues are handled in America — from which, to misquote George Bernard Shaw, we are separated

---

[2.] As a Fellow of the RSA, I was present at this lecture. It has been published in booklet form (1995) and is available from the RSA's Lecture Programme Office, 8 John Adam Street, London.

by a common legal system. In America, religious instruction and all forms of worship in state schools are arguably (a) illegal and (b) theologically undesirable.

II. THE ILLEGALITY OF CHRISTIAN EDUCATION AND WORSHIP IN AMERICAN STATE SCHOOLS

The First Amendment to the Federal Constitution states that "Congress shall make no law respecting an establishment of religion, or prohibiting the free exercise thereof." Concentrating on the "establishment" clause, one asks: What is the extent of the separation demanded?

In reference to the "School Prayer" issue (religious education and worship in state schools), conservatives have tried to argue either that the prohibition on religious establishment properly applies only to the Federal government and not to the States or that the original intent of the Founding Fathers was merely to prohibit the establishment of given *denominations*—not to keep the United States from being a distinctively Christian nation.[3] The first of these claims is now impossible to sustain in light of the Supreme Court's application of the Bill of Rights to the States by way of the 14th Amendment. As for the second, it raises the interesting hermeneutic question, which has always divided conservative and liberal constitutional constructionists, as to whether the meaning of the Federal Constitution (or, indeed, of any document) is equivalent to its author's original intention.[4]

How in fact does one know the "original intent" of the author or authors? One might well maintain that it is best discovered from the document itself—but this produces complete circularity of reasoning as to the determination of the document's meaning. Moreover, authors (not just Old Testament prophets!) sometimes do not

---

[3.] See, *e.g.*, various contributors to H. Wayne House's *Restoring the Constitution* (Dallas, Texas: Probe, 1987) and *The Christian and American Law* (Grand Rapids, Mich.: Kregel, 1998).

[4.] For the discussion to follow, cf. John Warwick Montgomery, "Legal Hermeneutics and the Interpretation of Scripture," in *Evangelical Hermeneutics*, ed. Michael Bauman and David Hall (Camp Hill, Pa.: Christian Publications, 1995), pp. 15-29.

really understand the meaning of what they have written: Sibelius, it is said, gave headaches to and destroyed appreciation of his *Finlandia* for those who listened to his "explanations" of the true meaning of the work.

Distinguished law professor and unsuccessful Supreme Court appointee Robert Bork endeavoured to get around the problem by suggesting that the issue is the meaning the document had for its original *audience*.[5] But the same questions arise here: How do we determine precisely what the original readers thought the document meant? (And this analysis assumes that we *can* identify that audience: the average man? educated readers? interested readers? some of the above? all of the above?)

Moreover, the strict constructionist's appeal to original intent, even if successful, would appear to be a Pyrrhic victory, since the most influential of the American Founding Fathers—those who had the greatest influence on the 18th century constitutional documents of the new nation—were generally not believing Christians at all. Franklin, Jefferson, Washington, Paine: they were Enlightenment deists at best.[6] And it was Jefferson who insisted on a strict "wall of separation" between religion and the state in general, both to protect religion from state interference and to prevent any form of state church to dominate the culture.

The legal consequences of the First Amendment separation of church and state have become evident only in the second half of the 20th century. In the 19th century, America was monolithically Christian and almost exclusively Protestant; religious conflict was limited in most cases to argument between Paedobaptists and Antipaedobaptists. But with the flood of immigration at the end of the century, much of it from Catholic countries of Europe (Ireland,

---

[5.] Robert Bork, interview in "Bork v. Tribe on Natural Law, the Ninth Amendment, the Role of the Court," *Life* (Fall Special, 1991), pp. 96-99. For his position in detail, see Bork, "Neutral Principles and Some First Amendment Problems," 47/1 *Indiana Law Journal* (Fall, 1971); Bork, *The Tempting of America* (New York: The Free Press, 1990); and cf. Ethan Bronner, *Battle for Justice: How the Bork Nomination Shook America* (New York: W.W. Norton, 1989).

[6.] See John Warwick Montgomery, *The Shaping of America* (corrected ed.; Minneapolis: Bethany, 1981), especially pp. 47-68.

Italy, Southern Germany, etc.) and subsequently from Eastern European lands where Jews fled various kinds of persecution, American demographics changed radically. And the 19th century also brought with it rising materialism, scientism, and secularism. By the 20th century, adherents of minority religions or avowed unbelievers in any traditional religion would no longer tolerate prayers in state school classrooms or any form of even passive proselytism for Christian faith. These concerns were given voice—and often exacerbated—by the work of the American Civil Liberties Union, an organisation of liberal political and religious persuasion which has always seemed to fight on the side of those trying to remove religion from the public square (though its purposes theoretically also embrace assistance to religionists persecuted for their faith or trammeled by government interference).[7]

A series of Supreme Court decisions put paid to the notion that it would be possible to retain religious (much less Christian) instruction or worship in the secular school context. Here is a summary of those major holdings:

- A state school curriculum must not be used to inculcate "the faith"—whether it be Protestantism, Catholicism, Judaism, Mormonism, or any other. (*McCollum v Board of Education*, 333 U.S. 203 [1948].)

- It is unconstitutional to require that the Bible be read or the Lord's Prayer be recited in a state school. (*Engel v Vitale*, 370 U.S. 421 [1962].)

- State-initiated, school-sponsored or teacher-led devotional exercises for public schoolchildren are barred by the First Amendment. (*School of Abington Township v Schempp*, 374 U.S. 203 [1963].)

- State-initiated programmes allowing students to lead in classroom devotional exercises violate the First Amendment. (*Karen B. v Treen*, 653 F.2d 897 [5th Cir. 1981]; aff'd 455 U.S. 913 [1982].)

[7.] William A. Donohue, *The Politics of the American Civil Liberties Union* (New Brunswick, N.J. and Oxford, U.K.: Transaction Books, 1985). See particularly the section titled, "Freedom from Religion," pp. 299-310, which contains the assertion: "The ACLU has interpreted the First Amendment to mean that there ought to be more than a wall between church and state—there ought to be an iron curtain."

- A daily moment of silence in state schools is likewise unconstitutional, since it was instituted (in Alabama) for the purpose of indirectly putting prayer in the schools. A policy entailing an entirely *neutral* moment of silence, allowing students to think about whatever they want, including God, probably would not violate the Establishment Clause of the First Amendment. (*Wallace v Jaffree*, 472 U.S. 38 [1985].)

- Allowing clergy to offer prayers as part of an official state school graduation ceremony is forbidden. (*Lee v Weisman*, 112 S.Ct. 2649 [1992].)

The above decisions, draconian as they may seem, do not, however, entirely eliminate religion from the American state school scene. The higher the age-level of the institution, the more likely the Court will allow for religious ideas to enter the picture. Thus student-organised and administered religious clubs on high school and state college campuses are allowed to function—as long as the institution has a policy to allow non-religious clubs to meet on campus (chess clubs, etc.). (*Widmar v Vincent*, 454 U.S. 263 [1981].) And the Federal Equal Access Act 1984 (20 U.S.C. secs. 4071-4074), upheld by the Supreme Court (*Board of Education of the Westside Community Schools District v Mergens*, 492 U.S. 917 [1989]), declared that high schools may not discriminatorily restrict the free speech rights of students by denying them the opportunity to hold religious club meetings on campus when they provide such opportunities to non-religious groups. It is noteworthy that this Federal law preempts state law on the issue.

These permissions apply *only* when the religious activity is *student-initiated*, to be sure: were it to be part of the official programme of the state school or initiated by a teacher or administrator or board of the school, it would constitute state-action, thereby falling under the axe of the Establishment Clause. Legally, in America, the state and its educational agents may not do *anything* to promote a given religious position, and it matters not what that religious position happens to be.

III. THE THEOLOGICAL UNDESIRABILITY OF RELIGIOUS EDUCATION AND WORSHIP IN AMERICAN STATE SCHOOLS

Wholly apart from the constitutional considerations just discussed, there are powerful theological factors militating against School Prayer and the promotion of religious positions in American state schools. These theological considerations were well brought to the fore in a Senate debate on 16 November 1981.[8]

Sen. John C. Danforth (R-Mo.) attempted to impale Sen. Jesse Helms (R-N.C.): "Let us assume that a teacher of, say, third-grade students, is a very devout Roman Catholic, and she goes into class one day and writes on the blackboard behind her desk the words of the 'Hail Mary.' She then announces, 'Children, we will now have a voluntary recitation of this prayer. Those of you who do not want to recite it need not recite it; those of you who wish to, please join with me.' Would it be the Senator's view that the Department of Justice, in such a case, should not go into court and a court should not entertain such a case?"

Helms replied : "I say to the Senator that the scenario he has concocted does not bother me at all. I am a Baptist. I would not object at all to my grandchildren being in a class where that happened, and I do not think the majority of the American people would." Pressed as to whether he would feel the same way if he were an orthodox Jew, Helms said that he would.

We find it remarkable that Danforth's realistic "scenario" did not "bother" Helms "at all." Theologically, it *ought* to bother serious Christians very much indeed. The New Testament insists on prayers *in the name of Jesus* (John 14:13-14; Col. 3:17). Thus, in the voluntary prayer atmosphere Senator Helms was promoting, children would have to be instructed by their Christian parents and their pastors not to participate whenever school prayers were biblically unjustifiable. This would also appear to apply to 'Hail Marys'

[8.] See John Warwick Montgomery, "School Prayers: A Common Danger," *Christianity Today*, 7 May 1982; and "School Prayer Born Again?," *New Oxford Review*, April 1995.

since "there is *one* mediator between God and men, the man Christ Jesus" (1 Tim. 2:5).

To be sure, Helms was thinking of a "theistic" (probably even evangelical) majority—as the Southern Baptists dominate so many communities south of the Mason-Dixon line. But that is not America from sea to shining sea at the end of the 20th century. In Boston, school prayers might well be Unitarian; in Salt Lake City, Mormon; and in San Francisco, directed at best to Vishnu, and at worst to Anton Lavey's Satan. Surely such a result would be an abominable confusion of Law and Gospel.

From the standpoint of serious theology, were religious promotion and worship to be allowed in the state schools of America, the result would be either (1) sectarian worship and instruction, which, considering the pluralistic character of the nation today, could well be non-Christian and non-biblical, or (2) generalised worship and instruction ("the God of the American Dream," "the Great Puff of Smoke on High," etc.). Serious Christian believers could not conscientiously participate in either and would thus need to opt out of such school activities. Result: bad theology and the fragmentation of the school system.

IV. SOME CONCLUSIONS AND LESSONS FOR THE ENGLISH SCHOOL SCENE

In America, where efforts were made by the early settlers to escape from the perceived miseries of European state churches, the country succeeded all too well: it got rid of denominational pressures and at the same time it got rid of Christian presence in the school system. The fact that it took two centuries for the latter to be implemented is interesting historically but not of great significance in principle. Church-state separation was but a cloud on the horizon of the nation in its early days; now it has become a whirlwind.

Future generations and their leaders receive their preparation for life in the state school system; and now they receive it with little or no awareness that it is in Christ that the whole creation holds together (Col. 1:12-20). It would be hard not to see the practical effects of such church-state separation in the increasing immorality and gun-toting violence of America's teenagers—and perhaps even in the blatant personal immorality of the country's immediate past President.

Two partial remedies are available in America. One is the parochial school system—and this is not to be found only within the Roman Catholic Church. Lutherans and Protestant evangelicals have developed extensive and intensive systems of parochial schooling, from kindergarten through high school, and, in the case of the Lutherans, these are backed by quality teacher training colleges for parochial school teachers. Church schools not only integrate Christ into the "secular" subject matter throughout the curriculum but also serve as important vehicles of evangelism for the parents of the enrolled children. Of course, the residual problem remains that parochial school children do not attend the state schools, or do so only for a part of their education, so Christian witness to the unchurched is reduced and the society suffers corresponding fragmentation.

The other partial remedy lies with the Christian teachers in the state schools. True, they must not conduct worship or engage in the evangelistic promotion of Christianity *per se*. But another avenue of witness is open to them—and is backed up by the Supreme Court itself! In the *Schempp* case, the Court expressly stated that the objective teaching of the Bible as literature and in history, art, music, etc., courses, and the teaching of comparative religion, are both permissible and desirable for a complete education. This means that the Christian teacher in America can and *should* demonstrate the central influence of the Christian gospel on the development of Western civilisation and the nation.

Science courses offer the possibility of discussing naturalistic theories of the cosmos ("Big Bang") vs. creation theory —via, *e.g.*, the Second Law of Thermodynamics; history and comparative religion courses provide the opportunity to discuss the historical claim of Christianity that its truth—and success in conquering the Roman Empire—depended on Christ's *de facto* resurrection from the dead; literature and art courses open the door to discussing the biblical motivations that inspired Dante, Bach, Händel, Milton, Bunyan,

Rembrandt, Christopher Wren, Pascal, Dr Johnson, Mendelssohn, T.S. Eliot, John Betjeman, C.S. Lewis, and J.R.R. Tolkien—to mention only a few. The "objective" presentation of Christianity also constitutes its defence, since the evidence for it lies in the realities of history, Christian faith being in the deepest sense a historical religion.

We give, simply by way of illustration, several passages which astute school teachers could profitably employ in presenting Christian faith within the framework of "secular" academic subjects:

- *Johann Sebastian Bach*

    "To turn from the Passion according to St. Matthew to the Mass in B minor is to step from the intimacies of personal faith and adoration into some great structure erected to the Glory of God, where man is a mere infinitesimal unit. Few of the solos have any touch of deep emotion, but chorus after chorus of the most immense magnitude, and demanding enormous powers of endurance, roll along until one is lost in amazement at the power of the human mind which could conceive and carry out such a stupendous plan. Some choruses are intensely introspective; no one can ever forget the tender poignancy of the *Qui tollis* and the *Et incarnatus* and the suffering of the *Crucifixus,* with its wonderful modulation at the end. Human joy seems to have reached its limits in the *Gloria,* the *Cum sancto spiritu,* and the *Resurrexit* The first part of the Sanctus is the noblest piece of music ever conceived, its strength is amazing, it moves along with overpowering majesty, and all the visions of glory of the Old Testament prophets are brought before our eyes; here, indeed, Bach seemed to have stepped from the finite into the infinite"—W.G. Whittaker.[9]

- *Dr Samuel Johnson: His Last Prayer*

    "Almighty and most merciful Father, I am now, as to human eyes it seems, about to commemorate, for the last time, the death of Thy Son Jesus Christ our Saviour and Redeemer. Grant, O Lord, that my whole hope and confidence may be in His merits, and Thy mercy; enforce and accept my imperfect repentance; make this commemoration available to the confirmation of my faith, the establishment of my hope, and the enlargement of my charity; and make the

---

[9.] Cf. Günther Stiller, *Johann Sebastian Bach und das Leipzig gottesdienstliche Leben seiner Zeit* (Berlin, 1970).

death of Thy Son Jesus Christ effectual to my redemption. Have mercy upon me, and pardon the multitude of my offences. Bless my friends; have mercy upon all men. Support me, by the Grace of Thy Holy Spirit, in the days of weakness, and at the hour of death; and receive me, at my death, to everlasting happiness, for the sake of Jesus Christ. *Amen."*

- *T.S. Eliot on the* Pensées *of Pascal*

"The Christian thinker—and I mean the man who is trying consciously and conscientiously to explain to himself the sequence which culminates in faith, rather than the public apologist—proceeds by rejection and elimination. He finds the world to be so and so; he finds its character inexplicable by any non-religious theory: among religions he finds Christianity, and Catholic Christianity, to account most satisfactorily for the world and especially for the moral world within; and thus, by what Newman calls 'powerful and concurrent' reasons, he finds himself inexorably committed to the dogma of the Incarnation."

- *John Betjeman on Christmas*

> "And is it true? And is it true,
>   This most tremendous tale of all,
> Seen in a stained-glass window's hue,
>   A Baby in an ox's stall?
> The Maker of the stars and sea
> Become a Child on earth for me?
>
> And is it true? For if it is,
>   No loving fingers tying strings
> Around those tissued fripperies,
>   The sweet and silly Christmas things,
> Bath salts and inexpensive scent
> And hideous tie so kindly meant,
>
> No love that in a family dwells,
>   No carolling in frosty air,
> Nor all the steeple-shaking bells
>   Can with this single Truth compare—
> That God was Man in Palestine
> And lives to-day in Bread and Wine."

What relevance do the American religious education problems have for the English situation? With an Established Church and no history of church-state separation, the English should not be suffering the difficulties constitutionally entrenched across the Atlantic. But the well-known siren call is heard to ape the American situation: get rid of Christian particularism in the schools (even though allowed, indeed encouraged, by law here): accommodate to pluralism. Remarkably, the English have never seemed to appreciate an old American frontier adage: "If it ain't broke, don't fix it." Let us hope that the Christian presence in the state school system here will not be eliminated on the specious ground that change is necessarily for the better. Abstract moral values do not survive in the absence of the theological foundations giving them a reality and an eternal sanction. Nations live on inherited capital only so long.

But, realistically, where pluralism cannot be stemmed, the Christian teacher in the English state schools can learn from his or her American counterpart. If a specifically Christian, biblical worship and instruction is not practical because of the local constituency, the indirect approach of presenting students with the truth and impact of historic Christian faith is always possible. This takes more than a little effort, dedication, and maturity; but why should one expect the carrying out of the Great Commission to be easy? The educational fields are also fields "white unto harvest."

Chapter 7

Church Remarriage After Divorce: A Third Way

I. THE DILEMMA

Britain has the sixth-highest divorce rate in the world; yet, paradoxically, the Anglican Church has one of the most stringent policies of any non-Roman Catholic ecclesiastical body against remarriage in the church of divorced persons whose previous spouses are still living. A recent letter to *The Times* from a clergyperson well expresses the concern:

> The bishops ... still ... do not see that the theoretical good achieved by the public maintaining of "Christian standards" is grossly outweighed by the pastoral damage done to those who are refused the new start our Gospel elsewhere so generously proclaims. For every couple whose marital resolve is strengthened by the Church's present policy, I meet a dozen who go away with a deep sense of rejection and disappointment.[1]

The problem, however, of upholding a high view of marriage and yet taking into account the frequency of marital breakup among believers as well as non-believers is by no means limited to the Church of England. It bedevils the Roman Catholic Church and the entire range of Protestant church bodies, whether free or established.

In this essay, after briefly surveying the two most common approaches to the issue of remarriage in the church, we concentrate our attention on a third (but by no means novel) way in which this exceedingly difficult issue can be treated.

---

[1]. The Revd Mrs Claire Wilson, Letters to the Editor, *The Times*, 24 September 1999.

II. THE STRICT AND THE FLEXIBLE ROUTES

In today's ecclesiastical climate, one generally encounters *either* the view that remarriage whilst a former spouse is still living is sinful in principle and must not be condoned by remarriage in the church (the Roman Catholic and the current Anglican position) *or* the view that the breakup of a marriage, though a result of the sinful human condition, is nonetheless forgiveable and thus should not constitute an impediment to remarriage in the church.

The Roman Catholic approach to the issue stems from its doctrine, first set forth officially by Pope Alexander II in 1159, that marriage between consenting persons (*sponsalis per verba de praesenti*) constitutes a sacramental union—even though the marriage were never in fact consummated. "Impediments" of two kinds, however, came to be recognised: prohibiting impediments, which imposed legal penalties but did not dissolve the marriage; and invalidating impediments, which gave grounds for canonically declaring that the marriage never took place at all. The former made possible legal separation (divorce *a mensa et thoro*), which did not permit remarriage; the latter allowed the parties subsequently to marry, but did not condone remarriage, since *de jure* they had never been married before. By a far wider application of the concept of annulment than exists in most secular legal systems, the canon law of the Roman Church has permitted a severing of marital relationships without compromising its theoretical position that marriage is indissoluble except by death.[2]

The Roman approach is replete with historical and contemporary difficulties. Annulment is so flexible a notion within the sys-

---

[2.] On the sociology and jurisprudence of divorce in the medieval period, see James A. Brundage, *Law, Sex, and Christian Society in Medieval Europe* (Chicago: University of Chicago Press, 1987); Frances and Joseph Gies, *Marriage and the Family in the Middle Ages* (New York: Harper & Row, 1987); and Christopher Brooke, *The Medieval Idea of Marriage* (2d ed.; Oxford: Clarendon Press, 1994). Brundage's work is by far the most comprehensive. The position of the Roman Catholic Church today on the indissolubility of marriage and the criteria for separation and for declarations of marital invalidity are set forth in the 1983 *Code of Canon Law*, can. 1141-1155; useful annotations are provided in the Latin-English edition published by Wilson & Lafleur, Montréal, 1993, and edited by E. Caparros *et al.*

tem that in practice it has been granted or withheld politically, thus often contradicting the very sacramental doctrine of marriage at the root of the Church's teaching. Thus—to take a notorious historical example—Henry VIII obtained a highly questionable papal dispensation to marry his brother's widow (Catherine of Aragon), but Clement VII refused to grant an annulment of that marriage to allow Henry to remarry so as to obtain a male heir even though canonically the marriage to his late brother's wife certainly qualified for annulment. The real reason for the Pope's refusal was that Holy Roman Emperor Charles V, Catherine's nephew, had imprisoned Clement and would not countenance such treatment of her.[3]

Today there are many Roman Catholic canonists who are unhappy with this history and with its present implications. At the same time, it is a sad fact that, because of the procedural complexity in obtaining an annulment in many cases today, that avenue, though open to all Roman Catholics in theory, may be available in practice largely to those with the financial resources to pursue the torturous process to its end. The time factor is such that some couples give up in disgust and simply remarry outside the Church or live together without benefit of clergy. Criticisms of the doctrine and the system have been rife within the Roman communion itself—many of these criticisms stressing *au fond* that even in the Orthodox Eastern Church the "indissolubility" of marriage has never been understood in the rigid terms insisted upon by traditional Roman Catholic theology.[4] And recent studies of the Early Fathers show that "there is only a shadowy teaching on the absolute indissolubility of the marriage bond until Augustine."[5]

[3.] See J. Gairdner's article on Catherine in the *DNB* and the references there given.

[4.] E.g., see William J.S. Wamboldt, "Canon Law on Indissolubility of Marriage in the Roman Catholic Church," 21 *Studia canonica* 265-70 (1987); Michael G. Lawler, "Indissolubility, Divorce and Holy Communion: An Open Response to Germain Grisez, John Finnis and William May," 76 *New Blackfriars* 229-36 (1995); William H. Woestman, "Too Many Invalid Marriages," 24 *Studia canonica* 193-204 (1990).

[5.] William F. Luck, *Divorce and Remarriage: Recovering the Biblical View* (San Francisco: Harper & Row, 1987), p. 270. I was privileged to serve as one of Professor Luck's teachers; in his dedicatory note, he wrote: "If this is any good, it is at least partly due to your efforts to teach me research techniques & logical argument. If it is not good, it is in spite of those good efforts."

Anglican Communions, as already noted, have traditionally followed the Roman Catholic approach in refusing ecclesiastical marriage to divorced persons having living ex-spouses. However, "the practice of the Church of England today varies from diocese to diocese," with only one in five dioceses adhering "strictly to the Convocation Resolutions."[6] At the moment, the Church is rethinking its position, and a news report notes that in the soon-to-be-published episcopal "teaching document" on the question it is acknowledged that the 16th century Reformers did not believe that Scripture taught that divorce is always wrong, so as to prohibit valid second marriages in the eyes of God—"nor was it taught in *The Book of Common Prayer* of 1662."[7] However, the success of the Bishops' endeavour is not especially presaged by the Working Party Report on "Marriage in Church After Divorce."[8] This Report, as I have pointed out elsewhere,[9] makes virtually impossible any principled theological amelioration of the divorce and remarriage issue, for it employs higher critical and redactive approaches to the New Testament teaching on the subject, thereby evacuating the Scripture of normative force:

> It is our belief that ... the form critics are right when they tell us that these words [Mark 10, 11 f] reflect the heightened Christian conscience of the early church in Rome, where Mark's Gospel was compiled, rather than the *ipsissima verba* of the incarnate Lord. The same may be said, *mutatis mutandis,* about other Biblical rules such as the Pauline privilege and the Matthaean exception, so that what matters is what the Spirit is now saying to the churches, and in particular the Church of England, on this question.

The Working Party's movement from Scripture to "what the Spirit is now saying to the churches" takes us to the other major approach to divorce and remarriage to be found in today's ecclesiastical circles: that of the charismatics and the broad-church liberals. In this view, the Spirit, working the the context of the individual heart

---

[6.] Norman Doe, *The Legal Framework of the Church of England* (Oxford: Clarendon Press, 1996), p. 378. For the survey, see A. Clarkson, *et al.,* "Marriage in Church after Divorce," 2 *Ecc. L.J.* 359.

[7.] Ruth Gledhill, "Church Closer to Marrying Divorcees," *The Times,* 21 September 1999.

[8.] 2 *Ecc. L.J.* 366.

[9.] 3 *Ecc. L.J.* 40; reprinted as Addendum to the present essay.

and/or the believing community, dictates an attitude of forgiveness and acceptance, such that no barriers should be raised to church marriage of previously divorced persons. Though charismatics are often associated with the conservative wing of contemporary Christianity, they in fact have much in common with religious liberals: for both, Scripture is not determinative; what *is* decisive is the experiential "leading of the Spirit." And the Spirit has a way of leading both charismatics and the broad-church in the direction of social accommodation and a good personal feeling-tone. Conclusion: divorce can't be all that bad and may well be an avenue to personal growth and a more "Spirit-filled life." Ken Crispin titles his book on the subject, *Divorce—The Forgivable Sin?*[10] and offers as one of the consequences of his "covenant principle" of marriage (genuine marriage exists only as long as the covenant between the parties is maintained):

> If a marriage becomes intolerable to one party in the sense that the conduct of the other party is such that a proper marital relationship is no longer viable, then a Christian husband or wife may proceed to divorce, that is, proceed to sever the marital relationship.... To the extent that a person is at fault for the breakdown of the marriage, that person will need to seek forgiveness. No matter how responsible they are for the termination of that marriage, however, God will forgive and that person will be free to remarry and to start a new life.[11]

The fundamental problem with this approach, to be sure, is that it operates with no objective standards for marriage, divorce, or remarriage. I have roundly criticised this libertarian error in public debate with the late Joseph Fletcher, father of the "situation ethics" movement; and the same applies, *mutatis mutandis*, to Paul Lehmann's "contextual ethics" and to the several kinds of "existential morality."[12] If, as Fletcher claims, "only one thing is intrinsically

---

[10.] Ken Crispin, *Divorce—The Forgivable Sin?* (London: Hodder & Stoughton, 1989).

[11.] Quoted with approbation by circuit judge Christopher Compston in his book, *Recovering from Divorce: A Practical Guide* (London: Hodder & Stoughton, 1993), p. 39. Judge Compston, himself divorced and remarried, "leads Divorce Recovery seminars at Holy Trinity Church, Brompton."

[12.] Joseph Fletcher and John Warwick Montgomery, *Situation Ethics—True or False? A Dialogue* (Minneapolis: Bethany House, 1972).

good, namely, love: nothing else," and there is no objective, revelatory guide to what is genuine love and what isn't, then the theology of marriage is set adrift on an infinite sea of personal experience with no compass at all.

The exact same problem exists for those charismatics who displace Scripture with Spirit—for, without an objective revelation to "test the spirits" (1 John 4:1), how is one to know that the inner guidance one is receiving, in a marriage or in the church, is the product of the *Holy* Spirit? Last we heard, many spirits are abroad, and not all of them are speaking a word from the Lord.[13] The view that a valid divorce and a God-honouring remarriage is available to all on the basis of repentance appears to be a classic example of what Bonhoeffer called "cheap grace"—or what the Reformers characterised as a confusion of Law and Gospel.

III. A THIRD WAY

Must the church choose either an inflexible, unqualified opposition to all divorce and ecclesiastical remarriage, or a completely open policy of accepting any and all remarriage of divorced persons whose spouses are still living? Are Christians doomed to legalism or cheap grace? We do not think so, and we suggest that a return to Reformation (and Biblical!) sources may offer a better roadmap through the thickets of the theology of marriage.

Luther, whilst holding to a very high view of marriage,[14] could not accept its sacramental character.

> For Luther, a sacrament consists in the combination of the word of promise with a sign, that is, it is a promise accompanied by a sign instituted by God and a sign accompanied by a promise. This means, first, that a sign or a symbol by itself is not yet a sacrament. Luther explains that every visible act can naturally mean something and be understood as a picture or an analogy of invisible realities.

[13.] See, *inter alia*, Michael G. Moriarty, *The New Charismatics: A Concerned Voice Responds to Dangerous New Trends* (Grand Rapids, Michigan: Zondervan, 1992), and John F. MacArthur, Jr, *Charismatic Chaos* (Grand Rapids, Michigan: Zondervan, 1992).

[14.] See William H. Lazareth's classic, *Luther on the Christian Home* (Philadelphia: Muhlenberg/Fortress Press, 1960).

> This is not enough, however, to make a symbolic act into a sacrament. The symbolic act must be instituted by God and combined with a promise. Sacramental character ultimately depends on the presence of a divine word of promise. Where this is missing, as in marriage or confirmation, one cannot speak of a sacrament. On the other hand, however, there are realties and deeds in the Christian life such as prayer, hearing and meditating on the word, and the cross, to which God has attached a promise. But they lack the characteristic of a sign or a symbol. This is the case, for example, in the so-called sacrament of penance. Strictly speaking therefore there are only two sacraments in the church of God: baptism and the Lord's Supper. For only in these is there both a sign instituted by God and the promise of the forgiveness of sins.[15]

If marriage is not a sacrament (and it is noteworthy that even in the Roman theology marriage is regarded as a sacrament created by the mutual promises of the couple, not by the act of the priest), then its human extent and the conditions for its lawful termination need to be sought in God's word, the Holy Scriptures. As early as 1522, Luther concluded that divorce and remarriage could scripturally be allowed only when adultery or abandonment had occurred.[16]

Here, two passages of the New Testament are decisive. First, Jesus' teaching in Matthew 19:9, and, secondly, Paul's admonition in 1 Corinthians 7:15. Of the former, Luther wrote in 1530:

> We have heard ... that death is the only reason for dissolving a marriage. And because God has commanded in the law of Moses that adulterers should be stoned [Deut. 22:22-24], it is certain that adultery also dissolves a marriage, because by it the adulterer is sentenced and condemned to death, and also because Christ, in Matthew 19 [:9], when he forbids married people to divorce each other, excepts adultery and says, "Whoever divorces his wife, except for unchastity, and marries another, commits adultery." ... Accordingly I cannot and may not deny that where one spouse

---

[15.] Paul Althaus, *The Theology of Martin Luther*, trans. Robert C. Schultz (Philadelphia: Fortress Press, 1966), pp. 345-46, with primary souce references to Luther's own writings.

[16.] Luther, *Vom ehelichen Leben*, WA [Weimarer Ausgabe, the standard, critical edition of Luther's writings] 10 II. Luther also sees impotence as a legitimate basis for severing the marital bond, but this really constitutes for him not divorce but evidence that the marriage was void *ab initio*. Cf. Thomas Max Safley, "Divorce," in *The Oxford Encyclopedia of the Reformation*, ed. Hans J. Hillerbrand (4 vols.; New York: Oxford University Press, 1996), I, 490-92.

commits adultery and it can be publicly proven, the other partner is free and can obtain a divorce and marry another.[17]

In his Commentary on 1 Corinthians 7 (1523), Luther writes concerning verse 15:

> Here the apostle releases the Christian spouse, once the non-Christian partner has separated himself or will not permit his mate to lead a Christian life, giving the former the right and authority to marry another partner. What St. Paul says here concerning a non-Christian spouse is also applicable to a false Christian; so that if such a one wanted to traduce his spouse to his unchristian ways and not permit the Christian way of life or would separate himself, then that Christian spouse would be free to marry another. If this were not permitted, the Christian spouse would have to follow after the non-Christian mate or live a life of chastity without the will and capability to do so, and he would thus be the prisoner of another's caprice and live in danger of his soul....
>
> But shouldn't the Christian mate wait until his non-Christian spouse comes back or dies, as has been the custom and canon law until now? Answer: If he wants to wait for his mate, that is up to his good will. For since the apostle proclaims him free and unbound, he is not obliged to wait for his mate but may change his status in the name of God. I wish to God that people had made use of this teaching of St. Paul or would begin to make use of it in cases where man and wife run away from each other or one leaves the other sitting, for much whoring and sin have resulted from them. This has been increased by the senseless laws of the pope, which, in direct contradiction to this text of St. Paul, compel and force the one mate not to change his status on pain of losing his soul's salvation, but to wait for the runaway spouse or the death of the same. This means that the brother or sister in such cases is truly bound in irons, because of the wantonness and wickedness of another, and for no cause is driven into the danger of unchastity.[18]

Does this mean that Scripture contradicts itself as to one and only one legitimate cause of divorce, namely, adultery? No, for malicious desertion is not a *cause* of divorce; it constitutes divorce in itself. The great Lutheran theologian of the second generation of the Reformation, Johann Gerhard, makes this clear:

---

[17] Luther, *Von den Ehesachen,* WA 30 III; trans. in Vol. 46 of the 55-vol. American edition of Luther's *Works* ed. by Jaroslav Pelikan and Helmut T. Lehmann.

[18] Luther, WA 12, 122-24; trans. in Vol. 28 of the American edition of Luther's *Works.*

> Christ's exclusive statement, which specifies adultery as the only reason for divorce, does not lose anything through the apostolic statement because the former is not dealing with one and the same question, nor with one and the same case, as the Apostle. Christ indicates the case of procuring a divorce; the Apostle indicates the case of suffering a divorce and becoming free again through unjust desertion. Christ speaks of one who procures a divorce; the Apostle speaks of one who suffers a divorce. Christ speaks of one who leaves his spouse; Paul speaks of one who is left by his spouse. Christ speaks of voluntary divorce; Paul speaks of involuntary divorce.[19]

This approach to divorce and remarriage became normative in Lutheran lands during the 16th and 17th centuries, and influenced civil legislation very widely. My doctoral professor at Strasbourg, the late François Wendel, in his treatise, *Le mariage à Strasbourg à l'époque de la Réforme,* observed that "l'ordonnance de 1530, qui vint enfin fixer officiellement les causes de divorce, ne cite que l'adultère et la désertion malicieuse."[20]

The resultant Lutheran doctrine[21] can be formulated in the following terms: (1) Marriage is ideally for life and any marital breakup is the result of sin. (2) Only one legitimate "cause" of divorce is recognised in Scripture: that of adultery. Here the innocent party has the option of staying in the relationship or of divorcing the guilty partner. (3) Malicious desertion by an unbelieving spouse constitutes divorce *per se*; here, the innocent spouse is freed from the marital bond by the desertion, but may choose to wait for the return of the deserting spouse and a reestablishment of the marriage with that person. (4) In the case of desertion, "unbelief" does not mean that an innocent spouse is freed from the marriage only if the deserting spouse is a professed non-Christian; conduct utterly inconsistent with Christian profession may properly relegate the deserter to the functional status of unbeliever for purposes of terminating the marriage. (5) Desertion may be actual or construc-

---

[19] Johann Gerhard, *Loci theologici,* VII (Berlin: Gust. Schlawitz, 1869), 407.

[20] François Wendel, *Le mariage à Strasbourg à l'époque de la Réforme* (Strasbourg: Imprimerie Alsacienne, 1928), p. 159.

[21] For a contemporary statement and justification of the Lutheran position, see the report on Divorce of the Commission on Theology and Church Relations of the Lutheran Church-Missouri Synod.

tive, the latter consisting, for example, of physical abuse or antisocial conduct of such seriousness that it forces the couple apart, or irrational refusal to enter into sexual relations (thus separating the couple on a fundamental level). (6) Even when neither adultery nor malicious desertion has occurred, it is conceivable (but rare) that a divorce can be ecclesiastically recognised on the ground that, though an evil, it is a lesser of evils.[22] (7) Whenever the divorce is theologically legitimate, remarriage is likewise legitimate and may be performed in the church and according to church rites.[23]

IV. EVALUATION OF THE "THIRD WAY"

The position on divorce and remarriage just described has not been characteristic only of Lutheran churches. Calvinist churches and their theologians have maintained an essentially similar view.[24] Where other Protestant churches have employed this approach, they have avoided the denigration of marriage on the one hand and, on the other, the kind of unscriptural legalism which so often ruins lives and alienates those outside the church. The "Third Way" prevents such sad situations as that described by Vander Lugt:

> A former pastor I know lost his position in a Christian organization when his wife left him and married another man. She admitted that he had been a good husband and father, but said his income level had been too low. He now is not permitted to serve as an elder because he is viewed as not meeting the "husband of one wife"

[22.] The "lesser of evils" principle is particularly characteristic of Lutheran theological ethics; see Adolf Köberle, *The Quest for Holiness,* trans. John C. Mattes (Minneapolis: Augsburg, 1938). That this is a far cry from Fletcherian "situation ethics" may be seen from the discussion in Montgomery, *Human Rights and Human Dignity* (2d ed.; Edmonton, Alberta: Canadian Institute for Law, Theology and Public Policy, 1995), pp. 178, 300 (n. 347) and 302 (n. 376).

[23.] "Both Testaments indicate that when divorce occurs ... right of remarriage is presupposed; in other words, when a marriage has been broken, divorce dissolves the marriage 'bond' and covenant; the Bible does not know legal separation witbout tbe possibility of remarriage"—David Atkinson, *To Have and to Hold: The Marriage Covenant and the Discipline of Divorce* (London: William Collins Sons, 1979), p. 126.

[24.] See, for example, systematic theologian John Murray's highly regarded work, *Divorce* (2d ed.; Phillipsburg, New Jersey: Presbyterian and Reformed Publishing Co., 1961), especially pp. 76-77.

requirement of 1 Timothy 3:2. This man, an innocent victim of his wife's greed, had been dealt with far more severely than many pastors who repented after immorality. This troubles me. A man thus divorced still meets the "husband of one wife" qualification even after a new marriage. The Greek expression is literally "a one-woman man." This refers to a man whose life as a husband was marked by fidelity to his mate. A good husband who remarries after his wife dies is also a "one woman man" in spite of having a second wife.[25]

A prime objection to the approach we have suggested needs, however, to be discussed briefly in conclusion. We are told that the classic Reformation approach is fatally flawed because it insists on locating fault in a marital breakdown, whereas fault can rarely be attributed to one marital partner alone; moreover, determining issues of fault commits church personnel and tribunals to messy and interminable hassles which can only be counterproductive, and which, in any event, give the impression that the church is in the business of judgment rather than of forgiveness and grace.

To which argument, we reply: (1) Fault issues (adultery, malicious desertion) are clearly set forth in the key biblical passages on the subject and, in the teaching of our Lord and in the Apostolic teaching, appear to be inseparably connected with their treatment of the morality or immorality of divorce and remarriage. The only way to eliminate the fault issue would seem to be no longer to consider these biblical passages as normatively binding on the church's practice.[26]

(2) It is simply not the case that one cannot generally identify the guilty party in a divorce situation. Here one is not dealing with guilt *in general* but with *immediate responsibility for the adultery or malicious desertion*. It may be that one spouse has irritating personal habits, but the decision to go off alone or with someone else as a consequence is the moral responsibility of the partner who commits adultery or deserts. Establishing which spouse has committed adultery or deserted should not be all that difficult.

---

[25] H. Vander Lugt, *Divorce & Remarriage* (Grand Rapids, Michigan: RBC, 1994), p. 25.

[26] Is this perhaps the reason why the Working Party takes such an approach? See our text at notes 8 and 9 *supra*.

(3) The argument that determinations of fault are messy has been central to the development of "no fault" divorce in many common law jurisdictions and the current trend is certainly in that direction. The problem here, however, is that "no fault" circumvents justice for the convenience of the tribunal: the wife who slaves to put her husband through medical school and is then dumped for a young nurse receives no more in the property settlement than the adulterous, deserting husband. The church ought not to sacrifice justice to convenience, even if the state falls into that trap.[27] All divorces are equal, perhaps, but some are certainly more equal than others.

(4) Does the determination of fault and the basing of remarriage in the church on such considerations make the church "judgmental"? Only if we absorb Law into Gospel and turn Jesus and the Apostles into purveyors of cheap grace. Perhaps the danger is not so much that the world will view the church as judgmental but that it will see the church as an organisation with as little moral backbone as the Elk's Lodge. To insist on high moral standards in marriage and outside of it will, in the long run, enure to the advantage of the church, not to its disadvantage. As Jesus put it, "Think not that I am come to destroy the law: I am not come to destroy, but to fulfil" (Matt. 5:17). His unmerited grace is available to all, but it does not abrogate the high view of marriage to be found from the beginning (Gen. 2:24) to the end (Rev. 21:2) of Holy Scripture.

[27.] Cf. Montgomery, "Commentary and Response," 35/1 *The Jurist* 4-5, 81 ff (1975).

Addendum*

MARRIAGE IN CHURCH AFTER DIVORCE

LETTERS TO THE EDITOR
From Dr John Warwick Montgomery

Dear Sir,

Appendix A to the Working Party Report on 'Marriage in Church After Divorce' (2 Ecc. L.J. 366) asserts: 'It is our belief that ... the form critics are right when they tell us that these words [Mark 10,11f] reflect the heightened Christian conscience of the early church in Rome, where Mark's Gospel was compiled, rather than the *ipsissima verba* of the incarnate Lord. The same may be said, *mutatis mutandis*, about other Biblical rules such as the Pauline privilege and the Matthaean exception, so that what matters is what the Spirit is now saying to the churches, and in particular the Church of England, on this question.'

Readers unacquainted with the Greek text of the New Testament should be informed that there are no substantive textual problems whatsoever with Mark 10,11f, nor—*mutatis mutandis*—with the Pauline privilege (1 Cor. 7,15) or the Matthaean exception (Mt 5,32). The form-critical argument in these instances is founded not on the exigencies of the text but (as is so frequently the case) on subjective considerations and extrinsic, deductivistic reasoning ('Jesus—or Paul—would not have taken such a viewpoint in light of the way we think doctrine evolves'; 'The Matthaean exception could not represent Jesus's own teaching, for it appears in only one Gospel'; etc.). The unscientific nature of such argumentation has been thoroughly documented; see, *inter alia*, Humphrey Palmer,

---

* First published in: *Ecclesiastical Law Journal* 3/12 (January 1993).

The Logic of Gospel Criticism (London: Macmillan, 1968), especially pp. 172-73, 185-91, 224; C.S. Lewis, 'Biblical Criticism', in his *Christian Reflections*, ed. W. Hooper (London, 1967), pp. 152-66; and Gerhard Maier, *The End of the Historical-Critical Method*, trans. Leverenz and Norden (St Louis: Concordia, 1977), *passim*.

Logically, if the key passages on marriage and divorce in the New Testament are not *per se* binding upon us, but are merely 'reflective of Christian conscience' at its early stage, then no objective criteria exist by which today's Church can pronounce on the very issues with which the Working Party is so properly concerned. Whether or not there can be 'marriage in church after divorce' becomes a *sociological* rather than a theological question—to be determined by the direction current societal and ecclesiastical winds are blowing.

A more serious route to lightening the burden of the church's blanket prohibition on ecclesiastical marriage after divorce would be to pay far more attention to the very texts the Working Party downplays. The Lutheran theology of the Reformation, which in many ways constituted the original thrust of the 16th-century Anglican Reform (see C.M. Jacobs, *The Lutheran Movement in England*, and N.S. Tjernagel, *Henry VIII and the Lutherans*) insisted—on the basis of the Matthaean exception and the Pauline privilege—that the ratio of the prior divorce must always be examined before refusing a church marriage. To paraphrase George Orwell, all divorces were considered equal but some were seen as more equal than others! In the view of the Continental Reformers, an innocent party to a divorce on the ground of adultery ought surely to be able to marry again in church. Likewise, the innocent party who divorces on the basis of desertion. Indeed, the Lutheran theologians recognised that there could also be such a thing as (legally) constructive desertion; thus cruelty might constitute constructive desertion, and Luther said that the persistent refusal of one partner to engage in sexual relations with the other could be tantamount to malicious desertion. To the objection of Anabaptists and pietists that none of this would apply if the guilty partner were a believer ('let the unbeliever depart' —1 Cor. 7,15), the Lutherans responded that no true

Christian would maliciously desert his or her mate, so the guilty partner could never legitimately hide behind the façade of Christian profession.

May we suggest that the Working Party might have more success in their endeavour if they attached their wagon not to the form-critical star but to the more biblically-serious approach of classic Reformation theology?

Yours faithfully,
Dr John Warwick Montgomery

CHAPTER 8

CAN BLASPHEMY LAW BE JUSTIFIED?*

I. INTRODUCTION

Contemporary opinion in the common-law world seems almost uniformly against retaining a legal prohibition against blasphemy. As will be observed from the following representative judgements, those dealing with the question do not mince their words:

> The use of the criminal law to assuage affronted religious feelings imperils liberty—not greatly, to be sure, because blasphemy laws have become legal relics in the Anglo-American world. But they are reminders ... that the feculent odor of persecution for the cause of conscience, which is the basic principle upon which blasphemy laws rest, has not yet dissipated. (Leonard W. Levy, Professor Emeritus of Humanities, Claremont Graduate School, California, concluding his 688-page survey, *Blasphemy: Verbal Offense Against the Sacred, from Moses to Salman Rushdie*.[1])

> The law of blasphemy remains a real constraint on freedom of speech. Moreover, by protecting only the tenets of the Christian church established in England, the law promotes religious discrimination favouring one religion against all others. (Anthony Bradney, University of Leicester, in his book, *Religions, Rights and Laws*.[2])

> The conclusions which Nicolas Walter draws do cogently reflect the view of a very significant body of public opinion that the law of blasphemy is wholly inappropriate today. (Peter M. Smith, Univer-

---

* An invitational presentation in the University College London's 4th colloquium ("Law and Religion") in the *Current Legal Issues* series, July 3-4, 2000.

[1] Leonard W. Levy, *Blasphemy: Verbal Offense Against the Sacred, from Moses to Salman Rushdie* (2d ed.; Chapel Hill: University of North Carolina Press, 1995), p. 579. The first edition was published by Alfred A. Knopf in 1993.

[2] Anthony Bradney, *Religions, Rights and Laws* (Leicester: Leicester University Press, 1993), p. 97. See also Bradney's article, "Taking Sides: Religion, Law and Politics," *New Law J.*, March 26, 1993, pp. 434, 443.

sity of Exeter Law Faculty, reviewing Nicolas Walter's book, *Blasphemy, Ancient & Modern*.[3])

To the amazement of many, blasphemy remains a part of our law, although to the fury of many others it is a weapon which can only be used to protect the Church of England.... It is an insult to Anglicans to suggest that their beloved forms of worship need to be supported by a criminal sanction. (John Mortimer, counsel for editor Denis Lemon in the *Gay News* case.[4])

It is as much for the ingloriousness of its legal history as for its lack of principle that I should wish the blasphemy law abolished, leaving public order laws to protect, as they amply do, the decent devotions of the faithful of all religions against scurrility or abuse. (Geoffrey Robertson, counsel for Gay News Ltd in the *Gay News* case.[5])

In the plural British society of the 1990s it is difficult to conceive of situations where blasphemy can be a necessary restriction on the right of freedom of expression. In the writer's view the sooner the offence is abolished the better. (Simon Stokes, citing the Law Commission's Working Paper 79 [1981], in the conclusion to his article, "Blasphemy and Freedom of Expression under the European Convention on Human Rights."[6])

God does not need the inadequate and barely credible protection of a confused Court or a frightened Board of Censors. (David Nash, Oxford Brookes University, concluding his historical survey, *Blasphemy in Modern Britain, 1789 to the Present*.[7])

---

[3] Peter M. Smith, Review in 3/13 *Ecc. L.J.* 126 (July 1993). Nicolas Walter's *Blasphemy, Ancient & Modern* was published in 1990 by the Rationalist Press Association, London.

[4] John Mortimer, *Murderers and Other Friends: Another Part of Life* (London: Penguin Books, 1994), p. 88.

[5] Geoffrey Robertson, *The Justice Game* (London: Vintage, 1999), p. 161. See also the critical treatment of blasphemy in Robertson's *Freedom, the Individual and the Law* (7th ed.; London: Penguin Books, 1993), pp. 248-54.

[6] Simon Stokes, "Blasphemy and Freedom of Expression under the European Convention on Human Rights: Two Recent Cases," 7/2 *Ent. L.R.* 90 (1996). The Law Commission's Working Paper 79 advocates abolishing the offence of blasphemy: *Offences Against Religion and Public Worship* (1981), p. 164, para. D.

[7] David Nash, *Blasphemy in Modern Britain, 1789 to the Present* (Aldershot: Ashgate, 1999), p. 277. The selective documentation provided by Nash is very useful, particularly in the areas of social history and linguistics.

But blasphemy continues as a criminal offence in this country: Lord Denning was a better lawyer than a prophet when he declared in 1949, "the offence of blasphemy is a dead letter."[8] Indeed, the notion is not even a dead letter elsewhere in the European Community. A *Times* report informs us that

> A national campaign against blasphemy is gathering force in The Netherlands....
>
> Anti-blasphemy lobbyists launched a protest campaign against a Korean car company which played with the Ten Commandments in its advertising. The offending advertisement was later withdrawn.
>
> The Association Against Cursing, which was set up in 1917 by Jan Baas, a Calvinist, now has 18,000 registered members and many sponsors (not only from the churches)....
>
> Rijk van de Poll ... would like to make the anti-blasphemy cause international.... "Only the Scots have followed our example, with a League for the Increase of Pure Speech," he says.[9]

Is Geoffrey Robertson correct that blasphemy law has an "inglorious" history, and, more important, lacks any "principled" justification today? We shall look again at these issues, beginning with questions of definition, then proceeding to existing legal and theological attempts to vindicate blasphemy law, and finally offering what may hopefully be regarded as a more adequate evaluation.

II. BLASPHEMY DEFINED THEOLOGICALLY

The second of the Ten Commandments declares: "Thou shalt not take the name of the Lord thy God in vain; for the Lord will not hold him guiltless that taketh his name in vain" (Exodus 20:7 and parallels).[10]

[8.] Alfred Denning, *Freedom Under Law* (London: Stevens, 1949), p. 46.

[9.] *The Times*, May 4, 1996.

[10.] This is the second of the Commandments in the Roman Catholic and Lutheran enumeration; for Anglicans, the Eastern Orthodox, the Calvinists and the Zwinglians, who split the first Commandment into two, it is the third of the Ten.

Blasphemy consists of violating this Commandment in a particularly egregious manner. It is "more than taking the name of God profanely. It is defamatory, wicked, and rebellious language directed against God (Ps. 74:10-18; Isa. 52:5; Rev. 16:9, 11, 21)."[11] *The Oxford Dictionary of the Christian Church* speaks of the offence in the following terms:

> Speech, thought, or action manifesting contempt for God. In moral theology it is commonly regarded as a sin against the virtue of religion, though St. Thomas Aquinas defined it as a sin against faith. It may be directed either immediately against God or mediately against the Church or the saints, and is by its nature a mortal sin. Blasphemy was punished by stoning in the OT (Lev. 24.16, I Kgs. 21.10), and the Code of Justinian, as well as the medieval canon law, also prescribed severe punishments.[12]

In the 1917 Roman Catholic *Corpus Iuris Canonici*, blasphemy is to be punished according to the decision of the Ordinary (can. 2323). The corresponding section of the 1983 Code consists of canons 1368-1369. Canon 1369 declares:

> A person is to be punished with a just penalty, who, at a public event or assembly, or in a published writing, or by otherwise using the means of social communication, utters blasphemy, or gravely harms public morals, or rails at or excites hatred of or contempt for religion or the Church.

The Latin-English (Montréal) edition of the 1983 Code, prepared by E. Caparros, *et al.*, comments that blasphemy here means "uttering words or committing an act with the intention of cursing or offending God, either directly or through some insult to the Blessed Virgin Mary or the saints."[13]

There is an obvious difference between the Protestant and the Catholic treatment of blasphemy, in that the Roman Church sees insulting words or behaviour toward Mary and the saints as consti-

---

[11] R. J. Rushdoony, *The Institutes of Biblical Law* (Nutley, N. J.: Presbyterian and Reformed Publishing Co., 1973), p. 108.

[12] F. L. Cross (ed.), *The Oxford Dictionary of the Christian Church* (corrected ed.; London: Oxford University Press, 1958), p. 177.

[13] *Code of Canon Law Annotated*, ed. E. Caparros, *et al.* (Montréal: Wilson & Lafleur, 1993), p. 853.

tuting *lèse majesté* vis-à-vis God himself and his Church, whilst Protestants place the gravamen of blasphemy specifically in contemptuous treatment of the Triune God, the Incarnate Christ, and the Holy Scriptures. But, for all Christians, there is a clear distinction between the serious act of blasphemy, on the one hand, and merely crude or scatological language—what the French refer to as *gros mots*.

III. BLASPHEMY DEFINED AT LAW

How is blasphemy to be understood legally? In the first day of the *Gay News* trial, John Mortimer began by asking the Court to consider "whether this law exists or not." His attempt to avoid the issue definitionally—and, indeed, "all the legal arguments" he put forward—did not succeed.[14] Though there may be "no single, comprehensive definition of the ... offence of blasphemy" in English law,[15] the authorities have had little difficulty in setting forth its meaning. Thus, Stephen's *Digest of the Criminal Law* offers the following definition, which received the approval both of Lord Scarman in the *Gay News* case and of Lord Justice Watkins in *Ex parte Choudhury*:

> Every publication is said to be blasphemous which contains any contemptuous, reviling, scurrilous or ludicrous matter relating to God, Jesus Christ or the Bible, or tbe formularies of tbe Church of England by law established. It is not blasphemous to speak or publish opinions hostile to the Christian religion, or to deny the existence of God, if the publication is couched in decent and temperate language. The test to be applied is as to the manner in which the doctrines are advocated and not as to the substance tbemselves.[16]

In point of fact, two closely related offences of blasphemy exist at common law: blasphemy *simpliciter* (oral and other non-perma-

---

[14.] Robertson, *op. cit.*, p. 139.

[15.] Law Commission, *Offences Against Religion and Public Worship*, No. 145 (1985), para. 2.1. Cf. also Law Commission, *Offences Against Religion and Public Worship—An Invitation for Views* (1981), para. 7.

[16.] James Fitzjames Stephen, *Digest of the Criminal Law* (9th ed., 1950), Art. 214. Cf. Stephen, *A History of the Criminal Law of England* (3 vols.; London: Macmillan, 1883), II, 468-76.

nent statements) and blasphemous libel (publication in permanent form, as in print, film, painting, sculpture, etc.). These distinctions parallel the common law of defamation in its two varieties, slander and libel. In English law, blasphemous libel (and possibly blasphemy itself), like civil defamation, is a *strict liability* offence, that is to say, no particular mindset *(mens rea)* need be proven to obtain a conviction. There must be an intent to publish, but there need not be an intent to blaspheme. If the words uttered or published are objectively blasphemous, the intent of the utterer is legally irrelevant. As is said in the law of defamation, "It is not what you aim at but what you hit" that counts!

A brief overview of the historical development of blasphemy law will assist in understanding its legal meaning.[17] The offence existed in the ancient common law of England. Blackstone says of it:

> Blasphemy [is] against the Almighty, by denying His Being or Providence; or by contumelious reproaches of our Saviour Christ. Whither also may be referred all profane scoffing at the Holy Scripture, or exposing it to contempt and ridicule. These are offences punishable at common law by fine and imprisonment, or other infamous corporal punishment: for Christianity is part of the laws of England.[18]

The offence of blasphemy was definitively brought within the jurisdiction of the King's Bench in *Taylor's Case* (1676). There the defendant had uttered the words that "Jesus Christ was a Bastard, a Whoremaster" and "Religion was a Cheat." He admitted as such (except for the word "bastard") but explained that he was only saying that "Christ was Master of the Whore of Babylon," in reference to the Book of Revelation. He was convicted, Chief Justice Hale declaring:

> That such kind of wicked Blasphemous words were not only an Offence to God and Religion, but a Crime against the Laws, State and Government, and therefore punishable in this Court. For to say,

---

[17] See, *inter alia*, Courtney Kenny, "The Evolution of the Law of Blasphemy," 1/2 *Cambridge L. J.* 127-42 (1922), and G. A. Jones's unpublished dissertation, "The Law of Blasphemy—A Comparative Study" (LL.M. in Canon Law, University of Wales Cardiff, 1995).

[18] Blackstone, *Commentaries*, IV.iv.4.

Religion is a Cheat, is to dissolve all those Obligations whereby the Civil Societies are preserved, and that Christianity is parcel of the Laws of England; and therefore to reproach the Christian Religion is to speak in Subversion of the Law.[19]

In the final years of the 17th century, the crime of blasphemy was made statutory; the Act defined the offence as follows:

> If any Person or Persons, having been educated in, or at any Time having made Profession of the Christian Religion within this Realm, shall by Writing, Printing, Teaching, or advised Speaking, deny any One of the Persons in the Holy Trinity to be God, or shall assert or maintain there are more Gods than One, or shall deny the Christian Religion to be true, or the Holy Scriptures of the Old and New Testament to be of Divine Authority...[20]

It will be observed that the Act specifically exempted those not brought up in or having professed the Christian faith within the Kingdom (thus the Act had no application to Jews or to members of other religions, unless they had apostasised from Christianity). This statute was repealed by the Criminal Law Act of 1967,[21] so that today blasphemy remains only as a common-law crime (in its two forms, blasphemy and blasphemous libel).

The significant case law has not involved a great number of prosecutions. In *R v Woolston* (1729),[22] the defendant maintained (much as modern-day redaction critics of the Bible!) "that the Miracles of Jesus were not to be taken in a literal Sense; for as such they were not great enough to prove his Divinity; but that they were to be understood in a Mystical and Allegorical Meaning." *R v Williams* (1797)[23] was directed at the English publisher of Thomas Paine's *Age of Reason*, the second part of which consists of an attempt to catalogue errors and contradictions in the Bible, thereby supporting

---

[19] 1 Vent. 293.

[20] 9 & 10 Will3, c.32 (1697-1698). "This statute was brought to the attention of the Virginia Legislature, and they proceeded to re-enact it in April, 1699, almost word for word"—Arthur P. Scott, *Criminal Law in Colonial Virginia* (Chicago: University of Chicago Press, 1930), p. 240.

[21] Criminal Law Act 1967, s.13 and schedule 4, pt 1.

[22] 1 Barn. KB 163.

[23] 26 St. Tr. 653.

Paine's deistic view that the "Book of Nature" is preferable to the superstitious and false claims of the "Book of Scripture."

In *R v Carlile (Richard)* (1819),[24] the Court (Abbott CJ) made for the first time the important distinction between the *content* of the utterance in question and the *manner* of uttering it: "You are not here called into question for having published any work containing a calm, serious, and dispassionate enquiry into the truth ... [but] for the publication of a work which reviles and calumniates it." Concern now begins to focus on the insulting nature of the utterance, not the utterance *per se*. Thus the *tone* of the attack on the Christian religion is central to the prosecution in *R v Hetherington* (1841),[25] and in *R v Ramsay and Foote* (1883)[26] Lord Chief Justice Coleridge declared: "If the decencies of controversy are observed, even the fundamentals of religion may be attacked without the writer being guilty of blasphemy."[27]

At the same time, the Court in *R v Gathercole* (1838)[28] followed Lord Hale in *Taylor's Case* in emphasising that since Anglican Christianity is established by law in this Kingdom, the law of blasphemy exists to protect the teachings of that Church and of other churches insofar as their doctrines are consonant with it:

> A person may, without being liable to prosecution for it, attack Judaism, or Mahomedanism, or even any sect of the Christian Religion, (save the established religion of the country); and the only reason why the latter is in a different situation from the others is, because it is *the form established by law*, and is therefore a part of the constitution of the country. In like manner, and for the same reason, any general attack on *Christianity* is the subject of criminal prosecution, because Christianity is the established religion of the country.

Twentieth-century cases invariably stress actual or potential breach of the peace as the gravamen of the crime. In *Bowman and*

[24.] 1 St. Tr. (n.s.) 1387, 1423 (App.D).

[25.] 4 St. Tr. (n.s.) 563.

[26.] 15 Cox CC 231, 238.

[27.] Coleridge's attempt in this case to dismiss the argument that blasphemy prosecutions are justified owing the integral connection between Christianity and English law was savaged by counsel for the appellant in *Bowman and Others v Secular Society*, AC 406, 412-13.

[28.] 2 Lewin 237, 254.

Others v Secular Society (1917),[29] the House of Lords defined the offence in terms of "such an element of vilification, ridicule, or irreverence as would be likely to exasperate the feelings of others and so lead to a breach of the peace." In 1922, Avery J. explicitly ruled (*R v Gott*)[30] that the prosecution need not show an actual breach of the peace: it is enough "if a person of strong religious feelings had stopped to read this pamphlet whether his instinct might not have been to go up to the man who was selling it and give him a thrashing, or, at all events, to use such language to him that a breach of the peace might be likely to be occasioned."

The famous (or notorious) *Gay News* case (1978)[31], which went to the House of Lords and to the European Court of Human Rights, marks the current state of the law. The defending periodical had published a poem of breathtaking offensiveness concerning Jesus (*inter alia*, ascribing to him homosexual practices with the Apostles) and Christian reformer Mary Whitehouse instituted a private prosecution.[32] In spite of distinguished counsel for Gay News and for its editor, the periodical lost both in the English courts and in Strasbourg. The trial judge, Alan King-Hamilton[33], instructed the jury that it would be sufficient for conviction if they were convinced that the publication vilified Christ: intention to publish, not intention to blaspheme, would be enough. On appeal to the House of Lords,[34] the lower court judgment was affirmed, blasphemous libel being a publication "calculated to outrage the feelings of Christians." Lord Edmund-Davies and Lord Scarman stressed that a tendency to cause a breach of the peace is not a necessary part of the prima facie case, and Lord Scarman called for Parliament to broaden the offence so as to protect religions other than Christianity. The defend-

---

[29] AC 406, 446 (Lord Parker); cf. p. 466 (Lord Sumner).

[30] 16 Cr App R 87, 89.

[31] [1978] 3 WLR 404 (CA); [1979] AC 617.

[32] For Mrs Whitehouse's position and reflections on the case, see her two autobiographies, *A Most Dangerous Woman* (London: Lion Books, 1982) and *Quite Contrary* (London: Sidgwick & Jackson, 1993).

[33] See his own account of the trial in his autobiography: Alan King-Hamilton, *And Nothing But the Truth* (London: Weidenfeld, 1982).

[34] [1979] 1 All ER 898 (HL); [1979] 2 WLR 281.

ants then took their case to the European Commission of Human Rights, arguing violations of Arts. 7, 9, 10, and 14 of the European Convention; the Commission, however, declined to admit the case, noting that the defendants had had sufficient protection of their rights under English law.[35]

Since *Gay News*, the only blasphemy case to elicit public attention has been *R v Chief Metropolitan Stipendiary Magistrate, ex p. Choudhury* (1990)[36], in which the applicant laid informations against Salman Rushdie and his publishers for issuing Rushdie's *Satanic Verses*, arguing that this publication blasphemed the God common to Islam and Christianity and constituted seditious libel. The application was rejected on the grounds that the English law of blasphemy protects only the Christian religion and that the applicant had not shown that the *Satanic Verses* constituted an attack upon Christian faith. In the ensuing press uproar, a number of writers and some scholars advocated, as had Lord Scarman in the Gay News case, that the time had come to expand the English law so as to protect non-Christian religious feelings.[37]

A further case, however, merits comment. In *Wingrove v United Kingdom* (1995)[38], Nigel Wingrove, a British film producer, filed an action in Strasbourg against the British government for having refused a licence for his film, "Visions of Ecstasy," in which St Teresa appears to display erotic ecstasy in contact with the crucified Christ. Wingrove invited the Court to "produce a judgment which declares the British blasphemy laws as unnecessary in theory as they are in practice in any multi-cultural democracy." In spite of hopes to the contrary by those opposing the English blasphemy law, the European Court of Human Rights ruled, deferring to the margin of appreciation given to Member States in the application of their own law, that there had been no violation of Art. 10 of the Eu-

---

[35] *Gay News Ltd and Lemon v United Kingdom*, [1982] 5 EHRR 123.
[36] [1990] 3 WLR 986; [1991] 1 QB 429.
[37] E.g., Bradney, *loc. cit.*, and Richard Webster, *A Brief History of Blasphemy: Liberalism, Censorship and ' The Satanic Verses'* (Southwold, Suffolk: Orwell Press, 1990).
[38] ECHR 19/1995/525/611: [1997] 24 EHRR 1.

ropean Convention of Human Rights (the Article guaranteeing freedom of speech).

A year earlier (1994), the European Commission and Court of Human Rights had ruled similarly (and on the merits) in the case of *Otto-Preminger Institute v Austria:* the Institute was unsuccessful in persuading Strasbourg that the censorship of their film "Das Liebeskonzil" for violating the Austrian Penal Code's prohibition against "disparaging religious doctrines" was contrary to Art. 10 of the European Convention of Human Rights. The Court employed its margin of appreciation doctrine so as to give latitude to the Austrian national authority in balancing the competing interests of preserving free speech and avoiding gratuitous offence to the public.[39]

What will be the future of blasphemy cases? The 1999 Edinburgh Festival fringe included a play, "Corpus Christi," in which Jesus is converted to homosexuality by Judas Iscariot. Protesters, according to news reports, failed to prevent its opening.[40] Is the production ripe for legal action under existing blasphemy law? It would appear that the answer is surely yes—if activists of the Mary Whitehouse variety are still on the scene.[41]

IV. A REHABILITATED BLASPHEMY LAW IN CONTEMPORARY LEGAL THEORY?

Our brief survey of the English blasphemy cases has shown a subtle change in emphasis across the centuries, though the law it-

---

[39] [1995] 19 EHRR 34, 38-39. The Regional Court in Innsbruck described the film as presenting God the Father "as a senile impotent idiot, Christ as a cretin and Mary the Mother of God as a wanton lady with a corresponding manner of expression."

[40] "Protest Fails to Stop Gay Jesus Playing the Fringe," *The Independent*, August 11, 1999. The play has since opened, at a small North London theatre, to the accompaniment of protest demonstrations both from Christians ("a quiet group holding candles") and from Muslims (yelling, "Dirty gays, you will die! Dirty queers, burn in hell!"): *The Times*, November 1, 1999.

[41] Only the English production would be subject to prosecution, since there is no comparable anti-blasphemy law in Scotland. It will be noted that we do not here deal with the American blasphemy cases. The most prominent (generally under the common law but also by statute in those jurisdictions which have enacted anti-blasphemy laws) are: *Commonwealth v Kneeland*, 20 Pick. (Mass.) 206; *Updegraph v Commonwealth*, 11 Serg. & R. (Pa.) 394; *People v Ruggles*, 8 Johns. (N.Y.) 290; *Andrew v New York Bible Society*, 4 Sandf. (N.Y.) 156; *State v Chandler*, 2 Harr. (Del.) 553; and *Vidal v Philadelphia*, 2 How. 127.

self has remained very much the same. In the early cases, the gravamen of the offence lay in undermining Christian faith and the established Church *per se*. Then, the focus moved to the *manner* of the insulting publication: the nature of the offensive remarks, whether reasonable and balanced or extreme and provocative. Finally, emphasis has been placed on the *consequences* of the words or acts: are they likely to produce a breach of the peace?

As noted at the outset, the continuation of blasphemy law has met with few advocates today. Those who do support its continued existence have various proposals for making it more palatable. Let us now look at these and evaluate them.

The majority of the Law Commission who dealt with the blasphemy issue advocated the abolishing of the offence as such, but a minority recommended the substitution of an offence of outraging any religious feelings.[42] This proposal is in accord with the sentiments of most critics of the present law; in essence, the argument is that only in this way will the protection of the law be evenhanded and non-discriminatory, taking into account all religions in today's pluralistic English society. The inability of Muslims to employ the present blasphemy law to deal with their *Satanic Verses* problem heightens, in the minds of some, the need to move in this direction.

Professor Elliott, in a trenchant article, notes the severe problems with this solution.

> The objections to this are: there are formidable problems of definition, and some views which would be classified as 'religious' may deserve criticism or ridicule in the strongest terms (for example Scientology), and as the majority point out, abuse and insult cannot be excluded as weapons of criticism, for example criticism of ritual slaughter and the treatment of dead bodies, both a cherished part of the beliefs of some religionists. All recognised religions would have to be covered, otherwise even-handedness would be lost, but covering them all would be an enormous encroachment on individual expression, and would still discriminate against non-religionists.[43]

[42.] Law Commission, No. 145 (1985), para. 2.48.
[43.] D. W. Elliott, "Blasphemy and Other Expressions of Offensive Opinion," 3/13 *Eccl. L.J.* 70, 84 (1993).

A second suggestion is to amend the Public Order Act 1986, sections 17-23, so as to include "religion" among the categories in reference to which the stirring up of hatred is prohibited. Elliott points out that, were this to be done, the result would be either "tightly drawn and interpreted" or left in a fairly loose state. If the latter, "it approximates to the previous proposal and shares its drawbacks." But if it is strictly handled, "it seems otiose, in view of the existence of the offence in section 4 of threatening or provoking violence."

Professor Elliott himself favours a retention of just section 4 of the Public Order Act, which criminalises threatening expressions—the advantage here being that section 4 "covers all matters, so does not discriminate between adherents of different religions or between adherents and non-believers. Moreover, with its requirements of threatened or provoked violence it comes within a universally accepted derogation of the right of free speech."

One might very well question whether such a derogation is indeed "universally accepted." Certainly, civil libertarians in the United States would regard such a restriction as untenable in light of the First Amendment to the Federal Constitution and corresponding protections in State Constitutions.[44]

It will be noted that all of the above alternatives to the present common law of blasphemy have a common denominator: they seek to move the crime into the realm of a generalised offence to religious sentiments, so as to prevent breaches of the peace and maintain public order. They echo the position of Hosking, J., who, in New Zealand's first blasphemy case, declared:

> The law of blasphemous libel is not intended to enforce religious doctrine, but to maintain peace and order in the community and enforce respect for things sacred, and to prevent the bitter feelings and breaches of the peace which might arise from malicious desecration.[45]

But in the course of making such a change in the law, one would necessarily evacuate that law of its original significance, which

---

[44.] See Samuel Walker, *Hate Speech: The History of an American Controversy* (Lincoln: University of Nebraska Press, 1994), *passim*.

[45.] *R v Glover*, reported in *The Times*, February 24, 1922.

146   *Chapter 8*

(whether or not one thinks it a good idea) had to do with supporting the fundamental beliefs of the Church legally established in this country. Moreover, if the point of the replacement is to prevent breaches of the peace, it would seem that existing criminal and tort law already adequately covers the field. And if the idea is to extend restrictions on free speech to the threatening or offending of members of all religions, then it does not seem possible that such legislation could survive the Human Rights Act, which incorporates into United Kingdom law the free-speech protections of the European Convention of Human Rights.

V. AN ATTEMPTED THEOLOGICAL JUSTIFICATION OF BLASPHEMY LAW

There is one remarkable effort on the contemporary theological scene to rehabilitate the criminalisation of blasphemy. Though the movement is not large, its influence is out of proportion to its size. We refer to "Christian Reconstruction" (also known as "Biblical Theonomy"), centred in but by no means limited to Calvinist, Reformed circles in the United States.

The leading thinkers of Reconstructionism are Drs R.J. Rushdoony, Gary North, and the late Greg L. Bahnsen. Their writings are prolific and their work has elicited not only scholarly critique but considerable media attention, including a prime-time American public television news special devoted to the movement and hosted by distinguished commentator Bill Moyers.

The primary tenets of Reconstructionism are: (1) The Calvinist starting-point of God's sovereignty as Lawgiver and source of eternal election, as contrasted with the Lutheran stress on the Incarnate Christ and the Arminian emphasis on freewill. (2) A presuppositionalist apologetic and a corresponding refusal to offer any kind of evidential basis for Christian faith. Rushdoony actually includes apologetic endeavours such as those of C.S. Lewis within the definition of blasphemy:

> God is thus the principle of definition, of law, and of all things. He is the premise of all thinking, and the necessary presupposition

for every sphere of thought. It is blasphemy therefore to attempt to "prove" God; God is the necessary presupposition of all proof. To ground a sphere of thought, life, or action, or any sphere of being, on anything other than the triune God is thus blasphemy. Education without God as its premise, law which does not presuppose God and rest on His law, a civil order which does not derive all authority from God, or a family whose foundation is not God's word, is blasphemous.[46]

(3) An insistence on deriving all civil and moral law from the Bible, not from natural-law sources.

Neither positive law nor natural law can reflect more than the sin and apostasy of man: *revealed law* is the need and privilege of Christian society. It is the *only* means whereby man can fulfil his creation mandate of exercising dominion under God. Apart from revealed law, man cannot claim to be under God but only in rebellion against God.[47]

(4) The conviction (shared by many English Calvinists of Commonwealth times and by New England Puritans of the 17th century) that the law given by God to Israel in the Old Testament should in general still be applied today, both within the Church (as the "New Israel") and in civil society. (5) An opposition to Premillennialism and to all theologies not operating with a "Covenant" approach to God's work in history. (6) A deep suspicion of democracy and a desire to reestablish "biblical theonomy" in which the laws of God, as set forth in Scripture, become the laws of the state.[48]

In particular, the Reconstructionists would reinstitute the criminal code of the Old Testament with its corresponding penalties. For example, with regard to adultery, Rushdoony asserts that "a godly law-order will restore the death penalty, but the church must live realistically with its absence and protect itself."[49] It goes with-

---

[46.] Rushdoony, *op. cit.* [in note 11 above], p. 127.

[47.] *Id.* at 10.

[48.] See Gary North and Gary DeMar, *Christian Reconstruction: What It Is, What It Isn't* (Tyler, Texas: Institute for Christian Economics, 1991), and the *Journal of Christian Reconstruction*.

[49.] Rushdoony, *op. cit.*, p. 399.

out saying that the same would apply to blasphemy: it should be criminalised and punished with utmost severity.

What can be said of this theology and approach to the blasphemy issue? Taking each of the points of the Reconstructionist system: (1) It confuses Law and Gospel: the Law is properly a "schoolmaster (Gk., *paidagogos*) to bring us to Christ" (Gal. 3:24), not an end in itself, and the centre of Christian theology needs to be the Christ who himself fulfils the Law for us and offers forgiveness and grace to a fallen world.[50] (2) If the use of evidence is to be rejected for choosing among contradictory religious truth-claims, how is the Reconstructionist position itself to be vindicated? The Theonomist's epistemological position is perfectly self-defeating.[51] (3) Natural law can hardly be denied, since the very Scriptures on which the Reconstructionist relies affirm that it exists: the law of God is written on the human heart (Rom. 1:19, 20; 2:14-16). The heart of man is indeed corrupted by sin, but the answer is not to denigrate the value of the natural law *per se*, but—as Blackstone did—to see special revelation as supplementing the natural law and correcting misunderstandings of it.[52] (4) The *moral law* given to the Israel of the Old Testament is indeed of universal application, but its *political and ceremonial law* was unique to that people; Reconstructionists commit a fundamental hermeneutic mistake when they confuse these categories and attempt to establish an Old Testament theocracy today. (5) Premillennialism, though often misused by Fundamentalists and Dispensationalists, is nonetheless clearly taught in Scripture and was believed by the early Church.[53] (6) Democracy may well reflect the majority opinions of a sinful and fallen race, but, as Churchill put it:

[50] Cf. Montgomery, *Law & Gospel* (2d ed.; Edmonton, Alberta: Canadian Institute for Law, Theology & Public Policy, 1994), especially pp. 5-10.
[51] See Montgomery, *Faith Founded on Fact* (Nashville: Thomas Nelson, 1978), *passim*; Montgomery, "Once Upon an A Priori," in *Jerusalem and Athens*, ed. E.R. Geehan (Nutley, N. J.: Presbyterian and Reformed Publishing Co., 1971), pp. 380 ff.; Montgomery, *Where Is History Going?* (2d ed.; Minneapolis: Bethany, 1972), pp. 141-81.
[52] Blackstone, *Commentaries*, Intro., ii.3-4.
[53] Montgomery, "Millennium," *The International Standard Bible Encyclopedia*, ed. G. W. Bromiley (2d rev. ed., 4 vols.; Grand Rapids, Michigan: Eerdmans, 1979-1988), III, 357-61.

Many forms of government have been tried, and will be tried in this world of sin and woe. No-one pretends that democracy is perfect or all-wise. Indeed, it has been said that democracy is the worst form of Government except all those other forms that have been tried from time to time.[54]

In the Reconstructionists' theonomous theocracy, who speaks for God? The Reconstructionists, presumably—which ought to give all of us pause.[55]

If no more satisfactory justification for blasphemy law can be offered theologically than that of the Theonomists, it is understandable that cries for its elimination are widespread, even within the churches.

VI. A BETTER JUSTIFICATION

Is there any sufficient rational ground for retaining blasphemy law? We shall endeavour to offer such in conclusion, but, first, let us eliminate a *poisson rouge*.

One continually hears the argument that blasphemy law should be rejected out of hand if only because it restricts freedom of speech and expression and runs into immediate conflict with Article 10 of the European Convention of Human Rights. However, we have already seen that the European Court allows to national law a significant margin of appreciation in this area, owing to the fact that a balancing of interests and rights is involved. In point of fact, no jurisprudence, common-law or otherwise, allows unrestricted freedom of speech and expression. As the great American Supreme Court Justice Oliver Wendell Holmes, Jr., put it:

> The most stringent protection of free speech would not protect a man in falsely shouting fire in a theatre, and causing a panic. It does not even protect a man from an injunction against uttering words that may have all the effect of force.[56]

[54.] Churchill in the House of Commons, November 11, 1947.

[55.] One of the most thoroughgoing critiques of Reconstructionism (dismissed, characteristically, by the major advocates of the movement) is Rodney Clapp's article, "Democracy As Heresy," *Christianity Today*, February 20, 1987, pp. 17-23.

[56.] *Schenck v United States*, 249 U.S. 47, 52 (1919).

Even the Rationalist Press Association's publication condemning blasphemy law admits that "every society, indeed every human group (if not every human individual), objects to some forms of expression for one reason or another; and every society imposes on such forms of expression limits of one kind or another"—and cites as examples treasonable, seditious statements; defamatory utterances; racist remarks; and obscenity.[57] The issue, then, is not the glories of untrammeled speech and action, but whether then is any good ground to maintain legal sanctions for blasphemous utterances and publications.

What would be the consequences of simply abolishing common-law blasphemy and blasphemous libel? Would there be no negative effects? Professor Elliott rightly observes that, owing to the protections for ethnic groups by way of the Race Relations Act 1976 and the interlocking of various minority faiths with ethnicity, abolishing the crime of blasphemy would leave "discrimination in favour of members of those religions and against Christians and non-believers, who are not identified with any ethnic group." Indeed, the existing "anti-discrimination provisions, because of their fuzzy identification of ethnic religions with ethnic groups, encourage the belief that ethnic groups have on account of their religion certain immunities from the ordinary laws which are denied to Christians and non-believers."[58]

The irony of this is, of course, that if *any* religious group ought to receive special treatment—"certain immunities"—one would think that the group would be, by definition, the established religion. This brings us to the heart of the problem.

As Paul Tillich so effectively argued in setting forth his concept of God as "Ultimate Concern," there are *no* atheists—either individually or collectively.[59] Every person and every nation has a "god"— an ultimate concern—a highest value. A state need not enshrine its

---

[57.] Walter, op. cit. [in note 3 above], p. 7.
[58.] Elliott, op. cit. [in note 43 above], pp. 84-85. Cf. Julian Rivers, "Blasphemy Law in the Secular State," 1/4 *Cambridge Papers* (December 1992).
[59.] See Montgomery, "Tillich's Philosophy of History," in his *Where Is History Going?* (op. cit. [in note 51 above]), pp. 118-40.

Ultimate Concern in the trappings of an established church, but that does not mean that the Concern is not there. It appears, perhaps, as what sociologist Robert Bellah has termed "Civil Religion," manifested in the identification of national interests (however obnoxious) with the will of God.[60] Should a nation determine that it wishes to make its Ultimate Concern explicit by establishing a particular faith or church, then it surely has the right specially to protect and encourage its value system by way of that faith or church—as long as this does not prevent other faiths and secular philosophical options from freely proclaiming their ideological wares in an open marketplace of ideas.[61]

The common law of blasphemy simply recognises the special character of Christian faith in England—and in particular the importance to the nation of that "Reformed part of the Holy Catholic Church established in this Kingdom."[62] By virtue of blasphemy law, special penalties are attached to the offensive denigration of Christian doctrine and Church practice, and, as we have seen, this protection extends automatically to any other Christian churches insofar as their teachings coincide with those of the established Church. The law serves to reinforce the nation's commitment to its Ultimate Concern as represented by its established Church, and informs all and sundry that those values must not be made the object of "contemptuous, reviling, scurrilous or ludicrous" treatment.

The nub of the matter, then, is not and never has been the blasphemy law *per se*. The central issue is the nation's value system: *if* it is still represented best by Anglican Christianity, then there is no legitimate argument requiring the elimination of the blasphemy law. But if (as those who want to disestablish the Church claim), the country is now, like many modern states, a pluralistic nation with

---

[60] Robert N. Bellah, "Civil Religion in America," in Donald R. Cutler (ed.), *The Religious Situation: 1968* (Boston: Beacon Press, 1968), pp. 331-93, and frequently reprinted.

[61] For a fuller development of this argument, see Montgomery, *The Repression of Evangelism in Greece: European Litigation vis-à-vis a Closed Religious Establishment* (Lanham, Maryland: University Press of America, 2001), especially chap. 4.

[62] Cf. Graham Routledge, "Blasphemy: The Report of the Archbishop of Canterbury's Working Group on Offences Against Religion and Public Worship: A Personal View," *Eccl. L.J.*, No. 4, pp. 27-32 (January 1989).

a secular, multiform value system, then *to be sure* there is no reason necessarily to continue to criminalise blasphemy and good reasons to eliminate it. Perhaps this acute opposition of national philosophies is the reason why the question of justifying blasphemy law continues to arise—and why it elicits such passionate judgments: the matter lies at the very borderland between two diametrically opposed philosophies of the nation.

> And beside all this, between us and you there is a great gulf fixed: so that they which would pass from hence to you cannot; neither can they pass to us, that would come from thence.[63]

[63.] Luke 16:26 (the parable of Dives and Lazarus).

CHAPTER 9

HUMAN DIGNITY IN BIRTH AND DEATH: A QUESTION OF VALUES*

Much of the ethical confusion experienced by physicians, nurses, hospital administrators, and their legal counsel in the health-care area derives from an attempt to deal with problem cases *ad hoc*—without considering fundamental principles. The all-too-natural tendency to "take each case as it comes" is exacerbated by the social pressures created through the spiralling costs of health care and the spectre of litigation. Like the anti-hero preacher of John D. McDonald's novel, *One More Sunday,* the health care professional too frequently finds herself reduced to getting past the current crisis, hoping that she can survive just "one more Sunday."

Even those to whom the practitioners look for guidance are not immune from losing the forest among the trees. Note the commentary offered on the following tragic malformed-infant case:

> *Case 3.* T.B., a 36-hour-old male, was transferred to a medical center for management of an imperforate anus. The product of a normal pregnancy of, and an uneventful vaginal delivery by, his 39-year-old mother, T.B. had been recognized as having the clinical features of Trisomy 21 (Down's Syndrome) shortly after delivery—flattened occiput, characteristic appearance to the eyes, slightly full and protruding tongue, a simian crease on both hands and feet, and diffuse hypotonia, plus a loud heart murmur on ausculation and extreme cardiomegaly on chest x-ray.
>
> Physical examination of the rectal area at the time of transfer demonstrated a thin veil of almost transparent tissue covering the rectal orifice. Surgical relief of the rectal problem was felt to be rela-

---

* Invitational keynote address at the Conference on Legal and Ethical Issues (Edmonton, Alberta, Canada, 2-4 May 1990).

tively simple to achieve, but the cardiac signs and symptoms were interpreted as indicative of a major cardiac defect likely to cause death in the absence of attempts at surgical relief.

At that point in time, the parents were presented with the perceived facts and the options available to them. They considered the alternatives overnight and then decided against surgical intervention. Then the involved attending physician, who had been ostensibly neutral, shifted and supported their position, as did the consultant surgeon. Other members of the medical staff disagreed totally with the decision against intervention. The nursing staff emphasized their "Catch 22" quandary: if they fed the child and he eventually aspirated, it could be considered as active euthanasia; if they withheld all fluids, it could be construed as intentional starvation, also an active euthanasia process. Much private one-on-one discussion and debate followed, but virtually no group discussion and/or meetings intervened. At the end of 48 hours, the child was transferred to a nursing home for terminal care. Some 10 years later, members of the staff who participated in the process continue to harbor unease about that situation and the mechanism of its management....

The point of concern is, of course, that the misery and antagonism embodied in such situations not be permitted to interfere with the already stressful environment of the hospital (and all its inherent potential for error) to precipitate inappropriate allegations of malpractice.[1]

To be sure, the commentator's subject is malpractice, but prior to all questions of possible litigation are such bedrock ethical issues as: Was the newborn human? What value did he (it?) have? Was the non-performance of the "relatively simple surgical relief" unethical and in violation of the physicians' oath? Should the parents make the life-or-death decision for the newborn?

Avoiding such fundamental ethical questions is fatal (both for patients and for those who treat them). Socrates put it this way: "The unexamined life is not worth living." And, in fact, no-one ever really avoids the ethical dimension. As in historical study, where everyone has a philosophy of history and the really dangerous historians are the ones who are unaware of the values they intuitively

---

[1] William O. Robertson, M.D., *Medical Malpractice: A Preventive Approach* (Seattle: University of Washington Press, 1985), pp. 73-74 (italics ours).

bring to their work,[2] so in health care the question is not whether one indeed has values but whether one is willing to bring them into the clear light of day where they can be subjected to analysis and rigorous criticism.

In this brief presentation, an attempt will be made to identify the fundamental value-questions which health-care professionals cannot avoid asking, and to examine the alternative responses available in answering them. My own preferences will be clear, but the object of the discussion is to encourage the reader to think through each of the six watershed questions for himself or herself—*before* the next crisis arises in the hospital, the office, or the home. The six value issues are:

1. How important are human beings?
2. How do you know it's human?
3. Are human beings equal in value?
4. How important is the individual?
5. Do individuals have the right of self-determination?
6. Are ethical standards absolute?

I. HOW IMPORTANT ARE HUMAN BEINGS?

Even misanthropes consider their own viewpoint on the subject important, and thus place a high value on themselves (if not on others). In general, everyone considers human beings, or some human beings, very important. The ways divide over whether the human being is, or is not, *all*-important.

Ho Chi Minh was quoted as saying that even if North Vietnam had its population devastated in war it made little ultimate difference, for "we can always grow more children." Classical Marxism has always regarded the Party's doctrine as more important than the welfare of particular persons; thus Socialist political trials have followed Lenin's view that the end justifies the means and the actual guilt of the accused is far less important than the "education" of

---

[2.] See John Warwick Montgomery, *The Shape of the Past* (rev. ed; Minneapolis: Bethany, 1975).

the populace by way of the trial.[3] In today's secular and capitalist West, success and accomplishment (building a bigger, more "successful" hospital or practice?) have not infrequently counted more than human values in pragmatic decision-making.

Over against the "limited importance" view of human worth is the Judeo-Christian conviction that human beings are unqualifiedly important. The European Civil Law tradition, stemming from the Christian Emperor Justinian's great 6th-century codification, and the Anglo-American Common Law, exemplified by Blackstone's fundamental distinction in his *Commentaries* between "persons" and "things," refuse on principle to subordinate human worth to any impersonal values. Thus in the Common Law of defense of property, one is not allowed to kill to prevent conversion or theft of personalty, whereas homicide may be justifiable if one's own life or the life of another is in jeopardy (self-defense, defense of others). In international human rights law, the conventions, instruments, and treaties almost invariably place the "right to life" first among all rights, and make that right non-derogable.

Why choose the Justinian-Blackstonian option? Practically, it may be enough to consider the personal consequences of being treated by a health-care provider who doesn't consider human beings all-important! But, in the final analysis, one's view will depend upon one's ultimate commitments. Kaptchuk has argued that the progress of Western medicine over against its oriental counterpart may best be seen as "a consequence of Judeo-Christian emphasis on an omnipresent, transcendent God."[4] I have maintained the same in reference to the foundations of human rights: without a transcendent Creator to establish and guarantee human dignity, man whistles in the dark when he tries to assert his ultimate worth (like a world congress of rabbits voting on the supreme

---

[3.] See John Warwick Montgomery, *The Marxist Approach to Human Rights: Analysis & Critique*, published as Vol. Ill (1983-1984) *of The Simon Greenleaf Law Review*, Anaheim, California.

[4.] Ted J. Kaptchuk, O.M.D., *The Web That Has No Weaver: Understanding Chinese Medicine* (New York: Congdon & Weed, 1983), p. 264.

worth of rabbithood). We must refer readers elsewhere to pursue this most basic of all value questions.[5]

II. HOW DO YOU KNOW IT'S HUMAN?

Even when we have made a decision as to human worth, we will be in grave difficulty if we cannot distinguish a human being from W.C. Fields' kumquat. Two approaches are available for resolving this all-important question.[6]

First, it is argued simply that a human being is to be defined and identified according to its *genetic-chromosomal makeup*.[7] On this view, one will not be able to justify on the grounds of "insufficient humanness" the killing of a fetus or a malformed neonatus.

Secondly, there is *the functional definition* of the human being: one is human only and insofar as one functions humanly. The most influential advocate of this viewpoint at the moment is philosopher Michael Tooley, who asserts: "An entity cannot be a person unless it possesses, or has previously possessed, the capacity for thought. And the psychological and neurophysiological evidence makes it most unlikely that humans, in the first few weeks after birth, possess this capacity."[8]

Problems are rife with the functional approach to personhood. Leslie Mulholland of the Memorial University of Newfoundland writes:

---

[5] See John Warwick Montgomery, *Human Rights and Human Dignity* (2d ed.; Edmonton, Alberta: Canadian Institute for Law, Theology and Public Policy, 1995).

[6] An example of particularly muddy thinking in this area is the Law Reform Commission of Canada's Working Paper 58, *Crimes Against the Foetus* (Ottawa, 1989). There we are informed (rightly) that "market research cannot provide a solution," and then - three pages later - given Angus Reid and Gallop poll results generally supportive of the authors' question-begging non-solution: "In conclusion, the foetus merits at least some protection, not necessarily of the same order as that accorded to those already born, but of a kind increasing as it develops" (pp. 10, 13).

[7] See John Warwick Montgomery, *Slaughter of the Innocents: Abortion, Birth Control and Divorce in Light of Science, Law and Theology* (Westchester, Illinois: Crossway Books, 1981), especially pp. 72-73, 87 ff.

[8] Michael Tooley, *Abortion and Infanticide* (Oxford: Clarendon Press, 1983), p. 421. Also: Helga Kuhse, *The Sanctity-of-Life Doctrine in Medicine: A Critique* (Oxford: Clarendon Press, 1987).

If every human being has the right to be a person, then there is still an important question to be asked: Does a human being who lacks the ability to exercise judgment still have the right to the status of a person? In considering such questions, the important thing is to avoid answering them by treating the questioner as if he/she were in a special privileged position to consider them. It can seem that the ability to engage in the answer puts one in a privileged position. However, we should not abstract from the education that allows one to be in this position. That is, no one could be in the position if others had not educated him/her. Thus the position of the educated individual, able to exercise reflection, is always acquired. The right to be educated and the right to exercise judgment cannot be a consequence of the education itself. Furthermore, it cannot be a consequence of the relative social position of the parents, etc., for their position still needs to be justified. It must pertain to the individual by virtue of being human alone.[9]

Moreover, if genetic-chromosomal makeup is insufficient to define the human being and to justify according him or her human value and worth, *who* precisely has the right to establish the additional, functional criteria? And who is to say if the candidate functions *well enough* to deserve to be treated as a human being? Tooley, a philosopher, declares that to be human one must *think*. (Descartes was more humble: he spoke of himself in his aphorism, *Cogito, ergo sum;* he did not thereby try to define others out of the human race by evaluating their thinking capacity.) But why use thinking ability alone? What about job skills and other socially useful attributes? Social planners have long been disturbed by the need to support social misfits. And note the applications of this approach to the end of life—when the (former?) person loses his ability to function productively. Since decisions in areas like this gravitate almost inevitably to government, Huxley's *Brave New World* raises its ugly head. Not only the fetus, the handicapped, and the aged suddenly find themselves in jeopardy, but so does everyone whose activity does not conform to current societal or political standards.

---

[9]. Leslie A. Mulholland, "The Innate Right To Be a Person," in *Ethique et droits fondamentaux,* ed. Guy Lafrance (Ottawa: Les Presses de l'Université d'Ottawa, 1989), p. 136.

May we suggest that humans do not become such by acting in a human way: they act (occasionally!) in a human way because they are *first of all human.*[10]

III. ARE HUMAN BEINGS EQUAL IN VALUE?

Once we have determined that our patient is indeed human and therefore of immense value, we are still faced with the awkward comparative question: how valuable is one human being in comparison with another? On the genetic-chromosomal basis, a fetus is just as human as his or her mother; what do we do, therefore, in those (admittedly rare, but no less agonizing) situations where the life of one or the other must be sacrificed?

Here we must make an important distinction. When asking, "Are human beings equal in value?" do we mean "equal in *inherent* value" or "equal in *social* value"? We have already dealt with the question of inherent worth, and we concluded that it is a sad philosophy which would reduce human worth to anything below infinite value. Robert Veatch, in an exceedingly important recent study,[11] has applied such reasoning to the handicapped; he argues that all human beings—including the retarded—are morally equal, for they are the special handiwork of an infinite and loving Creator.

As true as this is, it is not the whole picture. If we stopped here when faced with the life-of-the-fetus versus the life-of-the-mother, nothing could be done but to flip a coin (since each life has the exact same ultimate worth by virtue of its createdness). A further question needs to be asked—that of social value.

Though possessing exactly the same inherent value as its mother, the fetus lacks the nexus of social involvements, responsibilities, and dependencies that the mother possesses. Thus, for example, the mother's death will have a profound and concrete effect

---

[10.] See John Warwick Montgomery, "The Rights of Unborn Children," in 5 *Simon Greenleaf Law Review* (1985-1986), 23-72.

[11.] Robert Veatch, *The Foundations of Justice: Why the Retarded and the Rest of Us Have Claims to Equality* (Oxford: Oxford University Press, 1986).

upon her husband, her other children, her blood relations, her friends, her employer or employees, etc. The death of the fetus will also impact the lives of others (as a human being, even the fetus cannot be "an island unto itself"), but the impact will be minimal owing to the brevity of the fetus' contacts with human society. It would seem, therefore, that in the agonizing situation in which only one life and not the other can survive, the choice should be made in favour of the mother. By analogous reasoning, where either the hopelessly retarded or the "normal" individual cannot survive (e.g., when only one kidney dialysis machine is available), the choice may have to be made on the ground of relative social worth, i.e., the relative complexity of social dependencies.

Note, however, that such reasoning is applicable *only* in the life-versus-life scenario. To sacrifice one life for the non-necessary *convenience* of another person remains a monstrous act, devoid of ethical justification. Even if we were to try to reason that a retarded individual totally lacked social worth (a hard proposition to maintain, since those who take care of the severely retarded are the first to say how much they are impacted and often transformed by them), this would say nothing as to their inherent worth as human beings. Fascinatingly, great writers have often used the lunatic or the retarded as a prophetic figure or even a Christ-image. We devalue our own humanity when we seek to devalue theirs.

IV. HOW IMPORTANT IS THE INDIVIDUAL?

The mention of "social worth" leads inevitably to the ethical dilemma of the needs of the individual over against the needs of society. Suppose there is only so much money for hospital treatment, and it can be either divided up to help many patients or restricted to the very expensive costs of saving just one; how should the money be allocated?

The classic answer, representing the position of the French Declaration of the Rights of Man, the American Bill of Rights, and 18th-century Western political liberalism in general, is that except in cases of emergency it is never right to sacrifice the good of one human being for that of another. Each individual has inherent worth, and no individual's interests are to be subordinated to another's unless absolute necessity dictates. To be sure, the individual may *voluntarily* sacrifice his interests for those of another—and such acts are often ennobling in the highest degree (think of Sidney Carton in Dickens' *Tale of Two Cities);* but self-sacrifice is hardly identical to forced sacrifice.

The opposing viewpoint came on the ideological scene in the 19th century, and is generally termed utilitarian socialism. Its great advocates were Jeremy Bentham and James and John Stuart Mill. Here the watchword is "the greatest good for the greatest number". The individual should be subordinated to the body politic so that the level of the entire populace is raised. In health care, the utilitarian argues for the overall average benefit to the patient-pool.

The utilitarian-socialist approach seems to have much to commend it. Is it not true, for example, that even the most libertarian governments expropriate individually owned property for the good of the many (the widow's home is sold by court order to permit the motorway to be built), and that these same governments use compulsory military service to send unwilling individuals forth in war to be maimed or killed for the sake of the rest of the populace?

However, it will be noted that eminent domain is supposed to be used only as a last resort, and the property owner must in any case receive "just compensation" (in the United States this is mandated by the Fifth Amendment to the Federal Constitution, and the same principle is firmly embodied in the unwritten British constitution). As for compulsory military service, I am not particularly convinced that it *is* ethically justifiable—but even if so, it is surely to be regarded as an exception arising from necessity, not as the reflection of normal societal practices. The only reason for forcing an able-bodied person to die for his country is presumably that otherwise the entire society, including the weak, might be subject to wanton destruction.

Are medical dilemmas analogous to these limiting cases? We doubt it. If the utilitarian argument were to be applied in general to medical treatment, the results would be bizarre and offensive to ordinary moral sensibility. Thus, to achieve the greatest good for the greatest number, it would be legitimate to engage in forced organ transplants. If I am blind, and you have two eyes, it would be mandatory on utilitarian principles to take one of your eyes and give it to me. Compulsory organ banks would be a proper object of utilitarian-socialist medical legislation.

We recognize intuitively from such illustrations that the utilitarian approach demeans the individual. Because of the inherent worth of the person, he must not be used as a means to an end, even if that end is the presumed good of an abstract humanity. Human beings are ends in themselves, and must always be treated as such.

Bentham considered burial non-utilitarian, and so donated his embalmed corpse to University College, London, where he is visible today for the utilitarian edification of subsequent generations.[12] May we suggest that in this as in the application of utilitarianism to medicine, the whole idea suffers from exaggerated self-importance? A health-care facility, except in the rarest of dire emergencies, must never sacrifice the individual patient for a "higher general good." In point of fact, there *is* no higher medical good then the best interests of the individual entrusted to the health care provider.

V. DO INDIVIDUALS HAVE THE RIGHT TO SELF-DETERMINATION?

When we opt for the individual over against the "mass," are we saying at the same time that individuals always have the right to determine their own destiny—that they are the absolute "masters of their fate and the captains of their soul"? If so, we would be

---

[12.] On Bentham, see especially the writings of historian Gertrude Himmelfarb, e.g., her *Marriage and Morals Among the Victorians, and Other Essays* (New York: Random House Vintage Books, 1987), pp. 94-143.

adopting a viewpoint which has powerful contemporary support, and important applications in the medical-legal field.

Thus, the libertarian view argues in favor of "pro choice" in the abortion controversy: a woman has the absolute right to do as she wishes with her own body. The same approach is applied at the other end of life: one also has an absolute "right to death" and should not be kept on life-support machines a moment longer than one wishes. Indeed, analogous reasoning was employed by one Canadian Queen's Bench judge (now mercifully overruled) who argued that a provincial law requiring seat belts infringed on Section 7 of the Charter of Rights and Freedoms, since the individual allegedly has the freedom to make his own safety decisions and not be prosecuted for his choice.[13]

In sharp contrast with the libertarian approach is the viewpoint that individuals, though infinitely important, cannot be allowed to exercise their freedom of choice in an unrestrained manner. The very fact that each individual has the same inherent worth as each other individual creates a built-in restraint on a given person's choices and actions. "Your rights end where my nose begins" is a succinct statement of this ethical position.

In reference to the abortion issue, the "pro choice" advocate should be reminded that one cannot decide the question as if only the mother were present: the unborn person must also be taken into account. If the "right to privacy" is appealed to (as it has been in U.S. legal discussion from *Roe v. Wade* to the present), it is worthwhile noting that homicide in the Common Law never becomes justifiable because one commits it while protecting one's right to privacy. Thus, if I am plagued by a cheeky encyclopedia salesman who violates my right to privacy by shoving his literature through my open window day and night, I may obtain an injunction to stop this private nuisance—but I must not blow his head off with a sawed-off shotgun. If the fetus is a human being by genetic-chromosomal

---

[13.] "Seat Belt Legislation Unconstitutional, Says Judge," *HospitAlta*, February 1989, p. 6. The Alberta Hospital Association was a prime supporter of the (ultimately successful) seatbelt legislation.

definition, my right to absolute freedom of personal choice ends where his or her life is at stake.

What about the so-called "right to death"? The Common Law traditionally punished suicide as a criminal act, and aiding and abetting suicide is still criminalised in most jurisdictions. Blackstone explains the Common Law position as follows: "The law of England wisely and religiously considers, that no man hath a power to destroy life, but by commission from God, the author of it:... the suicide is guilty of a double offence: one spiritual, in evading the prerogative of the Almighty, and rushing into his immediate presence uncalled for: the other temporal, against the king, who hath an interest in the preservation of all his subjects."[14] Suicide is never really a "victimless crime," for the body politic is diminished by the loss of any of its members. "Never send to know for whom the bell tolls," wrote Christian poet and preacher John Donne, "it tolls for thee."

The same point applies to seatbelts, as the Alberta Hospital Association correctly reasoned and as the Canadian court system finally agreed. Those persons who refuse to wear or negligently do not wear seatbelts not only jeopardize their own lives and contribution to the community; they also cost the rest of society vast sums in medical care for the injuries sustained.

And cryonics? What about the recent effort (both in real life and on television) of the patient with a terminal brain tumor to have himself frozen now so that on being revived (hopefully!) at a later stage of medical knowledge his brain will have a better chance of treatment?[15] Assuming that this patient's brain would be destroyed by the time of his natural death, one could well argue that pre-death freezing would not in fact be suicide in the ordinary sense, since the object here is not the cessation of life but the (admittedly remote but nonetheless scientifically responsible) chance of restoring it.[16]

[14.] Wm. Blackstone, *Commentaries,* IV, xiv, 3.

[15.] Thomas Donaldson of Sunnyvale, California, had so petitioned the Santa Barbara County Superior Court to have himself frozen to death (28 April 1990); his attempt was featured in an episode of NBC's "L.A. Law" in January 1990.

Whatever one's position in the difficult and grey area of cryonic ethics, it should be plain that, in general, the inherent equality of individuals militates against the kind of unbridled individualism that would place no restraint on personal decision-making. As we opt for life over death, our life-and-death decisions must take others into account.

VI. ARE ETHICAL STANDARDS ABSOLUTE?

Throughout this essay we have been discussing standards of one kind and another. Now, in conclusion, we had better determine what degree of binding force standards ought to have. Two views of standards are common—the relativistic approach and the absolute viewpoint.

For the relativist, standards do not exist as moral absolutes over against the human decision-maker. *Contextual* ethicists, for example, see standards as arising from the very texture of group ethical discussion. *Existential* ethics (one thinks especially of Jean-Paul Sartre) focuses on the uniqueness of the ethical event and the active decision-making imposed by it. (To a Resistance fighter during World War II who came to Sartre for moral advice, the existential philosopher declared: "There are no omens in the world. ... DECIDE!") Joseph Fletcher tells us that ethics is *situational:* we should act in love, letting the end justify the means, and not think that the same moral rules are binding everywhere or for all time.

Ethical absolutists are not impressed by these positions. They note, first of all, that relativistic arguments always beg the question: one must begin with a non-relativistic premise in order even to be able meaningfully to state something relative. This is clear when one examines the assertion, "All is relative." Is *that* statement relative? (If so, it is no longer necessarily true. But if the statement is absolutely true, then relativism is perforce incorrect!)

[16.] Cf. John Warwick Montgomery, "Cryonics and Orthodoxy," *Christianity Today,* 10 May 1968, p. 48. See also John Warwick Montgomery, "Do We Have the Right To Die?," *Christianity Today,* 21 January 1977, pp. 49-50.

Relativistic viewpoints descend into hopeless subjectivity. Contextual ethics has been termed "morality by bladder control," for those able to sit the longest in the group discussion (without having to go to the toilet) influence the ethical discussion the most. Existentialism is purely *ad hoc* and therefore ethically arbitrary. The Resistance fighter who went to Sartre received no help whatever, for he *already* knew he had to make a decision—and Sartre on principle was incapable of offering any objective guidance to assist that decision. One man's existential decision can well be another man's poison, and no criteria exist (by definition) to arbitrate between them.

Fletcher's situationalism leaves love undefined and opens the floodgates to virtually any action that allegedly produces a good end. In my university debate with Professor Fletcher, I reminded the audience that since for my opponent lying was a legitimate means to a good end (and since he obviously considered their acceptance of situation ethics a good thing), they could discount the truth of anything and everything he said to them that evening![17] It is not accidental that Professor Fletcher is ethically untroubled by abortion on demand or by active euthanasia.

Medical decisions are fraught with such consequences for human life and dignity that one cannot afford the luxury of a relativistic ethic where they are concerned. Thus, in the international human rights field, efforts are focused on the preservation and promulgation of *inalienable, non-derogable* rights—rights that cannot be taken away by governments on the pretense that "national emergencies," changing socio-economic conditions, etc., may permit, for example, the torture of prisoners. Once we have justifiably arrived at ethical bedrock, let us not make the sad mistake of building our house upon the sands of relativism.

But is not ethical absolutism rigid and unfeeling? It *can* be, but this need not be the case. In the broken world we live in, even when moral issues are clearly seen, one must often face genuine conflicts

---

[17.] See Joseph Fletcher and John Warwick Montgomery, *Situation Ethics: Is It Sometimes Right To Do Wrong?* (2d ed.; Edmonton, Alberta: Canadian Institute for Law, Theology and Public Policy, 1999).

of principle and the necessity of choosing a lesser of evils. Such decisions are not compromises: they are rather a mature recognition of the problems inherent in a fallen world. Here, particularly, the theology represented by classical Christianity can be an incalculable boon, for at its heart is the Cross of Christ, offering forgiveness and hope as we struggle in the slough of ethical ambiguity, striving to apply sound principles to exceedingly complex and often heartrending individual cases.

One thing is certain. If we refuse to face the kinds of questions posed in this essay, we become a danger to the institutions which we represent and the patients and clients entrusted to our care. To paraphrase Socrates outrageously: "The unexamined hospital is not worth funding."

CHAPTER 10

WHOSE LIFE ANYWAY? A RE-EXAMINATION OF SUICIDE AND ASSISTED SUICIDE

I. INTRODUCTION

English common law is a conservative tradition. Judges are loath to play the role of legislators and Parliament is hesitant to enact legislation on controversial social issues. Thus law reform is not currently pending in the United Kingdom in regard to suicide or assisted suicide—in spite of the debates which such proposals and actual legislation have elicited in civil law and other common law jurisdictions. This chapter endeavours to determine whether, in principle, legal liberalisation ought in fact to be introduced for the benefit of those wishing to terminate their lives.

A generation has passed since the first appearance of Brian Clark's television play, *Whose Life Is It Anyway?* (1972), followed in 1978 by the moving stage production starring Tom Conti at London's Mermaid Theatre. The play turned out to be prophetic. Under the caption, "U.S. Courts Uphold Right to Assisted Suicide," the London *Times* reported on 9 April 1996:

> The right of terminally ill Americans to commit suicide with the help of a doctor has been upheld by two federal appeal courts. The landmark rulings on the East and West Coasts have brought a controversy that has long been simmering to the forefront. A national debate is emerging on the medical, legal and theological implications. The issue is almost certain to go to the Supreme Court where the justices will be asked to decide if the dying have a constitutional right to ask a doctor for assistance in ending their lives.... The federal appeal court in San Francisco voted 8-3 to annul a law barring assisted suicide that dated back 140 years in Washington state. The court said that competent adults have a constitutional

right to seek help in choosing "a dignified and humane death rather than being reduced to a child-like state of helplessness." The ruling was followed by a similar finding in New York.[1] The judges said it made no sense that doctors could pull the plug on life-support systems at a patient's request, but were not allowed to prescribe lethal doses of drugs for those who wanted them.

Clearly the issues at stake are of the most fundamental importance for human rights. Equally plain is the impossibility of treating the suicide/assisted-suicide question in a hermetically sealed legal compartment: root values are at stake, so there is no choice but to combine jurisprudential with serious ethical and theological analysis. The need for such treatment is particularly evident from the 9th Circuit (Washington) opinion, so we shall start there.

II. THE "COMPASSION IN DYING" JUDGMENT

The most striking aspect of the *en banc* opinion in *Compassion In Dying v State of Washington*[2] is not the substantive conclusions reached but the style of reasoning displayed. The Court by no means restricts itself to an analysis of precedents or to the funda-

---

[1] *Quill v Vacco*, 80 F. 3d 716 (2d Cir. 1996).

[2] 79 F. 3d 790 (9th Cir. 1996); 1996 WL 94848 (9th Cir. [Wash.]). The U.S. Supreme Court in early January 1997 heard oral arguments in an appeal against this decision and that in *Quill*, note 1 above. A United Press International release of 8 January 1997 reported:

> The Supreme Court indicates it might be a long way from approving physician-assisted suicide, as key justices suggest they have problems with the issue. The Supreme Court heard argument Wednesday on two lower court rulings that struck down bans on doctor-assisted suicide in New York and Washington states. Justice David Souter, considered a leader of the court's liberal wing, from the bench asked lawyers why the court shouldn't wait for society to resolve the issue politically. Souter told one lawyer advocating the right to doctor-assisted suicide, "Why not wait? We are not in the position to make the judgment now that you want. It would just be guesswork" without more information. Chief Justice William Rehnquist told lawyers that a ruling on physician-assisted suicide would bring on the same emotions as abortion, adding, "You're going to have those (pro and anti-abortion rights) factions fighting it out in every session of the legislature." And Justice Anthony Kennedy, usually a swing vote, said doctor-assisted suicide would cause "fear" among those who might be pressured to take their own lives. Citing a New York task force study on the issue that has been widely used in briefing the court, Kennedy told assisted-suicide advocates, "The autonomy (for the individual) that you seek is illusory.... In fact you will be introducing fear into medical facilities. That's what I get from that New York report."

On 26 June 1997, the U.S. Supreme Court did in fact reverse both decisions. Chief Justice Rehnquist delivered the Court's judgment, which was unanimous albeit with separate concurring opinions: 117 Sup. Ct. 2258.

mental Constitutional issues (due process, the state interest, the liberty interest, etc.): a painfully superficial overview of historical attitudes towards suicide provides the background for a discussion of "current societal attitudes." Here the Court gives considerable weight to polls and statistical surveys. We are informed, *inter alia*, that "polls have repeatedly shown that a large majority of Americans—sometimes nearing 90%—fully endorse recent legal changes granting terminally ill patients, and sometimes their families, the prerogative to accelerate their death by refusing or terminating treatment," that "polls indicate that a majority of Americans favour doctor-assisted suicide for the terminally ill," and that "according to a survey by the American Society of Internal Medicine, one doctor in five said he had assisted in a patient's suicide." Not surprisingly, the Court's venture into sociology concludes with a value-laden reference to the "growing movement to restore humanity and dignity to the process by which Americans die."

The Court is at pains throughout to emphasize its dependence on *Roe v Wade*, e.g.: "In examining whether a liberty interest exists in determining the time and manner of one's death, we begin with the compelling similarities between right-to-die cases and abortion cases."[3] One of the most "compelling similarities" between *Compassion In Dying* and *Roe v Wade* lies in the common sociological focus of the decision-making in the two cases. In *Roe*, shallow historicising (abortion has been opposed only by the Hippocratic school and by Christians, so it cannot be rejected out-of-hand in a pluralistic society today) is made the basis of sociological judgment: "This holding is consistent with the relative weights of the respective interests involved ... and with the demands of the profound problems of the present day."[4] No attempt is made to deal with the essential ontological question: "We need not resolve the difficult question of

---

[3.] Need it be pointed out that just as there is no unqualified U.S. Constitutional right to privacy justifying the taking of foetal life, so there is no unqualified "liberty interest" justifying the taking of one's own life or assisting others to do so? My right to privacy or to liberty is always limited by the effects of my actions on other individuals and on the body politic in general.

[4.] *Roe v Wade*, 410 U.S. 113, 165 (1973).

when life begins."[5] Just as *Roe* sacrifices the personhood of the foetus to the vagaries of contemporary sociological pressure,[6] so *Compassion In Dying* allows opinion polls to substitute for a principled determination of the worth of a dying patient's life.

Two observations need to be made concerning this common reasoning style. First: legal judgments are, by definition, "ought" statements; they do not describe a state of affairs but declare a binding standard. Thus whenever judges base their opinions on sociological or statistical considerations they commit the venerable naturalistic fallacy (sometimes termed, appropriately, the sociologist's fallacy): they suppose that one can derive the "ought" from the "is"—that the normative is derivable from the descriptive. But fifty million Frenchmen (or two-hundred million Americans) can be *wrong*—and often *are*. To allow abortion on demand because a majority of people favour it is the functional equivalent of decriminalising tax evasion because most people hate income tax. And to reason that because many people now think suicide or assisted suicide is permissible and that a certain number of physicians do in fact help the terminally ill on their way, such practices are legally justifiable, is utterly fallacious. *Vox populi* has never been, and has not suddenly become, *vox Dei*.

Secondly, the jurisprudence of *Roe v Wade* and *Compassion In Dying* is not classic common-law jurisprudence at all, but a relatively recent deviant, which, however, has virtually captured the field in America. The greatest exponent of so-called American Legal Realism, Karl Llewellyn, argued that since (in his view) law is but a means to social ends and courts are in reality engaged in a process of rationalising precedent and principle to achieve contemporary social goals,[7] judges should substitute for the nineteenth century "formal style" (where the real grounds for decision are concealed behind an appeal to formal reason and supposedly objective

---

[5]. *Id.* at 159.

[6]. J.W. Montgomery, "Abortion and the Law: Three Clarifications," in *New Perspectives on Human Abortion*, Hilgers, Horan, and Mall eds. (1981) 281-92; *Slaughter of the Innocents* (1981); "The Rights of Unborn Children," 5 *Simon Greenleaf Law Review* (1985-1986) 23-72.

[7]. K. Llewellyn, *Jurisprudence: Realism in Theory and Practice* (1962) 55-57.

values) the "grand style" (where one straightforwardly identifies the roots of the law in social needs). Llewellyn was convinced that by the 1960s the grand style had come to prevail, at least in American appellate courts.[8] Recently, Atiyah of Oxford and Summers of Cornell, in a major comparison of the English and American common law traditions, have distinguished two visions: the classic English "formal vision" in which courts rely on precedent, commit themselves to principled decision-making, and leave law-making to the legislature (Parliament); and the modern American "substantivistic model" in which judges confidently make law based on policy-orientated considerations.[9] Ronald Dworkin has pointed out the extreme dangers of policy-orientated, judicial lawmaking, where judges become deputy legislators and policy rather than principle comes to prevail on the bench.[10] *Compassion In Dying* would appear to represent the latest example—and a particularly egregious one—of this sad trend in the higher courts of America.

But if principle rather than social policy is to be our proper guide, then we must look in depth at the jurisprudential background of the suicide and assisted-suicide question.

III. THE LAW OF SUICIDE AND ASSISTED SUICIDE

The common law traditionally punished suicide as a criminal act, and aiding and abetting suicide is still criminalised in most common law jurisdictions. The grounding for the legal doctrine was to be found in both civic and theological principle. Sir Matthew Hale wrote in his authoritative *History of the Pleas of the Crown* (late seventeenth century):

> *Felo de se* or suicide is, where a man of the age of discretion, and *compos mentis*, voluntarily kills himself by stabbing, poison, or any

---

[8.] K. Llewellyn, *The Common Law Tradition: Deciding Appeals* (1960) 35 ff.

[9.] P.S. Atiyah and R.S. Summers, *Form and Substance in Anglo-American Law: A Comparative Study of Legal Reasoning, Legal Theory, and Legal Institutions* (1991).

[10.] R. Dworkin, *Taking Rights Seriously* (1978) 82-92; *Law's Empire* (1986) 221-24, 244. On Dworkin's approach to the abortion issue, as set forth in his book, *Life's Dominion*, see J.W. Montgomery, "New Light on the Abortion Controversy?," 60/7 *New Oxford Review* 24-26 (1993).

other way. No man hath the absolute interest of himself, but 1. God almighty hath an interest and propriety in him, and therefore self-murder is a sin against God. 2. The king hath an interest in him, and therefore the inquisition in case of self-murder is *felonicè & voluntariè seipsum interfecit & murderavit contra pacem domini regis.*[11]

Sir William Blackstone, in the first general textbook of the English common law, the *Commentaries* (eighteenth century), made the same points with greater eloquence:

> The law of England wisely and religiously considers, that no man hath a power to destroy life, but by commission from God, the author of it: ... the suicide is guilty of a double offence: one spiritual, in evading the prerogative of the Almighty, and rushing into his immediate presence uncalled for: the other temporal, against the king, who hath an interest in the preservation of all his subjects.[12]

And, at the beginning of the nineteenth century, East declared in his *Treatise of the Pleas of the Crown:*

> The last kind of felonious homicide is that against a man's own life, which denominates the party slaying himself *felo de se.* This is where any one wilfully or by any malicious act causes his own death. The law regards this as an heinous offence, though the party himself may at first view appear to have been the only sufferer: for as the public have a right to everyman's assistance, he who voluntarily kills himself is with respect to the public as criminal as one who kills another. It is equally an offence against the fundamental law of society, which is protection. The law has therefore ordained as severe a punishment for it as the nature of the case will admit of, namely, an ignominious burial in the highway with a stake driven through the body; and a forfeiture of all the offender's goods and chattels to the king.[13]

As for assisted suicide, Sir James Fitzjames Stephen states the historic common law position:

> Suicide is held to be murder so fully, that every one who aids or abets suicide is guilty of murder. If, for instance, two lovers try to

---

[11.] Hale, *P.C.* I, 411-12 (chap. xxxi). Cf. W. Hawkins, *P.C.* I, 67-69 (chap. xxvii) (1716).
[12.] *Bl. Com.* IV, xiv, 3. For theological selections from Blackstone and Hale, see J.W. Montgomery, *Jurisprudence: A Book of Readings* (4th ed. 1992) 277-81, 331-38.
[13.] East, *P.C.* I, 219 (chap, v, sec. 5).

drown themselves together, and one is drowned and the other escapes, the survivor is guilty of murder.[14]

In that connection Stephen makes comparative reference to the nineteenth century German *Strafgesetzbuch*, Art. 216, "which, in providing for the punishment of various cases of homicide, says:—'If a person is induced to kill another by the express and serious request of the person killed, he must be imprisoned for not less than three years' (and by Article 16 not more than five)."[15]

The deterrent of forfeiture of lands or goods belonging to the one who kills himself was removed in 1870 as a result of the abolishing of forfeitures for felony in general (33 & 34 Vic. c. 23). The custom of interring the suicide at a public crossroads also disappeared in the nineteenth century, again as a result of legislation (4 Geo. 4, c. 52; 45 & 46 Vic. c. 19).

The twentieth century has seen suicide reduced from a felony to a misdemeanour and ultimately decriminalised entirely in most common law jurisdictions; in England the latter occurred as late as 1961 by way of the Suicide Act of that year. *Attempted* suicide has also been decriminalised; Glanville Williams makes the pregnant comment:

> Although it is now universally conceded to be useless and harmful to punish those who attempt suicide for any reason, because the punishment of one who attempts suicide can only increase his depression and render a renewed attempt more likely, prevailing opinion still holds that it is right and efficacious to punish those who assist suicide (or who kill with consent), even though they act from the strongest humanitarian motives. This seems to show that the more relaxed attitude toward the person who attempts his own suicide is based on limited pragmatic considerations and does not signify any abandonment of the traditional condemnation.[16]

Where suicide itself does not exact any legal opprobrium, there is a certain superficial logic (we shall later see how superficial it indeed is!) to the view that assisting suicide should also be free of

---

[14.] J.F. Stephen, 3 *A History of the Criminal Law of England* (1883) 104.
[15.] *Id.* at 106.
[16.] G. Williams, "Suicide," 8 *Encyclopedia of Philosophy* 44 (P. Edwards ed. 1967).

legal penalties. Thus the distinguished nineteenth-century French criminalist Faustin Hélie wrote:

> La loi n'a point incriminé le suicide. Le fait de complicité est-il punissable? La negative est évidente, puisqu'il n'y a pas de participation criminelle à un fait qui ne constitue en lui-même ni crime ni délit.[17]

Glanville Williams sees clearly the resolution of this apparent paradox that "if one person can lawfully commit suicide, why should it be an offence for another to help him?"—it is "because we still think suicide immoral."[18]

Indisputably, however, secular, pluralistic Western societies at the very end of the twentieth century are less and less inclined to regard suicide as immoral—and so they are more and more inclined to decriminalise aiding and abetting the suicide of others. The Netherlands offers a well-known case in point. Though Article 293 of the Dutch Penal Code classes voluntary euthanasia as one of the "serious offences against human life" in Title XIX of the Code, assisted suicide is known to have become an established part of medical practice in the Netherlands since the early 1970s. Two court decisions in 1986 (one from the Hague Court of Appeal, the other from the Dutch Supreme Court) have created a defence of "necessity," absolving physicians from prosecution as long as the voluntary euthanasia conforms to certain guidelines.[19] And now we have the two U.S. federal appeals court decisions which would, but for their reversal by the U.S. Supreme Court, have provided parallel death-on-demand possibilities in America—to operate in tandem with abortion-on-demand as established throughout the United States in 1973.

Clearly there are value questions of gigantic proportion to be faced in determining whether such a trend ought to be supported

---

[17] F. Hélie, *Pratique criminelle des cours et tribunaux, résumé de la jurisprudence sur les Codes d'instruction criminelle et pénal*, pt. 2 ("Code pénal"), (1877) 299.
[18] G. Williams, *Textbook of Criminal Law* (1978) 531. Cf. his *The Sanctity of Life and the Criminal Law* (1957).

or opposed. Let us now turn to such an evaluation.

[19.] See J. Keown, "The Law and Practice of Euthanasia in the Netherlands," 108 *Law Quarterly Review* 51-78 (1992). According to the London *Times* (1 April 2002), "The Netherlands becomes the first country to legalise mercy killings and assisted suicides when euthanasia law takes effekt today. It allows doctors to help to end the lives of patients suffering from an unbearable, terminal illness, but only under stringent procedures."

The London *Times* reported (13 April 1996) that by the time Australia's Northern Territory's euthanasia act entered into force on 1 July 1996, a physician in Darwin should have developed a software program making it possible for a terminally ill patient to take his own life by pressing the return key on his laptop computer (the subject will be connected to a syringe driver, linked in turn to the laptop; when the appropriate command is activated, a lethal dose of barbiturate will be injected into the subject's bloodstream). "The Church and prolife lobbyists fear that the law will make Darwin the death capital of Australia, if not the world, attracting hundreds of terminally ill people to the Northern Territory." Church Net UK News Service announced on 16 August 1996 that the "NSW [New South Wales] Council of Churches has called on the Prime Minister to examine ways to establish a uniform, national anti-euthanasia policy, far beyond the perimeters proposed in *The Territories (Protection of Human Life) Act 1996* [A Federal Private Member's Bill to overturn the Northern Territory legislation]. Council President, Rev. Ross Clifford said today, 'The Council of Churches fully supports the draft content of the proposed private members Bill but for any anti-euthanasia legislation to really work effectively, a national perspective must be adopted through the co-operation of all states and territories exercising their own legislative power.' ... He added, 'Without a unified policy, any move to reverse the Northern Territory legislation would be thwarted if any other State passing pro-euthanasia legislation allowed people from other States to freely access the Act.'"

Mr. Clifford, who is also a NSW and Northern Territory Solicitor and Barrister, provides the following updated information on the Australian situation (fax of 28 November 1996 to this author): "With respect to the Northern Territory of Australia Rights of the Terminally Ill Act the Supreme Court of the Northern Territory dismissed the appeal. As a consequence a member of our Federal Parliament (Mr Andrews) has presented to our Federal Parliament the Euthanasia Laws Bill 1996 to overturn the Territory Euthanasia provisions. The House of Representatives, our Lower House and where the power resides, is still debating the Bill (maybe they will vote in December). Our Senate which is made up of senators from our states has referred the matter to a committee, one reason being the question of state rights—the power of the Federal Parliament to overrule a state/territory. The committee will not report before February 24, 1997 and no vote in the Senate will take place before then. Commentators feel the Lower House will support the Andrews Bill but the Upper House is doubtful. Our Federal High Court has determined not to hear the issue until the parliamentary process is complete. As a matter of interest our New South Wales parliament had a debate on the issue (no Bill just a debate) and voted overwhelmingly against euthanasia. Our Premier, Mr Carr, has written to me as President of the NSW Council of Churches, to indicate 'after the debate I cannot see euthanasia legislation being enacted in our State.' He expressed a strong public voice against euthanasia." For Mr. Andrews's first reading speech on the Federal Bill, see the Addendum to this chapter. The House of Representatives passed the Bill (see *The Times*, 10 December 1996), as did the Senate (see the *Financial Times*, 25 March 1997), overturning the Northern Territory euthanasia legislation.

IV. A THEOLOGICAL PERSPECTIVE

It is not by chance that the decriminalisation of suicide and (much more recently) of assisted suicide coincides with the modern post-Reformation era of Enlightenment secularism. Voltaire regarded the suicides of Brutus, Cassius, and Marc Antony as victories over nature.[20] Montesquieu (*Considérations sur les causes de la grandeur et de la décadence des Romains* [1734]) admired the Roman practice of suicide which allegedly "gave every one the liberty of finishing his part on the stage of the world in what scene he pleased."[21]

David Hume—better known for his attempt to undercut all arguments from miracles, such as Christ's resurrection from the dead, as proofs of religious truth—elaborated Montesquieu's arguments. In his *Essay on Suicide* (1783) he concluded that "the life of a man is of no greater importance to the universe than that of an oyster"[22]—a position directly contradictory to that of Jesus, not so incidentally, who declared that "you are of more value than many sparrows" (Matthew 10:31).

Schopenhauer, in his treatise *On Suicide*, claimed that taking one's own life should be regarded neither as a crime nor as a sin since "it is quite obvious that there is nothing in the world to which every man has a more unassailable title than to his own life and person."[23] (Note how this argument parallels that of the Pro-Choice advocate who claims that a woman has an absolute right to do as she wishes with her own body.)

In our time, atheist Antony Flew defends suicide and assisted suicide on the twin grounds that to keep sufferers from a quick death is ethically cruel and that no human being can disregard the

---

[20] Voltaire, "Of Suicide," 17 *Works* 165 ff. (4th ed. T. Smollett transl. 1772).
[21] Montesquieu, 3 *Complete Works* (1777) 86-87.
[22] D. Hume, 2 *Philosophical Works*, T.H. Green and T.H. Grose eds. (1874-1875) 406 ff. For a critique of Hume's argument against miracles, see J.W. Montgomery, *The Shape of the Past* (1975) 288-98 and *Faith Founded on Fact* (1978) 43-73.
[23] A. Schopenhauer, *Studies in Pessimism* (2d ed. T.B. Saunders transl. 1891) 43-73.

aspirations, wishes, and interests of another human being without denying that person's true worth, even when the consequence is the cessation of the other's life.[24] Humanist philosopher Sidney Hook argues:

> We may define the good differently, but no matter what our conception of the *good* life is, it presupposes a physical basis—a certain indispensable minimum of physical and social well-being—necessary for even a limited realisation of that good life. Where that minimum is failing together with all rational probability of attaining it, to avoid a life that at its best can be only vegetative and at its worst run the entire gamut of degradation and obloquy, what high-minded person would refuse the call of the poet *mourir entre les bras du sommeil*? We must recognise no categorical imperative "to live," but "to live well."[25]

The problem with such views is that, stimulating as they may be, they do not necessarily represent more than the opinions of the thinker who sets them forth. Wittgenstein was surely correct in principle when he observed that "ethics is transcendental,"[26] that is, any genuine ethic would have to rise above the level of human opinion and have an absolute justification for the values it proclaims. Inevitably, therefore, we must go beyond philosophical opinion to the consideration of religious—theological—answers to the question of whether life ought to be terminated by the individual himself, with or without the aid of others.

But what religion or theology can assist us here? Religious claims are hardly identical and indeed are often mutually incompatible.[27] Moreover, not a few religious positions have historically

---

[24.] A. Flew, "The Principle of Euthanasia," 4 *The Plain View* 189-90 (1957). My critique of Flew's antimiraculous argumentation may be found in J.W. Montgomery, *Faith Founded on Fact* (1978) 52 ff.

[25.] S. Hook, "The Ethics of Suicide," 37 *International Journal of Ethics* 173 ff. (1927). Such sentiments are commonly expressed in the popular pro-euthanasia literature, e.g. D. Humphry, *Final Exit: The Practicalities of Self-Deliverance and Assisted Suicide for the Dying* (1991).

[26.] L. Wittgenstein, *Tractatus Logico-Philosophicus*, para. 6.41-6.421 (1971). For the implications of this truth in jurisprudence and legal ethics see J.W. Montgomery, "The Case for 'Higher Law,'" 6/2 *Pepperdine Law Review* 359-80 (1979) and *Law and Morality: Friends or Foes? An Inaugural Lecture* (1994).

[27.] See J.W. Montgomery, *The Suicide of Christian Theology* (1970) and *Christianity for the Toughminded* (1973).

been indifferent to the value of individual human life[28] and little concerned with what modernly we call human rights.[29] Greco-Roman polytheism, for example, had no difficulty with suicide—or, for that matter, infanticide by the exposing of unwanted children.[30]

We turn to Christian theology both on the ground that it offers a defensible case for transcendent revelation[31] and because it has provided the basic value system for the entire Western culture and, at least from the time of Justinian in the sixth century, the ethical foundations of both the common and the civil law traditions.[32] To ignore the Christian perspective on suicide and assisted suicide, therefore, would be folly, for it would entail cutting ourselves off not only from our heritage but also from the most fruitful potential source for resolving these very difficult value questions.

Biblical revelation is directly opposed to suicide, on the twin and related grounds that human life is infinitely precious and that it comes about as a gift of the divine Creator and Redeemer of mankind, who therefore alone has the right to terminate it.[33] "All they that go down into the dust shall kneel before Him: and no man hath quickened his own soul" (Psalm 22:29-30, Book of Common Prayer). "Naked came I out of my mother's womb, and naked shall I return thither: the Lord gave, and the Lord hath taken away; blessed be the name of the Lord" (Job 1:21, AV). Every instance of suicide in Scripture is related to spiritual collapse, from Saul to Judas (I Samuel 31:4; II Samuel 17:23; I Kings 16:18-20; Matthew 27:5; Acts 1:18).

---

[28]. J.W. Montgomery, *Giant in Chains: China Today and Tomorrow* (1994) 101-36.

[29]. J.W. Montgomery, *Human Rights and Human Dignity* (1986) 105 ff.

[30]. This was also the position of Epicureanism and (with the exception of Cicero, whose natural law views and ethic had close affinities to biblical religion) Stoicism. Seneca argued, for example, that "just as I shall select my ship when I am about to go on a voyage, or my house when I propose to take a residence, so shall I choose my death when I am about to depart from life" (*Epistolae morales* LXX, 11).

[31]. J.W. Montgomery, *Where is History Going?* (1969), *Human Rights and Human Dignity* (1986) 131-60.

[32]. See H.J. Berman, *Law and Revolution: The Formation of the Western Legal Tradition* (1983), especially chapter 4 ("Theological Sources of the Western Legal Tradition").

[33]. J.W. Montgomery, "Do We Have the Right to Die?," *Christianity Today* 469-79 (January 21, 1977), and "Human Dignity in Birth and Death: A Question of Values" (Chapter 9 in the present volume).

The contrast with contemporary secular thought could hardly be greater. As in the case of abortion, the modern secularist here insists on the autonomy of the individual. One's personal choice is the absolute, before which all other considerations may be sacrificed. Such a viewpoint is well illustrated by the closing exchange in *Whose Life Is It Anyway?* between the judge and the tetraplegic seeking to have his life-support machine shut down:

> *Judge:* But wouldn't you agree that many people with appalling physical handicaps have overcome them and lived essentially creative, dignified lives?
>
> *Ken:* Yes, I would, but the dignity starts with their choice. If I choose to live, it would be appalling if society killed me. If I choose to die, it is equally appalling if society keeps me alive.
>
> *Judge:* I cannot accept that it is undignified for society to devote resources to keeping someone alive. Surely it enhances that society.
>
> *Ken:* It is not undignified if the man wants to stay alive, but I must restate that the dignity starts with his choice. Without it, it is degrading because technology has taken over from human will.[34]

The classical theologians of orthodox Christianity, such as Augustine, have set themselves firmly against such autonomous reasoning: man does not exist for himself alone, but for his God and for others, as in our Lord's well-known summary of Old Testament teaching (Matthew 22:37-40, and parallels):

> Thou shalt love the Lord thy God with all thy heart, and with all thy soul, and with all thy mind. This is the first and great commandment. And the second is like unto it, Thou shalt love thy neighbour as thyself. On these two commandments hang all the law and the prophets.

Thus, as might be expected, any limited support in today's church for voluntary euthanasia has come from situationists who do not recognize the existence of absolute biblical principles (e.g. Joseph Fletcher, *Morals and Medicine*).[35] St. John-Stevas so well summarises the Christian theological position that he deserves to be quoted *in extenso:*

---

[34] B. Clark, *Whose Life Is It Anyway?* (1978) 78.

[35] See J. Fletcher and J.W. Montgomery, *Situation Ethics: True or False* (1972).

> Christians put forward three arguments for condemning euthanasia. The basis of the Christian position is not, as is sometimes stated, that life has an absolute value, but that the disposal of life is in God's hands. Man has no absolute control over life, but holds it in trust. He has the use of it, and therefore may prolong it, but he may not destroy it at will. A second point made by Christians is that no man has the right to take an innocent life. "The innocent and just man thou shalt not put to death," says Exodus 23:7.... The only occasion when a Christian may take the life of a human being, is when he is an unjust aggressor against an individual or the common good.
>
> Suffering for the Christian is not an absolute evil, but has redeeming features. It may be an occasion for spiritual growth and an opportunity to make amends for sin. Lord Horder in the House of Lords debate in 1950 drew attention to this aspect of pain. "To call the function of a doctor who helps a patient to achieve that degree of elevation of spirit an intolerable burden—as the euthanasia advocate is apt to call it—seems to me to be disparaging one of the very important duties that a doctor has to perform." At the same time the Christian recognises suffering as an evil in the natural order, and is under a duty to relieve it where possible, although not at any price....
>
> A third cause of Christian opposition to euthanasia is the "wedge" argument. In its strict form, this states that an act which if raised to a general line of conduct would injure humanity, is wrong even in an individual case. In its more popular sense, it means that once a concession about the disposability of innocent life is made in one sphere, it will inevitably spread to others.[36]

To be sure, Christian theology has been well aware of the moral ambiguities that plague the suicide issue—as they do all ethical issues in a sinful and fallen world. What about martyrdom—or the giving of one's life to save the lives of others? Scholastic theologians have employed the so-called "doctrine of double effect," noting that the good result in such instances can be seen to derive not from the suicide itself but from the motivation or objective act that led to it. This rather convoluted reasoning should not, however, be allowed to obscure the basic theological point: suicide is always an evil, never a good. In certain limited circumstances, it may be a lesser of

---

[36.] N. St. John-Stevas, *Life, Death and the Law* (1961) 271-73.

evils, but a lesser evil is never somehow magically transmuted into a positive good.

The Christian position on suicide and assisted suicide is grounded in an acidly realistic view of fallen human nature. Because of the self-centredness characteristic of all human beings since the Fall of our first parents, to normalise or legalise the aiding and abetting of suicide is an act of utter naivety and folly. Owing to original sin, we are all subject to fallibility, laziness, and perversity. Where voluntary euthanasia is allowed, a gilt-edged invitation is provided for the manifestation of these characteristics. The patient and/or the physician may err in diagnosis of the true medical condition and the chances of survival. The patient and/or his loved ones may simply tire of life and of the care needed to sustain it. Those who will survive the patient may even be motivated by greed or by the potential benefits accruing to them from the patient's early demise.

All of these considerations are particularly magnified in our modern secular society, with the intense psychological and social pressures it puts on its members: the supposed absolute right to health, success, and happiness. No-one should have to endure a moment of unnecessary suffering! High suicide rates in the Scandinavian welfare states illustrate the neurotic side of the problem today, and the increasing number of teen suicides in America should make us attentive to the need societally to restrain rather than approve the facile termination of life. In this area as in all others, the secularist suffers from a high dose of naive rationalism: he assumes that suicide and the aiding and abetting of suicide will occur for the best of reasons. In point of fact, precisely the opposite is far more likely, given the self-centredness characteristic of us all. Perhaps the last thing we need is unlimited autonomy where matters of life and death are concerned.[37]

Are we saying that the Christian position is unqualifiedly condemnatory of assisted suicide—that no concessions are warranted even when extraordinary means are being employed to keep a patient alive? As already noted, Christian ethics is perfectly willing to recognise that in a sinful and fallen world suicide, unassisted or assisted, may rarely constitute a lesser of evils (e.g. in war, where the suicide of a captured prisoner might be preferable to a period of torture during which he would surely reveal strategic information leading to massive loss of other lives; or, medically, where only one life-support machine is available and the only way for it to benefit a young person in need is for it to be disconnected from a willing, terminally-ill elderly patient). But these limiting cases do not ever yield a principled justification of suicide or assisted suicide *per se*—nor sufficient ground for legislative approval of such acts. Hard cases still make bad law.

As for "pulling the plug"—removing extraordinary means of keeping a patient alive—one faces the tremendous difficulty of defining what is in fact "extraordinary." Surely the use of a feeding tube, so as to keep a dying patient alive, is not abnormal medical treatment, any more than is the bringing of a tray of food to a patient whose legs have been amputated. In the English case involving the removal of life support from comatose Tony Bland,[38] the Court's opinion has been rightly criticized on this very ground:

> Lord Goff's reasoning is, with respect, vulnerable to at least three major criticisms. First, why is pouring food down a tube "medical treatment"? What is being treated? Further, the analogy between tube-feeding and mechanical ventilation is unpersuasive. A ventilator assists a patient to breathe but a tube does not assist a

---

[37.] A particularly sad example of misplaced autonomy was the death of the seven-year-old child pilot Jessica Dubroff in April, 1996. The London *Times* reported (13 April) that in spite of criticisms that allowing her to pilot a plane in severe weather conditions to break a record displayed "bad adult judgment" and raised the spectre of "the motives of highly ambitious parents," her mother justified the little girl's choices in these words: "She should have been up there. She had a freedom which you can't get by holding her back.... She went with her joy and her passion, and her life was in her hands.... I beg people to let children fly if they want to."

[38.] *Airedale NHS Trust v Bland* [1993] AC 789.

Slavery was a highly disputed religious question, but should the state therefore have stood neutrally apart, permitting those who saw nothing the matter with slavery to keep their slaves?[45] The right to life is enshrined in international covenants and conventions as the most fundamental of human rights; we must not let it be eroded by jurisprudential indifferentism. Argues Keown:

> The notion of a worthless life is as alien to the Hippocratic tradition as it is to English criminal law, both of which subscribe to the principle of the sanctity of human life which holds that because all lives are intrinsically valuable, it is always wrong intentionally to kill an innocent human being. This principle is, by contrast, rejected by the so-called "new" (consequentialist) morality which openly espouses the notion of the "life not worth living."[46]

B. Victimless Act or Harming Others

It is said that suicide and assisted suicide are "harmless acts"—acts that impact only the terminally ill patient—and therefore should be subject to his absolute and untrammelled control. Stephen notes the common view (though he feels uncomfortable with it) that "suicide is the only offence which under no circumstances can produce alarm."[47] This is essentially the position of Joel Feinberg, who in Chapter 27 of his influential *Harm to Self* (Volume III of *The Moral Limits of the Criminal Law*)

> ... examines from a special perspective the problem of voluntary euthanasia. In particular it [the chapter] considers the effects on voluntariness of "understandable depression," and concludes that depression need not vitiate the voluntariness even of a choice of death, provided certain other conditions are met, and that only a kind of defective reasoning—the "catch 22 arguments"—can seem to show the contrary. On the larger question of the moral permissibility of active euthanasia generally, after considering the role of living wills and durable power of attorney, the chapter concludes that the only possible reason for maintaining the present absolute prohibition is that it is necessary to prevent mistakes and abuse. If

---

[45.] See T. Sutton, "Christians as Law Reformers in the Nineteenth and Twentieth Centuries," *Christian Perspectives on Law Reform* (P.R. Beaumont ed. 1998) 13-15.
[46.] J. Keown, 52 *Cambridge Law Journal* 211 (1993).
[47.] J.F. Stephen, 3 *A History of the Criminal Law of England* (1883) 107.

there is no such necessity then there is no morally respectable reason to interfere with the liberty of an autonomous person to dispose of his own lot in life, even if his choice is for death.[48]

Though Glanville Williams regards suicide as "a practice freely consented to that does not harm others,"[49] he concedes that assisted suicide could well have a dark side to it: "There is a case for punishing those who assist suicide by young people (who may go through a temporarily difficult phase, and whose suicide is a cruel blow to parents), or who *persuade* others to commit suicide, or use fraud, or assist the act for selfish reasons."[50]

The mention here of parents suffering from the suicide of their children should remind us that suicide never occurs in a social vacuum. Indeed, because of the interlocking character of human life—the fact that man is inherently a social animal—there are strictly no immoral acts that hurt only the perpetrator. "Harmless wrongdoing"[51] is a contradiction in terms, as even lighthearted playwright Noël Coward fully recognised.[52] One of the most touching testimonies to this truth where suicide is concerned is found in the first of Lord Chancellor Hailsham's autobiographies, and it warrants much reflection:

> I am moved at this stage to add a footnote about suicide. I had thought of remaining reticent on the subject, but I am impelled to write about it in the hope that at some time someone will read, and heed, my words. My dear brother Edward committed suicide, and there is a sense in which I have never recovered from the blow. He was in every way a delightful person, brave and talented beyond the lot of man. He rowed for Leander, was President of the Oxford Union, earned and received a Double First, was MP for Eastbourne, the author of at least one best-selling book, and a rising member of the Bar. He could not have failed, had he lived, to play an important,

[48.] J. Feinberg, *Harmless Wrongdoing*, xix (1988).

[49.] G. Williams, 8 *Encyclopedia of Philosophy* (P. Edwards ed. 1967) 44.

[50.] G. Williams, *Textbook of Criminal Law* (1978) 531.

[51.] Joel Feinberg's title to Volume IV of his *The Moral Limits of the Criminal Law* (see note 48 above).

[52.] This is one of the central themes of Coward's frequently revived play, *Present Laughter* (acting ed. 1949), e.g. at 25-26:

> *Garry:* I don't do any harm to anybody.
>
> *Liz:* You do harm to yourself and to the few, the very few who really mind about you.

perhaps even a decisive, part in the history of the country. He killed himself one spring day in our home in Sussex with my 20-bore shotgun which, when I had been a little younger, had been my most prized possession. I will not waste time discussing what led him to do it, except to say that the last phase was insomnia, or to say why I have never failed to blame myself without mercy for my failure to prevent him doing it. I only write this in order to express my profound and passionate conviction that suicide is always wrong if only for the misery it inflicts on others. Bereavement is one thing. The pain at bereavement is the price we pay for love, and high as that price is, it is not one which one grudges paying when bereavement is suffered. But bereavement by suicide is something altogether different and leaves an incurable wound. If only Edward had known the pain he was inflicting on us all who were left behind, and the ceaseless and incurable self-condemnation we all felt so that even now forty years later I cannot bear the burden of it, he would never have done what he did and, if by reading this some other unhappy family may be saved from woe so intolerable, this book will not have been in vain. As it is, Edward is in the hands of God, and no doubt he is wholly forgiven, since if our poor natures can wholly forgive him as we do, how much more will the infinite compassion of the Saviour take him to his arms. But suicide is wrong, wrong, wrong, and Christians were amongst the first to recognise the fact. Their spiritual insight is to be recognised as among the proofs, as well as the consolations, of Christianity.[53]

C. Pluralism and the Risks and Consequences of Assisted Suicide

Finally, we are told that, even granting the moral power of Christian objections to suicide and assisted suicide, one has no right to impose such views on a pluralistic society. One might reply, in the words of the Psalmist (16:4, *Book of Common Prayer*): "They that run after another god shall have great trouble." If the Christian world-view is correct in its understanding of human nature—both as to man's inherent dignity and as to his existing corrupted state of selfishness—then to disregard these facts societally, even in a pluralistic society, is to court disaster. Professor Kamisar, a non-Christian, has shown on purely secular, pragmatic grounds that the

[53.] Hailsham, *The Door Wherein I Went* (1975) 60-61. *Cf.* his more recent *A Sparrow's Flight: The Memoirs of Lord Hailsham of St Marylebone* (1990), and the chapter devoted to him in R. Clifford, *Leading Lawyers' Case for the Resurrection* (1996) 70-81.

biblical prohibitions against suicide and assisted suicide are fully warranted. He points up the difficulty of establishing genuine consent when the patient is suffering from severe pain; the risk of incorrect diagnosis—with, in this case, irreparable consequences; and the real possibility of carrying out euthanasia on a patient who could subsequently have been cured by new medical developments. Kamisar further elaborates the classic "wedge" argument: to condone euthanasia is inevitably to reduce respect for the sanctity of human life in general.[54]

The practical soundness of these arguments—and the confirmation they offer of the validity of the Christian stance on suicide and assisted suicide—comes from the most detailed study to date of the legally sanctioned practice of euthanasia in the Netherlands. Here there is ample empirical evidence of the slippery slope, practically, logically, legally, and ethically. The study concludes that in the Netherlands, with "standards" (note well!) roughly the equivalent of those advocated by the Compassion In Dying organisation and other American euthanasia groups,

> ... euthanasia is being practised on a scale vastly exceeding the 'known' (truthfully reported and recorded) cases. There is little sense in which it can be said, in any of its forms, to be under control. As Leenen has observed, there is an "almost total lack of control on the administration of euthanasia" and "the present legal situation makes any adequate control of the practice of euthanasia virtually impossible."[55]

The same considerations have been shown to apply to the so-called "living wills." Jerome Wernow of the University of Leuven, Belgium, has irrefutably demonstrated that

---

[54] Y. Kamisar, "Some Non-Religious Views Against Proposed 'Mercy-Killing' Legislation," 42 *Minnesota Law Review* 969-1042 (1958). Glanville Williams characteristically attempted to refute Kamisar's arguments in "Mercy-Killing Legislation—A Rejoinder," 43 *Minnesota Law Review* 1-12 (1958).

[55] J. Keown, "The Law and Practice of Euthanasia in the Netherlands," 108 *Law Quarterly Review* 51-78 (1992). See our text at note 19 above. For an updated treatment of Keown's material in book form, together with valuable essays on the subject by other specialists, see L. Gormally (ed.), *Euthanasia Clinical Practice and the Law* (1994). Keown's latest treatment of the subject is his article, "Euthanasia in the Netherlands: Sliding Down the Slippery Slope?," 9 *Notre Dame Journal of Law, Ethics & Public Policy* 407 ff. (1995).

The current content and legal acceptance of these documents is largely a product of what once was known as the Euthanasia Education Council, now called Concern for Dying. A scrutiny of their rationale for the use of the living will exhibits a presuppositional strain of thought similar to that espoused by the proponents of suicide throughout history. Tenets like self-determination and primacy of health as life's essential values are similar to the bases for advocacy of suicide found in Seneca, the Stoics, the Humanist Movement and Social Darwinism.[56]

D. Conclusion

And where do such philosophical conceptions take us? A concluding story—true, but no less parabolic for that—may provide an answer.

Some years ago when I served as Director of Studies at the International Institute of Human Rights, founded by René Cassin, in Strasbourg, France, one of the guest lecturers was a New York lawyer who delivered a series of lectures on "The Right to Die." She expected a very positive response from the avant-garde student audience. She was shocked to find just the opposite reaction, particularly among international students from the Third World. Their point was that in their countries the struggle for the right to life had hardly been won—after ages of paganism in which the individual counted for next to nothing. Anything that would facilitate death at the expense of life was therefore anathema.

The 9th Circuit opinion in *Compassion In Dying* is well aware that life issues are interconnected: voluntary euthanasia is linked with abortion throughout the opinion. What the Court appears blissfully ignorant of is that, because of the seamless garment of human dignity, facilitating death in any way facilitates it in every way. Owing to human selfishness, there is a built-in tendency toward social entropy: we find it easier and more convenient by far to kill than to keep alive. The law is supposed to protect us from ourselves in this respect, not make it easier for us to destroy each other or ourselves. If we err, let us err on the side of preserving life.

[56.] J.R. Wernow, "The Living Will," 10 *Ethics & Medicine* 27-35 (1994).

Law reform is not *per se* a positive good. Its value depends squarely on the value of the changes proposed. The absence of current UK legislation or serious legislative proposals to facilitate dying may not be most helpfully explained by the conservative temper or alleged lack of philosophical reflection on the part of legislators and the English legal community. Rather, it is best seen as signifying a deeper appreciation than one encounters today in many other legal contexts that the life one saves (societally and individually) may be one's own.

Addendum

EUTHANASIA LAWS BILL 1996 (AUSTRALIA) PRESENTED

CURRENT HOUSE HANSARD (AUSTRALIA), 9 SEPTEMBER 1996. PAGE: 3670 (PROOF)

Bill presented by Mr Andrews.

Mr ANDREWS (Menzies) (12.54 p.m.)—Mr Acting Speaker, I presented the Euthanasia Laws Bill 1996. Last year, the Northern Territory became the only place in the world to legalise what proponents describe as voluntary euthanasia—in reality, intentional killing and assisted suicide. Whether intended or not the act, passed by a legislature representing less than one per cent of the national population, has a direct impact on other Australians.

Far from its operation being limited to Northern Territory residents, people have travelled from elsewhere seeking to use the act. This then is a national issue. Let there be no doubt about what the Northern Territory has done.

The Northern Territory act is not about the discontinuance of futile or heroic treatment. It is not about the refusal of burdensome or unwanted medical attention. It is not about the appointment of an agent to make decisions about treatment for an incompetent person. And it is not about the provision of modern, pain-relieving palliative care. The Northern Territory act is about one thing—the use of a lethal injection to bring about the immediate death of another. This, Mr Acting Speaker, is a Commonwealth bill to stop lethal injections.

Four reservations expressed about the draft bill have been met. The new bill does not single out the Northern Territory; it enacts a law to the extent of the Commonwealth's power. The bill does not invalidate the Territory's Natural Death Act. This bill is solely about euthanasia and no other matter. And this new bill has no retrospective effect.

The bill restates two clear principles about the treatment of the dying and the disabled in our society. First, the bill states that the legislative assemblies have no power to make laws which permit or have the effect of permitting the form of intentional killing of another called euthanasia—which includes mercy killing—or the assisting of a person to terminate his or her life. Secondly, the bill confirms that the legislative assemblies do have power to make laws with respect to the withdrawal or withholding of medical or surgical measures for prolonging the life of a patient, and of medical treatment in the provision of palliative care to a dying patient—but not so as to permit intentional killing.

These principles reflect the state of the law throughout Australia, with the notable exception of the Northern Territory. Every other state and territory has laws which proscribe intentional killing and assisted suicide. Where these issues have been addressed in recent years—in Victoria, South Australia and the ACT—euthanasia has been rejected. Plans to legalise it in New South Wales were dropped in the face of overwhelming parliamentary opposition. The national approach to rejecting the intentional killing of the terminally ill and assisted suicide is therefore reflected in this Commonwealth bill.

By enacting its legislation, not only has the Northern Territory rejected this national approach; it has ignored the findings of every major committee of inquiry in the world, it has cast aside the ethical principles of the world medical profession, it has rejected the tenets of every major religious group, it has ignored the concerns of its own Aboriginal people, and it has turned a blind eye to the evidence of widespread abuse of euthanasia in the Netherlands. The Northern Territory has also failed to do two things which could reasonably be expected of a legislature concerned about caring for the dying.

First, there has been no attempt to introduce modern refusal of treatment legislation as in Victoria and South Australia. Instead, the

CHAPTER 11

THE EMBRYO CLONING DANGER IN EUROPEAN CONTEXT

Summary: So-called "therapeutic" embryo cloning (to provide stem cells which can develop into tissue, organs, etc. for allegedly curative purposes) necessarily entails the destruction of the embryos so created. These embryos have all the genetic characteristics of the human being. Even if we were in doubt as to their nature, the mere possibility that they are human should deter us from killing them. But, wholly apart from the wrongfulness of violating human dignity by experimenting on human subjects (reminiscent of Nazi medical activity during the Third Reich), there is no necessity for such experiments, since umbilical cords can provide stem cells and very soon such cells will be able to be obtained from adult subjects. Moreover, evidence now exists that the use of embryo-derived treatments for Parkinson's disease (supposedly a main beneficiary of embryo research) can produce horrific worsenings in the condition of the patient. We simply do not know enough about the effects of cloning to warrant our employing it. Scientific evidence and ethical considerations thus unite to condemn therapeutic embryo research. Governments have a moral responsibility to forbid it.

At the moment the United States faces one of the most agonising and crucial ethical issues in the history of medical science: whether to permit experimentation and treatment by way of embryo research. Recent developments in the British and European context[1] can perhaps assist the American executive to arrive at a proper position vis-à-vis this phenomenon.

I. THE NATURE OF HUMAN CLONING

What, precisely, is being proposed in the cloning debate? The following helpful summary appears in a recent publication of a British lawyers' society:

[1.] See appended summary of current European national and community law.

> Cloning is carried out by a process known as "cell nuclear replacement." The nucleus of a human egg cell is removed and replaced with the nucleus from a cell of the animal from which, or of the person from whom, the "clone" is to be produced. The cell is then artificially stimulated so that it begins to develop into an embryo in the same way that a fertilised egg develops....
>
> The grim reality is that both reproductive and therapeutic cloning involve the creation of new human beings, who, being very small and at an early stage of development, should be accorded the extra special protection of the law. The only difference between therapeutic and reproductive cloning is that, in the former, the human embryo is broken up at an early stage, when he or she is known as a "blastocyst." ... At this stage the cells are "undifferentiated," but thereafter, if they are allowed to develop, the cells in the blastocyst will begin to develop into different organs, some developing into bone or liver or skin, and so on.
>
> What scientists wish to do is to take these "stem cells" from a broken-up blastocyst and experiment on them to see if they can encourage these individual cells to grow into particular types of tissue which might possibly, so they claim, be used to replace or repair damaged tissue in an older patient....
>
> Some may think that in many respects therapeutic cloning is even more barbarous than reproductive cloning since it involves deliberately tearing to pieces a specially created human embyro.[2]

What is being advocated, therefore, is the use of specially created, cloned embryos as sources of stem cells for the treatment of various medical conditions, including heart failure and, in particular, Parkinson's disease—even though in principle such cells can also be harvested without the destruction of embryos from umbilical cord blood or in the very near future from adult bone marrow or blood.

Unless anti-rejection drugs are used, the body rejects cells taken from someone else. Thus, in short, those favouring cloning propose that clones of the patient himself or herself be allowed to live for a short time as a source of matched stem cells. Normally, some six cloned and aborted fetuses are required to yield enough cells for a single patient.

---

[2]. Association of Lawyers for the Defence of the Unborn, *News and Comment*, No. 88 (Winter 2000/2001).

II. A RECENT DECISION OF THE BRITISH PARLIAMENT

On 22 January 2001, the House of Lords, by a majority of 120, approved the therapeutic cloning of human embryo cells no older than fourteen days, thereby legalising such research in the United Kingdom.[3] In a December session of the House of Commons, MPs had passed the cloning bill by a free vote supporting (366 to 174) an amendment to the British Human Fertilisation and Embryo Act. Labour's Public Health Minister, Ms Yvette Cooper, in defending the cloning bill in the Commons, distinguished stem-cell cloning from reproductive cloning (in which the embryo is allowed to develop into a baby, and which remains illegal in the United Kingdom). She maintained that the new law did not constitute an ethical "slippery slope" and that "there are immense potential benefits from allowing this research to go ahead, particularly for those suffering from dreadful chronic diseases."

By no means were all of the Parliamentarians convinced. Dr Fox, a former general practitioner, spoke for many when he declared: "Medical revolution carries with it moral, ethical and philosophical consequences and our ability to deal with these matters sometimes lags behind our technical knowledge. Just because we can do something does not mean that we have to. We need to establish a clear framework within which to operate."[4]

What in fact are the "moral, ethical and philosophical consequences" of stem-cell embryo research, and what can the United States learn from the British and the European attitudes toward it?[5]

---

[3] *The Times* [London], 24 January 2001.
[4] *The Times* [London], 20 December 2000.
[5] As will be seen from the Addendum to this paper, the European nations do not take a uniform position on the cloning issue. A "liberal" approach characterises not only Britain but also Denmark, Finland, Greece, and the Netherlands; Belgium, France, Italy, Spain, and Sweden treat the matter in a mediating fashion; Portugal has not yet arrived at any national view; and Austria, Germany, and Ireland ban such research entirely.

III. THE ARGUMENTS PRO AND CON

On the positive side, the argument is very straightforward. Proponents of the use of embryos to obtain stem-cells argue for the unique medical value which will allegedly follow from such research in the treatment and cure of intractable ailments, principally Parkinson's disease. Any moral difficulties attendant on such research are met with utilitarian reasoning: human misery will be lessened as a direct result of allowing research to be done involving embryos which have not yet developed recognisably human features such as a central nervous system.

Negatively, there are a plethora of arguments ranging from weak to very powerful against the proposed embryo research. These deserve the most careful attention, particularly by statesmen in a position to determine national policy.

The Luddite Argument. It is maintained by some that to engage in any embryonic research is to fly in the face of Nature, which must remain inviolate. The problem here, to be sure, is that virtually all scientific and medical research has modified that natural state of affairs in one way or another. It would be most unfortunate if the case against stem-cell embryo research were to take on the character of those who held, in the early days of aviation, that "if the Lord had wanted us to fly, he would have put wings on our backs." From the religious viewpoint, it appears that mankind is to "subdue the earth," not succumb to it. The issue, then, is not the avoidance of new research techniques, but a determination of what kind of "subduing" of nature is proper, and what improper.[6]

The Slippery Slope Argument. Must stem-cell embryo research lead inevitably to reproductive cloning and to the Frankenstein monster scenarios often painted by journalists? The answer is, simply, that we do not know. In theory, it should be possible by carefully drawn legislation to carve out permissible, as opposed to

---

[6.] It is also worth emphasising that those who disagree with embryro research of the kind approved by the British Parliament are not in any way compelled to fight against the Human Genome Project and similar efforts to understand more fully the human makeup. Francis Collins, the world leader of the Genome Project, has stated that in his view the Project is engaged in no less a task than the mapping of Divine Creation.

illegitimate, areas of research. At the same time, hardly had the British Parliament passed its new law but a team of Italian research scientists announced (9 March 2001) that they are ready to proceed with the cloning of babies. But the issue is not what *might* transpire in the future; it is whether the use of embryos to provide stem cells *in the present* is desirable or undesirable.

The Right-to-Life Argument. Analysts of the embryo research issue have consistently pointed out its connection with legalised abortion. "The context of experimentation on the human fetus is plainly provided by liberal abortion.... That liberalisation both made fetuses more widely available and, more important, marked a change in the public (and medical) perception of the fetus."[7] Indeed, "it has been argued (with some reason) that for a society which allows the abortion of the maturing fetus on (often) trivial grounds to object to the careful experimental use of the zygote is both illogical and hypocritical."[8]

The fundamental question, therefore—as uncomfortable as it may be—turns on the nature of the embryo. Even prior to 14 days of its existence, what precisely do we have here? Tissue and no more than tissue, or a human being? If the former, experimentation on it may well be not only permissible but in fact a societal duty; if the latter, such research takes on an entirely different moral character. So which view is correct? This will depend squarely on one's definition of "human," or, more precisely, on whether one defines the human being by his or her *genetic-chromosomal makeup* or by some *functional criterion*.

For the functionalist, one is human only and insofar as one functions humanly—and the young embryo does not so function. The most influential advocate of this viewpoint at the moment is philosopher Michael Tooley, who asserts: "An entity cannot be a person unless it possesses, or has previously possessed, the capacity for

---

[7.] Nigel M. de S. Cameron, "Man As Experimental Subject: Embryo Research and Its Context," in Ian L. Brown and Nigel Cameron (eds.), *Medicine in Crisis* (Edinburgh, Scotland: Rutherford House, 1988), p. 52.

[8.] *Id.* at 42. The same point has been made by Sir John Peel in his essay, "After the Embryo the Fetus?," in Nigel M. de S. Cameron (ed.), *Embryos and Ethics* (Edinburgh, 1987).

thought. And the psychological and neurophysiological evidence makes it most unlikely that humans, [even] in the first few weeks after birth, possess this capacity."[9]

But if genetic-chromosomal makeup is insufficient to define the human being and to justify according to him or her human value, worth, and protection, *who* precisely has the right to establish the additional, functional criteria? And who is to say if the candidate functions *well enough* to deserve to be treated as a human being? Tooley, a philosopher, declares that to be human one must *think*. But why use thinking ability alone? What about job skills and other socially useful attributes? Social planners have long been disturbed by the need to support social misfits. Nazi eugenics and concentration camp medical experimentation were based on precisely such a philosophy.[10] And note the applications of this approach to the end of life—when the (former?) person loses his or her ability to function productively.[11] Since decisions in areas like this gravitate almost inevitably to government and political decision-making, Huxley's *Brave New World* raises its ugly head. Not only the fetus but also the handicapped and the aged suddenly find themselves in jeopardy—as well as all those whose activity does not conform to current societal or political standards.

May we suggest that humans do not become such by acting in a human way: they act (occasionally!) in a human way because they are *first of all human*. And when do they begin being human? When they acquire the genetic-chromosomal character of humans, and that occurs—if it occurs at all—at the moment of conception. One of Europe's foremost microbiologists put it this way:

---

[9]. Michael Tooley, *Abortion and Infanticide* (Oxford: Clarendon Press, 1983), p. 421. Also: Helga Kuhse, *The Sanctity-of-Life Doctrine in Medicine: A Critique* (Oxford: Clarendon Press, 1987).

[10]. See John Warwick Montgomery, *Slaughter of the Innocents* (Westchester, Illinois: Crossway Books, 1981); *Human Rights and Human Dignity* (Edmonton, Alberta, Canada: Canadian Institute for Law, Theology and Public Policy, 1987); and his essay, "Abortion and the Law: Three Clarifications," in Hilgers, Horan, and Mall (eds.), *New Perspectives on Human Abortion* (Frederick, Maryland: University Publications of America, 1981), pp. 281-92.

[11]. John Warwick Montgomery, "Whose Life Anyway? A Re-Examination of Suicide and Assisted Suicide" (Chapter 10 of the present volume).

> The first cell [formed by sperm-and-egg union] is already the embryo of an autonomous living being with individual hereditary patrimony, such that if we knew the nature of the spermatozoid and the chromosomes involved, we could already at that point predict the characteristics of the child, the future colour of his hair, and the illnesses to which he would be subject. In his mother's womb, where he will grow, he will not accept everything she brings to him, but only that which is necessary to his existence: thereby he will realise his hereditary patrimony. In that first cell the profound dynamism and the precise direction of life appears.... In spite of its fragility and its immense needs, an autonomous and genuinely living being has come into existence.... It is rather surprising to see certain physicians speak here of "potential life" as if the fertilised egg began its real life when it nests in the uterus. Modern biology does not deny the importance of nidation, but it sees it only as a condition—indispensable, to be sure—for the *development* of the embryo and the *continuation* of a life already in existence.[12]

But if the embryo, from the moment of conception, is indeed a genuine human being, then the experimental use of that entity—although for the high purpose of benefiting others medically—must be regarded as a legal offence to the person and thereby ethically repellent.

The Dignity of the Human Person Argument. Even if one is unwilling to take the eminently logical and scientific position that the embyro is in fact a human being and therefore deserving of legal protection, there is strong reason to oppose fetal experimentation. "While opposition to the use of the human embryo for purposes of deleterious research has largely come from those who regard the human embryo as a human person, it should be noted that the minority on the [British] Warnock Committee who dissented from any experimental use of the embryo did not do so on that ground. Theirs was a more limited case.... The *potential* character of the early embryo, as forerunner of the personal human being, is—it can be argued—itself sufficient reason to grant it respect and protection."[13]

---

[12] Jules Carles [French National Centre for Scientific Research], *La Fécondation* (Paris: Presses Universitaires de France, 1967), pp. 81-82. Our translation; author's italics.

[13] Cameron, "Man As Experimental Subject" (*op. cit.*), pp. 42-43.

There is no way to deny that if the embryo is allowed to develop naturally the result will be an additional person on the planet. It follows that every embryo used for medical experimentation destroys human life. And it should be kept in mind that, just as the successfull cloning of the sheep Dolly required a long series of failures, so (as pointed out earlier) it requires at least six aborted fetuses to provide enough stem cells to treat a single patient. "Man's abuse of his own kind for experimental purposes must rank as the most dreadful of all his abuses of himself. The disinterested character of (some of) those involved, far from lessening and justifying what they do, serves to heighten its significance by underlining the degradation to which man is putting his fellow, treating as a mere laboratory artefact one who bears the divine image."[14]

This was essentially the position of the Legal Affairs Committee of the European Parliament in 1990. The Committee chairman, German Euro-MP Willi Rothley

> maintained that fertilised human eggs already had 'human potential" although he acknowledged that EC member states had been unable to define whether the embryo is a legal entity. He asserted: "The use of human embryos for research purposes which deny their human nature and subject them to arbitrary goals is an infringement of the dignity of man. The freedom to carry out research may also conflict with the right of a person to self-determination.... A human can never be a thing, but will always have a personality. The underlying principle of our legal and political system places an absolute prohibition on one person being at the total disposal of another. It must also be the primary consideration when assessing research on embryos."[15]

The Committee's Italian vice-chairman, Carlo Casini, took an even stronger position: "Human life begins, without doubt, from fertilisation, and develops without any qualitative leaps in a continuous process until death." The negative stance of this Committee was in sharp contrast to the British approach, as reflected in the

---

[14.] *Id* at 55.
[15.] Arthur Rogers and Denis Durand de Bousingen, *Bioethics in Europe* (Strasbourg, France: Council of Europe Press, 1995), pp. 56-57.

creation of Frankenstein monsters, the fact is that animal cloning has on occasion produced bizarre and frightening genetic results. We simply do not know what may be the consequences of meddling with the human genetic makeup. Fear of the unknown ought not to deter scientific progress—but where the very nature of the human being is in the balance the greatest caution should surely be exercised. Mistakes here could produce the most terrible of consequences.

Moreover, it has been assumed in all the arguments in behalf of legalising stem-cell embryo research that this scientific activity will in fact produce positive medical benefits. It now appears that this is not at all necessarily the case. Our ignorance in this area is evidently far greater than anyone had imagined. The esteemed *New England Journal of Medicine* has reported that "a carefully controlled study that tried to treat Parkinson's disease by implanting cells from aborted fetuses into patients' brains not only failed to show an overall benefit but also revealed a disastrous side effect."[18] In some 15 percent of the patients, the implantations produced uncontrollable movement ("writhing, twisting, jerking"); moreover, there is no way to deactivate or remove the transplanted cells.

Dr Paul E. Greene, a neurologist at Columbia University's College of Physicians and Surgeons, was reported as saying, "It was tragic, catastrophic, a real nightmare. And we can't selectively turn it off." His conclusion: "No more fetal transplants." Dr William Weiner, the director of the Maryland Parkinson's Disease and Movement Disorder Centre now says: "If a patient came to him today seeking advice, he would say, 'The bottom line is that human fetal cell transplants are not currently the best way to go.... My advice is you ought not to do this.'"

As a result of this horrendous setback in his research, Dr Curt R. Freed of the Colorado Health Sciences Centre in Denver, one of the

[18.] *The New York Times*, 8 March 2001. The original research report appeared as "Transplantation of Embryonic Dopamine Neurons for Severe Parkinson's Disease," under the joint authorship of Curt R. Freed, Paul E. Greene, Robert E. Breeze, Wei-Yann Tsai, William DuMouchel, Richard Kao, Sandra Dillon, Howard Winfield, Sharon Culver, John Q. Trojanowski, David Eidelberg, and Stanley Fahn (344/10 *New England Journal of Medicine* [8 March 2001]).

two directors of the failed project, is now "implanting less fetal tissue and putting the tissue in a different area of the brain." And yet he says that "it would be a mistake to stop doing the surgery altogether: to say that you can't do or shouldn't do human research because the research has uncertain outcomes, I think would be a bad decision."

IV. CONCLUSION

We profoundly disagree. Human cloning for the purpose of stem-cell embryo research (a) is an affront to human dignity, (b) is not the only means of achieving its proponents' objectives, (c) is not well enough understood to be trusted as a curative mechanism, and (d) appears to carry with it the most dangerous and irreversible side-effects and may not in fact have any significant curative properties. Responsible governments should outlaw it and devote national resources to medical activity not saddled with the enumerated devastating disadvantages.[19]

We conclude with a letter published in the London *Times* during the controversy over this issue in Great Britain. It was written by religious leaders but expresses (or should express) the concerns of all citizens who respect human life and responsible medical treatment.

> While the end—research into new treatments for disease using stem cells—is good in itself, the means being proposed are quite immoral. To create and destroy human lives simply to extract cells for research is wrong. Such procedures use human lives as disposable objects.
>
> Such research is also unnecessary. Recent advances in stem cell research from adults are proving highly promising. A large body of scientists acknowledge that it is not possible at present to say whether embryonic or adult stem cells will ultimately prove to be of greater value therapeutically.
>
> In these circumstances, is it not better to concentrate on research which can command wide public acceptance and support, rather

---

[19.] Cf. Leon Kass, "The Wisdom of Repugnance: Why We Should Ban the Cloning of Humans," in Glenn McGee (ed.), *The Human Cloning Debate* (Berkeley, California: Berkeley Hills Books, 2000).

than blaze a trail that is morally unacceptable and may well prove to be scientifically unnecessary?[20]

And, may we add—positively harmful?

---

[20] *The Times* [London], 14 December 2000.

Addendum

HUMAN CLONING REGULATION IN EUROPE

Overview

The birth on 6 July 1996 in the UK of "Dolly the sheep," cloned by the transfer of a nucleus from an adult lamb, led the European Commission to request an opinion on the ethical implications of such techniques from the Group of Advisers on the Ethical Implications of Biotechnology[21] (GAEIB) in February 1997. The European Parliament (EP) responded by adopting a resolution in March 1997 urging Member States to ban the cloning of human beings and calling on the Commission to examine the ethical and legal implications of such technology.

The EP reiterated its call for a legal ban on human cloning by adopting a resolution in January 1998, supporting the Council of Europe's Bioethics Convention and additional protocol. An EP/Council directive setting out intellectual property rights and what cannot be patented, including human cloning, followed. This directive, however, was undermined when the European Patent Office granted a patent which could be used to cover human cloning, causing the EP to issue another resolution condemning this decision.

The UK came under renewed scrutiny when its government showed support for cloning with "therapeutic" ends. This led the EP to address the issue of human cloning again in a resolution of September 2000, which repeated the call for voting legislation banning research into human cloning. This did not alter the UK decision on therapeutic cloning, which British MPs and the House of Lords approved in December 2000 and January 2001 respectively.

[21.] The GAEIB is an informal group of advisers, created by the European Commission; it is now called the European Group on Ethics: http://www.europa.eu.int/comm/secretariat_general/sgc/ethics/en/index.htm

The September EP resolution also addressed the setting up of a Temporary Committee on Human Genetics to investigate the ethical and legal issues raised by new developments. Proposals for this committee were adopted in December, specifying that, over a period of twelve months, it should report on new and potential developments in human genetics, identify the ethical, legal, social and economic implications and, if appropriate, make recommendations to guide the EP in its decision-making in this area. The committee has to have regard to the positions already established by resolutions of Parliament.

The Temporary Committee on Human Genetics held its first meeting on 16 January 2001. Since that time, the committee has been involved in hearings with a range of experts, corresponding committees in national parliaments and representatives of civil society.

Cloning Regulation in the Council of Europe

A. Council of Europe Convention on Human Rights and Biomedicine

This convention is supposed to put the interest of human beings before the interests of science or society. That mandatory principle applies except in certain circumstances where "public health or safety are at risk or where crime prevention or the rights and freedoms of others may be seriously jeopardised."

Article 18 – research on embryos *in vitro* - provides that "Where the law allows research on embryos *in vitro*, it shall ensure adequate protection of the embryo. The creation of human embryos for research purposes is prohibited."

The future additional protocol on embryo protection may, however, considerably weaken the force of this article.

The convention was opened for signature in Oviedo on 4 April 1997. It entered into force on 1st December 1999 in Denmark, Greece, San Marino, Slovakia and Slovenia (the first five states having ratified it). It entered into force for Spain on 1 January 2000 and will enter into force for Georgia on 1st March 2001. Twenty-two other states have signed it.

B. Council of Europe Protocol banning human (reproductive) cloning

The Protocol on the Prohibition of Cloning Human Beings entered into force on the 1st of March 2001, after the required five ratifications—from Slovakia (22.10.98), Slovenia (05.11.98), Greece (22.12.98), Spain (24.01.2000) and Georgia (22.11.2000).

This Additional Protocol to the Council of Europe Convention on Human Rights and Biomedicine is designed to prevent abuses of such techniques by applying them to humans, banning "any intervention seeking to create a human being genetically identical to another human being, whether living or dead," i.e., reproductive cloning.

The Protocol leaves it to countries' domestic law to define the scope of the term "human being."

Cloning of cells and tissues for research purposes covers three situations: cloning of cells as a technique, use of embryonic cells in cloning techniques, and cloning of human beings. The third situation is the prohibition of cloning human beings, which is within the scope of this Protocol. The second situation will be examined in a protocol on embryo protection (still under process in the CDBI).

The Protocol has been signed by 24 countries: Croatia, Cyprus, the Czech Republic, Denmark, Estonia, Finland, France, Hungary, Iceland, Italy, Latvia, Lithuania, Luxembourg, Moldova, the Netherlands, Norway, Poland, Portugal, Romania, San Marino, Sweden, Switzerland, the former Yugoslav Republic of Macedonia and Turkey.

C. Future Additional Protocols to this Convention

Drafting work on protocols, done by an intergovernmental group (CDBI), concern:

- **protection of the human embryo and fetus.** Here, the CDBI has huge difficulties in reaching agreement. The United States of America sends observers to this group and may have access to all its documents.

- **biomedical research.** This draft is currently being finalised and should soon be declassified for public consultation.

- **transplantation of human organs and tissue.** This draft has been sent to the Parliamentary Assembly for a second debate at a Plenary Session. It must then be submitted to the Committee of Ministers for final adoption.

- **genetics.**

Cloning Regulation in the Particular European Union Countries

A. Countries with "liberal" legislation

United Kingdom

The Human Fertilisation and Embryology Act 1990 created a regulatory authority responsible for licensing the practice of embryo research. Licences were issued only for research conducted before the "primitive streak" at 14 days. In January 2001 the House of Lords voted in favour of allowing the Human Fertilisation and Embryology Authority, a public and independent authority supervising research into embryos and IVF techniques, to authorise research into therapeutic cloning.

Denmark

The Ethics Committee accepted therapeutic cloning by way of Law No. 460 of June 1997 which regulates artificial fertilisation in connection with treatment, diagnosis and research. Article 25 of the Law states that embryo research can take place only where the purpose is to improve *in vitro* fertilisation techniques or preimplantation diagnosis. All research projects are subject to the approval of ethics committees.

Netherlands

In September 2000 a bill governing intervention on human gametes and embryos (the "Embryos Bill") was put before Parliament. The Bill contains a number of bans on procedures involving gametes and embryos—such as the production of genetically identical individuals, the production of human/animal combinations and the application of sex-selection techniques. Other procedures involving gametes and embryos are made contingent on certain conditions (i.e., consent, therapeutic purposes). Research must satisfy specific criteria (listed in the Bill) and must not be performed without a research proposal having first been approved. The Bill includes the provision that, as soon as is deemed appropriate and under strict conditions, the total ban on the creation of embryos for research purposes can be replaced by a ruling which permits it.

Finland

The April 1999 Medical Research Act establishes a 14-day time limit on embryo research, subject to the prior consent of the progenitors. Section 13 states that the creation of embryos purely for the purposes of research is prohibited. Chapter 3 specifies that research can be performed only by agencies with the appropriate licence from the National Authority for Medico–Legal Affairs. Section 14 states that research on a fetus must be done only with the written consent of the pregnant woman. Section 15 explicitly prohibits any research which has the objective of modifying the genetic line

patient to digest, and it replaces, rather than assists, swallowing. Moreover, the withdrawal of a ventilator does not prevent the patient from breathing spontaneously but the withdrawal of tube-feeding results in certain death. And if the delivery of food by tube is medical treatment, is the removal of waste products by catheter and enema also medical treatment? Secondly, even if tube-feeding is medical treatment, why is it futile? Is it not achieving its purpose of nourishing the patient? To hold that the treatment is futile because the patient will not recover consciousness is surely to confuse the worthwhileness of the treatment with the worthwhileness of the patient's life.[39]

Arthur Hugh Clough, a fairly muddy-minded English poet of the nineteenth century, wrote the oft-quoted couplet:

> Thou shalt not kill; but need'st not strive
> Officiously to keep alive.

But what is "officious"? The usual response is that anything beyond self-support is artificial, mechanical, and therefore legitimately disposable. Thus, in *Whose Life Is It Anyway?*:

> *Judge:* Certainly, you're alive legally.
>
> *Ken:* I think I could challenge even that.
>
> *Judge:* How?
>
> *Ken:* Any reasonable definition of life must include the idea of its being self-supporting. I seem to remember something in the papers—when all the heart transplant controversy was on—about it being alright to take someone's heart if they require constant attention from respirators and so on to keep them alive.[40]

In principle, however, the "artificiality" of life-sustaining procedures does not alter the suicide or assisted-suicide scenario in the slightest. Would it be any less murder if, instead of shooting a person, we deprived him of his iron lung or of his insulin on the ground that these are "artificial" means of keeping him alive? If doing such things to another would be homicide, then doing them to oneself would just as certainly be suicide. A little reflection on the question of "dependence" will reveal that no-one—at any stage of

[39] J. Keown, "Doctors and Patients: Hard Case, Bad Law, 'New' Ethics," 52 *Cambridge Law Journal* 210 (1993).
[40] B. Clark, *Whose Life Is It Anyway?* (1978) 76.

his or her existence—is really independent of others or of the environment, "natural" or "artificial" (if the distinction really has any meaning). We depend upon others, including manufactured devices, for our very survival. (If you doubt this, try not using your boiler this winter.) Far more unites the terminally ill patient, the foetus, and the healthy, adult reader of this chapter than separates them. All three are dependent, and their dependency, instead of offering a potential ground for destruction or self-destruction, is a common bond. "Never send to know for whom the bell tolls," John Donne reminded humanity: "it tolls for thee."[41]

V. THREE OBJECTIONS AND A CONCLUSION

Several major objections can be raised to the position espoused here but they are all readily answerable.

A. Private Morality or Public Concern for the Right to Life

H.L.A. Hart maintains that the suicide and assisted-suicide issue should remain a matter of private morality—that such sensitive ethical decisions should not be legislated.[42] This is precisely the approach Ronald Dworkin takes to abortion: as a religious question, it should not be subjected to the interference of the state or its laws.[43] But, as I have argued over against Dworkin,[44] where life is in the balance, the state and its law must intervene in order to prevent egregious violations of human rights.

[41.] It may be that the judicial confusion on the legitimacy of doing nothing so as to allow a patient to die versus the culpability involved in stopping a proper medical treatment derives from the unfortunate Common Law doctrine of nonfeasance: the notion (rejected in the Continental Civil Law) that one can with impunity refuse to assist a person in peril—that culpability attaches only when one commences to assist and then negligently does not continue to do so. This distinction is as conceptually bad and ethically immoral as the effort to distinguish between "active" and "passive" euthanasia. See A. D'Amato, "The Conflict Between Legal and Moral Obligation: the 'Bad Samaritan' paradigm," in *his Jurisprudence: A Descriptive and Normative Analysis of Law* (1984) 287-303, and J.W. Montgomery, *Human Rights and Human Dignity* (1986) 186-87.

[42.] H.L.A. Hart, *Law, Liberty and Morality* (1962).

[43.] R. Dworkin, *Life's Dominion* (2d ed. 1994).

[44.] See note 10, above.

Northern Territory clings to its Natural Death Act, antiquated legislation which originated in America two decades ago. Hence there are no provisions for the appointment of agents to make medical decisions on behalf of a person who becomes incapable of doing so. Secondly, the standard of palliative care in the Northern Territory is totally inadequate.

Instead, the Northern Territory chose to bypass a caring response for all dying people and to legalise assisted suicide for a few. The Commonwealth parliament clearly has the constitutional power—and, I believe, the duty—to enact this bill. I commend it to all honourable members. I present the explanatory memorandum.

Bill read a first time.

Mr ACTING SPEAKER—In accordance with standing order 104A, the second reading will be made an order of the day for the next sitting.

Warnock report which laid the basis for the current permissive British legislation.

But what about the utilitarian claim that, after all, embryos without consciousness and incapable of pain are able to assist in the curing of diseases which shorten the lives and reduce the quality of life of suffering adults? The answer to this is that (in the felicitous expression used by legal philosopher Ronald Dworkin and many other critics of utilitarianism) fundamental human rights "trump" the use of humans as means to others' ends.

It is never right to hurt one human, without his or her permission, to reduce the difficulties of another. The classic analogy is that of the "eye bank." Suppose eye transplants became possible: would it then be legitimate, on utilitarian and democratic grounds, to force those with two eyes to undergo the removal of one of their eyes so as to give sight to the totally blind? Of course not; the very idea is monstrous and an affront to the dignity of the person. But stem-cell embryo research proposes exactly this kind of activity: the life of the unborn (whether regarded as human or potentially human) is sacrificed without personal consent for the benefit of other persons. Surely a civilised society must avoid at all costs such a denigration of the human being. People—no matter how young and undeveloped—must not be reduced to means for the sake of others' ends, or respect for human life in general will be so diminished that no-one will be safe from majoritarian tyranny.[16]

The Argument from Human Ignorance. In his book defending right-to-life, *Abortion and the Conscience of the Nation,* President Ronald Reagan spoke to those who are agnostic as to the nature of the fetus and who base their willingness to abort on this lack of knowledge. His point applies in every respect to the issue we are addressing here. President Reagan posed the situation in which he is out hunting and sees something at a distance which *might* or *might not* be another hunter. Would he be right to fire his gun, on

---

[16.] Cf. the case against "situation ethics": John Warwick Montgomery versus the late Joseph Fletcher: *Situation Ethics—True or False. Is It Sometimes Right To Do Wrong?* (reprint ed.; Edmonton, Alberta, Canada: Canadian Institute for Law, Theology, and Public Policy, 1999).

the chance that it is a deer? The answer, of course, is *certainly not*. In cases of ignorance as to whether we might kill a human being, we do not take that chance. To do so would be criminal negligence at best and, more likely, culpable manslaughter on the ground of sheer recklessness. Even if we are not sure whether the embryo fully qualifies as a human person, any doubt must be resolved in the direction of the human, and therefore nothing must be done which could result in harm to a possible human subject.

The Alternative Means Argument. Even if one concedes that presently intractable human ills could conceivably be ameliorated by stem-cell embryo research, this fact in itself would not necessarily justify such research activity. Since it is unarguable that there is irreversible harm to the fetus produced by such research, its justification would only be possible in principle if it could be shown that no other, less harmful means is available to bring about the same benefits. Ethically and practically, no-one could seriously support a more harmful over a less harmful remedy for the same disease! What is the situation in this instance? In point of fact, stem cells do not have to be obtained from embryos. They can at present be harvested from umbilical cords at birth, and, according to the best scientific opinion, in a very few years they will readily be able to be obtained from adult bone marrow or blood.[17]

The Unknown Danger Argument. In spite of admittedly overblown journalistic characterisations of cloning as the prelude to the

---

[17.] "Stem cells extracted from adult bone marrow proved beneficial at saving heart tissue damaged by heart attack, according to a new study. Scientists at Columbia Presbyterian Medical Center who injected the cells into rats say that the treatment may one day prove lifesaving for people with damaged heart muscle. A second study, by the National Human Genome Research Institute and New York Medical College, isolated stem cells from the bone marrow of male mice and injected them into the hearts of 30 female mice, in which heart failure had been induced. Over an average of nine days, the stem cells turned into heartmuscle cells, filling in 68 percent of the damaged areas in the hearts of 12 mice. The cells also turned into smooth muscle and blood vessel cells.... The research aims to harness a patient's own restorative powers to reverse the damage done by heart attacks. Using adult stem cells also would enable researchers to sidestep the controversial use of stem cells extracted from human embryos.... Trials using the procedure in humans are being designed and could begin this year, said Itescu, director of Columbia's transplant immunology program in the department of surgery. Because a heart patient's own marrow would be used as the stem cell source, the body's immune system would not reject them" (*Newsday*, 3 April 2001).

unless undertaken for the purpose of preventing or curing a serious hereditary disease.

Greece

Embryo research is not subject to explicit regulation, but falls under the terms of the General Council for Health Statement of 1988, which specifies that embryo research is permitted until 14 days post conception with the approval of the appropriate ethics committee. The statement explicitly prohibits cloning.

B. "Moderate" Countries

France

Law No. 94-654 of 29 July 1994 and its amendments restrict the use of reproductive technology to procreative cases. Research can be carried out only where it is seen to offer direct benefit to the embryo or to reproductive medicine. This has been supplemented by Decree No. 97–613 of 27 May 1997, inserting a new section into Division 2 of the French Public Health Code. The consent of both donors is required, and a 7-day time limit with specific prohibitions on certain types of research is imposed.

The National Ethical Consultative Committee for Life and Health Sciences (CCNE), established in 1983, expressed opposition to Directive 98/44/EC on the patenting of biotechnological inventions, but accepted with a very small majority therapeutic cloning (2001-01-18).[22] The French prime minister, Lionel Jospin, also gave his support to therapeutic cloning. President Jacques Chirac has an ambiguous position: he rejects cloning on new embryos, preferring to use adult stem cell techniques.

Every five years, the "bio-ethic " law of 29 July 1994 will be re-voted.

[22.] See : http://www.ccne-ethique.org/english/start.htm

Belgium

Belgium does not have a legislative framework for therapeutic cloning. Research touching on this type of cloning, like other human experimentation, is not subject to any national protocol, but research projects are under the control of local ethics committees.

Yvon Englert, Vice-President of the Consultative Committee on Biothethics, has suggested that Belgium could be inspired by recent British legal developments. There are current proposals to allow research on embryos under very stringent conditions.

Italy

In September 2000 the Minister of Health created a committee presided over by Nobel Prize winner Renato Dulbecco. It aimed to monitor research from a scientific and ethical perspective. In December 2000, the committee published its conclusions. Its opinion was divided: some members absolutely rejected all research on embryonic stem cells, whilst others highlighted the "potential benefits" of such research.

Spain

The 1988 Law on Techniques of Assisted Reproduction states that research can take place within the first 14 days with the progenitor's consent. However, it must be applied research of a diagnostic character or have a therapeutic purpose. Non-therapeutic research is permitted "on non-viable embryos and where it cannot be undertaken on an animal." Section 20 prohibits human cloning. The Spanish Committee of Experts on Cloning published a report in June 1999 supporting legislation to lift the existing ban on cloning in order to allow the creation of tissue to cure certain diseases. It strictly opposed the legalisation of reproductive cloning of human beings.

Sweden

Embryo research is governed by two statutes, the Swedish *in vitro* Fertilisation Act 1988 and the Act Concerning Measures for Research or Treatment Involving Fertilised Human Ova 1991. The 1988 Act regulates the practice of assisted reproduction and permits some research on human embryos. The research must be performed within 14 days of fertilisation and can be carried out only with the consent of the progenitors. Any research which seeks genetically to modify the embryo is prohibited. Once the research process has been completed the embryo must be destroyed. The implantation of a research embryo *in utero* is absolutely forbidden.

The 1991 legislation addresses the issue of embryo storage. The period for which an embryo may be cryopreserved is extended from one year to five years following amendments to the law of 1988.

C. "Conservative" Legislation

Austria

Embryo research is tightly constrained by the 1992 Act on Procreative Medicine. The central principle of this legislation is that reproductive medicine is permissible only within a stable heterosexual relationship for purposes of procreation. Embryo donation is forbidden and the number of ova that can be fertilised is restricted.

The current government will not change this legislation.

Germany

The 1992 Embryo Protection Act is a criminal statute imposing sentences of up to five years imprisonment upon those who breach its provisions. The law prohibits all forms of commercial research on human embryos and it is an offence to attempt to fertilise an egg for any purpose other than bringing about a pregnancy. The law, however, covers only *in utero* implantation and, while expressly forbidding human cloning, does not outlaw the removal of embryonic stem cells from cadaveric fetuses.

Germany has promised to support the French in their demand for the revision of Directive 98/44/EC on the patenting of biotechnological inventions. Julia Nida-Rümelin, Federal Minister of Culture, has taken a controversial stand maintaining that the cloning of embryos does not undermine human dignity. Gerhard Schröder is advocating a debate in Parliament on this issue.

Ireland

The 8th Amendment to the 1983 Constitution acknowledges the right to life of the unborn, with due regard to the equal right to life of the mother. This is interpreted as an absolute prohibition on embryo research.

D. No Official Position Taken

Portugal

Portugal does not have any legislation regulating medically assisted procreation or the status of the *in vitro* embryo. However, on 1 April 1997, the National Council on Ethics for the Life Sciences (CNEV) adopted Opinion 21/CNEV/97 on the ethical implications of cloning, following a formal request from fifteen representatives of the National Parliament (27 February 1997). The Opinion recommended that cloning should be prohibited.

CHAPTER 12

THE ALLEGED MYTH OF THE MAFIA*

Summary: *One of the most influential and prolific contemporary criminological scholars is Gordon Hawkins, co-editor of The Pursuit of Criminal Justice, collecting seminal essays produced during the first twenty years of activity in the Center for Studies of Criminal Justice at the University of Chicago. It is Hawkins' contention that the notion of a "nationwide crime syndicate" and of "a Mafia in particular" is a species of myth, analogous to theological claims about the existence of God. Both, it is said, are epistemologically unverifiable—species of technical nonsense or meaninglessness (in the sense in which these terms are used in Analytical Philosophy). The aim of the present paper is to show why this is not the case and why proper epistemological analysis leads in the very opposite direction: to a serious consideration of national, and indeed international, criminal activity and the need to combat it with the most sophisticated ideological and material efforts.*

I. THE HAWKINS THESIS

In his classic and clever essay, "God and the Mafia"[1] Gordon Hawkins argues that "a large proportion of what has been written [about organised crime] seems not to be dealing with an empirical matter at all. It is almost as though what is referred to as organised crime belonged to the realm of metaphysics or theology."[2]

Hawkins finds several parallels between Mafia-claims and God-claims. In both instances, the very existence of the phenomenon proves "on examination to consist of little more than a series of dog-

---

* Invitational keynote presentation at the Seventh International Anticorruption Conference, held in Beijing, China, 6-10 October 1995.

[1] Originally published as a journal article in 14 *The Public Interest* 24-51 (1969) and reprinted in *The Pursuit of Criminal Justice*, ed Gordon Hawkins and Franklin E. Zimring ("Studies in Crime and Justice"; Chicago and London: University of Chicago Press, 1984), pp. 157-84. Citations of the essay in the present paper will in all instances refer to the latter (reprint) edition.

[2] *Ibid.*, p. 157.

matic assertions."[3] Thus, the Final Report of the California Special Crime Study Commission on Organised Crime (1953)

> falls back on the argument that "The study of these crimes over the years shows a definite pattern, the repetition of which in case after case cannot be laid to coincidence." This incidentally bears an extraordinary resemblance to one of the best known arguments for the existence of God: that is "the argument from design" in the form in which it was used by the eighteenth- and nineteenth-century rationalist theologians. But it is neither probative nor particularly persuasive.[4]

Like God-claims, assertions concerning organised crime in general and the Mafia in particular do not inform us as to "what would be regarded as constituting significant counter evidence"—i.e., these claims apparently offer no meaningful possibility of disconfirmation: they are compatible with anything and everything, and therefore say nothing. The famous "Kefauver Committee" (the Senate Crime Committee) thus declared: "Almost all the witnesses who appeared before the committee and who were suspected of Mafia membership, either denied that they had ever heard of the Mafia, which is patently absurd, or denied membership in the Mafia."[5] The Mafia reminds one of those ghosts who are only present when a trained psychical investigator is absent!

The terms attributed to the Mafia "imply divine attributes, such as invisibility, immateriality, eternity, omnipresence, and omnipotence." What we are in fact left with is folklore and mythology—the product of a desire to introduce some kind of explanatory order into the bewilderingly diverse phenomena of our complex, modern world. Anthropologist Ruth Benedict is quoted in support: "Man in all his mythologies has expressed his discomfort at a mechanistic universe and his pleasure in substituting a world that is humanly motivated and directed."[6]

[3.] Ibid., p. 158.
[4.] Ibid., p. 159.
[5.] Ibid.
[6.] Ibid., p. 164. It may be worth noting that Benedict's scientific status, at guru level when Hawkins' article was originally written and published, has suffered an immense decline in recent years, owing to the discovery that she used faulty methodologies and tainted evidence.

The notion of a massive crime confederation or syndicate reduces, then, to "an article of faith, transcending the contingent particularity of everyday experience and logically unassailable; one of those reassuring popular demonologies that, as William Buckley has remarked, the successful politician has to cherish and preserve and may, in the end, come to believe."[7] This is true because, for the true believer in the Mafia, "precisely those features that in ordinary discourse about human affairs might be regarded as evidence in rebuttal are instantly assimilated as further strengthening the case *for* the hypothesis."

Hawkins concludes his philosophical-theological critique of the Mafia "myth" with the inevitable reference to the astronomer Laplace who, when asked by Napoleon why God was not mentioned in his *Traité de la mécanique céleste,* replied: "Sire, I had no need for that hypothesis." This response should "also obtain in the more mundane field of criminology: there are hypotheses that we do not need."

II. A WORD ABOUT VERIFIABILITY

Although Hawkins does not mention the fact in his article, his critique of organised crime theory is based squarely on the so-called "Verification Principle" set forth by philosophers of the contemporary Analytical School.

In a brief paper such as this, it would be impossible to discuss the history of this Analytical movement, arising from the pioneering *Principia Mathematica* of Russell and Whitehead, extending through the "logical atomism" of Wittgenstein's amazing *Tractatus Logico-Philosophicus,* and culminating in the (misnamed) "logical positivism" of von Mises and the "linguistic analysis" or "ordinary

---

[7.] *Ibid.,* pp. 183-84. Other opponents of the notion of a "nationwide crime syndicate" are: Daniel Bell, *The End of Ideology* (New York, 1962), especially chap. 7; Francis A. J. Ianni, *A Family Business: Kinship and Social Control in Organised Crime* (New York: Russell Sage Foundation, 1972); and Dwight C. Smith Jr, *The Mafia Mystique* (New York: Basic Books, 1975).

language philosophy" of the later Wittgenstein and Ryle.[8] But, in very general terms, the conclusions of these analytical thinkers can be summarised in regard to the problem of verifiability:

> The criterion which we use to test the genuineness of apparent statements of fact is the criterion of verifiability. We say that a sentence is factually significant to any given person if, and only if, he knows how to verify the proposition which it purports to express—that is, if he knows what observations would lead him, under certain conditions, to accept the proposition as being true, or reject it as being false.[9]

This "Verifiability Criterion of Meaning" arose from the discovery (set forth by Whitehead and Russell in the *Principia*) that assertions in mathematics and deductive logic are tautologous, i.e., they state nothing factual about the world, but follow from the *a priori* assumptions of the deductive system. Such "analytic" sentences can be verified without recourse to the world of fact, since they say nothing about the world; but other assertions (non-tautological, or "synthetic" affirmations) must be tested by the data of the real world if we are to discover their truth or falsity.

Thus any propositions, upon inspection, will fall into one of the following categories: (1) Analytic sentences, which are true or false solely by virtue of their logical form, *ex hypothesi*. Such assertions, though essential to thought and potentially meaningful, are often termed "trivial," since they never provide information about the world of experience. Example: "All husbands are married," whose truth follows entirely from the definition of the word "husband." (2) Synthetic sentences, which are true or false according to the application of the Verifiability Criterion set forth above. Such sentences are sometimes termed "informative," because they do potentially

---

[8.] For an introduction to these movements, see Victor Kraft, *The Vienna Circle*, trans. Arthur Pap (New York: Philosophical Library, 1953); G.J. Warnock, *English Philosophy since 1900* (London: Oxford University Press, 1958); and J.O. Urmson, *Philosophical Analysis* (New York: Oxford University Press, 1967).

[9.] A.J. Ayer, *Language, Truth and Logic* (New York: Dover Publications, [1946]), p. 35. Since the publication of the first edition of his work (1936), Ayer has somewhat refined his statement of the "Verifiability Principle" (see his Introduction to the new edition, pp. 5-16); however, in substance, his original statement remains unaltered and its classic simplicity warrants its continued use.

give information about the world. Example: "Jesus died at Jerusalem," which can be tested through an examination of historical evidence. (3) Meaningless sentences, embracing all affirmations which are neither analytic nor synthetic. Such sentences are incapable of testing, for they neither express tautological judgments (they are not statements whose truth depends on their logical form) nor do they affirm anything about the real world which is testable by investigating the world. Example: the philosopher F.H. Bradley's claim that "the Absolute enters into, but is itself incapable of, evolution and progress." Such a statement is clearly not tautologous, for it is not deduced from the *a prioris* of logic, nor is it capable of any test which could conceivably determine its truth or falsity. Thus it is meaningless or nonsensical (in the technical meaning of "nonsense," i.e., without verifiable sense).

The importance of the analytic approach to questions of truth and falsity cannot be overestimated. As a result of its application, vast areas of philosophical speculation and argument have been shown to lie in a never-never land of meaninglessness—a land where discussion could continue for ever without any possibility of arriving at truth or falsity. The analysts have successfully cleared the philosophical air of numerous positions about which discussion of truth-value is a waste of time, because their verifiability is impossible in any case.[10]

The Verification Principle thus constitutes an epistemological tool of great utility, and Hawkins' employment of it *per se* subjects

---

[10.] Attempts have been made, of course, to destroy the Verifiability Criterion. Few traditional, speculative philosophers have been happy with Feigl's remark that "Philosophy is the disease of which analysis should be the cure!" But the Verifiability Principle still stands as the best available road map through the forest of truth-claims. One of the most persistent attempts to refute the Criterion has been the effort to show that it is itself a meaningless assertion, being evidently neither an analytic nor a synthetic statement. However, this objection has been effectively met both by Ayer, who argues that the Criterion is actually a definition (*op.cit.*, pp. 15-16) and by Hempel, who shows that it, "like the result of any other explication, represents a linguistic proposal which itself is neither true nor false" ("The Empiricist Criterion of Meaning," published originally in the *Revue Internationale de Philosophie*, IV [1950], and reprinted, with newly appended remarks by the author, in *Logical Positivism*, ed. A.J. Ayer [Glencoe, Illinois: Free Press, 1959], pp. 108-129).

him to no legitimate criticism whatsoever. The issue before us is not the validity of the Verifiability Criterion of Meaning (would we really want to believe in something which no evidence could even in principle confirm or disconfirm?), but whether or not organised crime fails the verifiability test.

III. IS THE MAFIA ANALYTICALLY MEANINGLESS?

Clearly, the existence of massive organised crime is not a definitional question: the assertion "the Mafia exists" will never be true or false by virtue of its logical form. The truth or falsity of such a claim depends entirely on empirical evidence. The claim is at least potentially "informative," purporting to give information about the world; whether it in fact does so can only be determined by investigating the real world of criminal activity. Is it fair to apply to the nationwide crime syndicate, as Hawkins does in the prefatory quotation to his article, the line from Ibsen's *Peer Gynt*, "And if any more proof is needed, I possess invisible horns"? Just how visible are the horns of organised crime?

Answer: appallingly visible.

At the end of his detailed survey, *Crime Inc.: The Story of Organised Crime*, Martin Short summarises an interview with law professor Robert Blakey:

> Professor Robert Blakey, director of the Notre Dame University Institute on Organised Crime, is the man who drew up the three federal laws which are now being applied so successfully against organised crime (the RICO statute, and the laws governing electronic surveillance and witness protection). Blakey regards the Mafia as the only enduring criminal organisation of all those groups that have ever been active in America. "The single strongest group happens to be people of Italian descent. The Sicilians put it together in the 1930s when they beat every single group and it is still together in the 1980s. There are emerging groups. Many of them have Mafia characteristics but only the Mafia has the cohesion, the wealth, the access to violence, the access to lawyers and to political corruption. That's a fact."[11]

[11.] Martin Short, *Crime Inc.: The Story of Organised Crime* (London: Thames Methuen, 1984), p. 345.

The factual nature of massive Mafia activity in the United States is patently clear from Moquin's anthology, *The American Way of Crime: A Documentary History*, which chronicles its rise to power and national prominence during Prohibition and its diversification into racketeering, white collar crime, and drugs in the half century that followed. Moquin is impressed by the arguments of Hawkins, and agrees that "organised crime operates primarily on a local basis." However, he is unwilling to cast aside the expression "national crime confederation" as employed by Senator Kefauver and others.[12] "Although it may not be a formal nationwide organisation, a loose confederation can consist of local syndicates, each a law unto itself, cooperating with the others in enterprises that cannot be carried off so well alone, such as narcotics traffic."[13]

Former U.S. Attorney General Ramsey Clark came to much the same conclusion in his important study, *Crime in America: Observations on its Nature, Causes, Prevention and Control*. Cautioning that "organised crime is a very small part of America's crime" taken as a whole,[14] since it does not account for the vast number of juvenile, race, and local crimes, Clark nonetheless stresses that "major organised crime in America is committed by large cohesive groups exhibiting similar patterns of activity in cities separated by hundreds or even thousands of miles—New York, Las Vegas, Chicago, Miami. They are essentially a loose confederation."[15] Though loosely confederated, not monolithic, they are characterised by "vertical integration" and "diversification."[16] Organised crime may be a "limited empire"—to use one of Clark's chapter titles—but it is an empire nevertheless.

Those with serious doubts as to the scope and extent of organised crime in general and the Mafia in particular should consult a comprehensive reference work which is virtually guaranteed to

---

[12.] Cf. Estes Kefauver, *Crime in America* (New York: Doubleday, 1951), *passim*.

[13.] Wayne Moquin (ed.). *The American Way of Crime: A Documentary History* (New York: Praeger, 1976), p. x.

[14.] Ramsey Clark, *Crime in America: Observations on Its Nature, Causes, Prevention and Control* (New York: Pocket Books, 1971), p. 66.

[15.] *Ibid.*, p. 58.

[16.] *Ibid.*, pp. 55-56.

remove the subject from the realm of mythology. Jay Robert Nash's 624-page *World Encyclopedia of Organised Crime* (1992) is based on meticulous field research and the consultation of thousands of published sources, the general bibliography alone running to some twenty double-column pages. The geographical section (divided into "regions of the world in which organised crime has established a stronghold") is 137 pages in length, whilst the main body of the work covers, alphabetically, the gamut of persons and organisations in the modem history of organised crime.

Nash concludes his detailed general article on the Mafia with this judgment:

> The U.S. Mafia, by the 1980s, had invested billions of its illegal earnings from gambling, prostitution, and especially drug trafficking into legitimate businesses that produced even more profits. Today the Mafia in the U.S. is enormously rich and powerful and its tentacles reach into almost all areas of U.S. business. It works in cooperation with non-Sicilian criminals who are members of the same crime cartel known as the Syndicate, which was once aptly described by one of its leading exponents, Meyer Lansky: "We are bigger than U.S. Steel."[17]

As for the Syndicate itself, created in the 1930s "to eliminate gang warfare, facilitate communication, and maximise profit among several mobs," and which later came to be "almost wholly controlled by the Mafia," neither its methods not its interests altered significantly during the ensuing half-century.

> The main business ventures of the thirties included gambling, vice, union racketeering, and narcotics—the repeal of Prohibition had put the mobsters out of the bootlegging business. Its biggest money makers today remain narcotics and gambling.[18]

In the 1980s, however, Syndicate criminal activity took on an international dimension undreamed of by its earlier practitioners.

> By the late 1980s, the syndicate was no longer dominated by the old Mafia leaders and had become a polyglot organisation into

---

[17] Jay Robert Nash (ed.), *World Encyclopedia of Organised Crime* (New York: Paragon House, 1992), p. 271. The general article on the Mafia covers pp. 264-72, with cross-references to twenty-eight related articles.

[18] *Ibid.*, p. 376 (article: "Syndicate, The").

whose ranks any nationality or race was admitted (although the hierarchy has remained basically white and of Italian-Sicilian background). Blacks, for instance, began to retake rackets they had originated in Harlem in the 1920s, such as policy (numbers). Mexican and South American crime lords, with the expansion of drug trafficking from those areas from the 1960s onward, came into greater power, so that the U.S. syndicate was forced to share in the supply and distribution of drugs and their huge profits with such foreign organisations as the Medellin drug cartel and other foreign drug organisations in France, Sicily (the mother country of the Mafia), China, and even Japan, where the vast and fanatical Yakuza crime organisation dominates the country to the highest political levels.

From its crude beginnings of thousands of Italian and Sicilian immigrants held in almost slave labour by ganglords of the 1920s as they worked handmade alky cookers to produce illegal liquors and beer, to the present day where the syndicate reaches into almost every worldwide business—from vending machines to the cleaning of restaurant tablecloths and the production of video tapes— the history of organised crime is one replete with mass murder, wholesale corruption of public officials, and staggering power, the kind of seemingly unchallengeable power that keeps John Gotti in New York and Sam Anthony Carlisi in Chicago on their respective syndicate thrones. Next to the federal government itself, the syndicate is the most powerful organisation in America, feeding upon the public's appetite for the illegal, and being fed by it while it goes about its insidious business of crime. Its counterparts around the world exist in evil harmony, controlling, to a great degree, the economic and political destiny of nations and peoples— as corruptive as the venal force that drove humanity from Eden into the lands of darkness.[19]

Rhetorical as it may be, this summation is fully supported by the content of Nash's encyclopedic work.

And the saga by no means stops there. The international expansion of organised Mafia activity has been the subject of London *Times* news reports, which detail the entrance of the Mafia into the British drugs and banking scene and the impact of the linking of the Mafia and South American drug cartels on cocaine traffic in Western Europe.[20]

[19.] *Ibid.*, p. ii ("Foreword").
[20.] See London *Times* articles of 29 December 1993 and 5 May 1995.

In the face of such evidence, one can hardly maintain the "myth" of the Mafia—much less the dismissing of its membership as (in the words of a character in one of Scott Turow's legal novels) "just a bunch of dark Mediterraneans who didn't finish high school"— "the most overpublicised group in history."[21]

But what accounts for such flights from reality, when the empirical evidence weighs so heavily in favour of the reality of the phenomenon? Perhaps the analogy of comparable attempts at using the Verification Principle to de-empiricise can be helpful.

Norman Cohn, a distinguished historian of ideas who has specialised in millennialisms, argues that witches' covens and sabbats never in fact existed. Montague Summers and other specialists in the history of the occult who claim that they did are "unable to produce any credible evidence for that view."[22] Secret societies of witches are simply an unverifiable myth. Yet, in point of fact, Summers offers considerable primary source data in support of his position.[23]

Or consider Hawkins' own prime analogy: the existence of God. Far from there being no empirical evidence which can count for or against this claim, God's existence is supportable, *inter alia*, by (1) the Second Law of Thermodynamics (an atheistic universe would already have reached maximum entropy: heat death)[24] and (2) the historical facticity of the resurrection of Jesus Christ from the dead, confirming his self-affirmation of Deity.[25]

[21.] Scott Turow, *Pleading Guilty* (New York: Warner Books, 1993), pp. 266-67.
[22.] Norman Cohn, *Europe's Inner Demons* (rev, ed.; London: Pimlico, 1993), p. 161.
[23.] John Warwick Montgomery, *Principalities and Powers* (rev. ed.; Minneapolis: Bethany Dimension Books, 1975), especially pp. 34, 45, 209.
[24.] John Warwick Montgomery, *The Suicide of Christian Theology* (Newburgh, Indiana: Trinity Press, 1998), especially pp. 251-66; *Evidence for Faith: Deciding the God Question* (Richardson, Texas: Probe Books, 1991), *passim*.
[25.] John Warwick Montgomery, *History and Christianity* (Minneapolis: Bethany, 1986) (also available in Chinese: P.O. Box 13-144, Taipei, Taiwan); *Human Rights and Human Dignity* (2d ed.; Edmonton, Alberta: Canadian Institute for Law, Theology and Public Policy, 1995).

Since both covens and divine existence are in principle verifiable, and thus analytically meaningful, why are they summarily relegated to the domain of mythology by thinkers who otherwise display considerable scholarly ability? The answer is undoubtedly that the strangeness of the phenomena (the occult, the Deity) makes one feel so uncomfortable—so threatens one's settled world view—that one finds it easier to eliminate the whole idea as analytically nonsensical than to engage in the detailed empirical investigation required for actual confirmation or disconfirmation of the thesis.[26]

Perhaps the same underlying psychology operates in the relegation of massive organised crime to the realm of mythology. The whole idea seems incredible to our ordinary experience and a threat to the neat, controlled world in which we function. How convenient, then, if we can summarily classify Mafia confederations as untestable mythologies! But empirical reality, whether of organised evil or transcendent good, has a way of demanding our attention. We ignore facts in any sphere to our extreme peril.

IV. COUNTERACTING CRIMINALITY AND CORRUPTION

In what Marshall McLuhan termed the "global village" at the onset of the 21st century, where both communication and crime have become well organised and international, what is to be done to reduce the incidence of massive corruption? Three requisites appear to be absolutely mandatory.

First, as our discussion to this point should have made patently clear, *criminal activity must be treated with utmost seriousness*. Remedies are never taken seriously when the disease is regarded as trivial. An ailment which is considered purely local will inevitably be the object of limited, local curative measures. Only when we come

---

[26.] Cf. John Warwick Montgomery, "A Philosophical-Theological Critique of the Death of God Movement," in Bernard Murchland (ed.), *The Meaning of the Death of God* (New York: Random House Vintage Books, 1967), pp. 25-69; and *La Mort de Dieu* (Strasbourg, France: Editions Oberlin, 1971), *passim*.

to appreciate the massive extent of organised crime, both nationally and internationally—only when we see it as it is, a cancer eating away at society in general—will we employ budgetary and human resources on a sufficient scale to meet its challenge. Needless to say, such a realistic perspective on the nature of contemporary criminal activity entails the recognition that crime and corruption are by no means restricted to or the product of limited ethnic groups (Italians, Sicilians, etc.): *every* society and *every* individual is potentially capable of criminality and corruption. Crime knows no geographical or national boundaries.

Secondly, to combat modern crime and corruption, *the most comprehensive investigative techniques and the most innovative legal measures consistent with the due process of law and the civil liberties of the subject need to be employed.* Fears of losing national sovereignty must not be allowed to impede the growth of international police work (such as Interpol). Computerised files on criminals and criminal activity must be made more and more internationally accessible. "Sting" operations need to be expanded—without, of course, degenerating into entrapments (which, rather than catching criminals, actually create them!). Indirect prosecutorial approaches need to be considered, such as the use of tax-evasion statutes to apprehend criminals (Al Capone and other mafiosi, it will be remembered, were finally brought down by violations of the U.S. Internal Revenue Code when prosecuting them on more "substantive" criminal charges proved impractical or impossible). Draconian penalties, such as confiscation of all property obtained as a fruit of illegal activity (e.g., hotels and other businesses financed by criminal operations) or all property used to carry on a criminal activity (e.g., boats used to transport drugs) can be useful economic deterrents to crime—especially when one remembers that the prime motivation for organised crime and corruption is greed.

Thirdly, modern criminal activity and corruption will only be fought effectively when their *etiological complexity is recognised.* In a recent address in Edinburgh, Scotland, Sir John Crofton, who forty years ago found the cure for tuberculosis by developing an innovative mix of anti-tuberculosis drugs, correctly argued that the disease of crime likewise constitutes a "spectrum" and can only be treated by a spectrum of responses. Not to recognise this complexity, in Sir John's opinion, is simply "medieval."[27] But the tendency toward causal reductionism in the analysis of crime and corruption is so widespread and so devastating to the proper understanding of the phenomena that we must focus on this issue in detail in the concluding pages of our essay.

Crime and corruption have three causal dimensions, no one of which can be neglegted if we wish to understand and counteract these evils: the *social*, the *governmental*, and the *individual*. We can diagram them thusly:

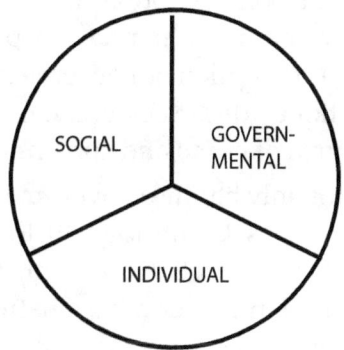

The Etiology of Crime/Corruption

Let us discuss each in turn.

1. *The social dimension.* Crime and corruption are societally related. Marxist theory (in its doctrine of "base" and "superstructure") quite properly emphasises the socio-economic sources of criminal activity, as have Western criminologists, whether of a socialist or of a more liberal persuasion. It is undeniable that miserable living conditions and the lack of opportunity to escape from ghettos to a better economic existence create the seedbed in which much crime and corruption are generated. Ramsey Clark identifies the problem clearly:

[27.] Reported in the *Times Higher*, 7 April 1995, p. 4.

> Helpless and hopeless, the poor urban slum dweller is the natural prey of organised crime which thrives in his environment....
>
> Who in our society is more likely to seek the escape offered by narcotics than the poor who live in the devastating misery of urban slums? Drugs will temporarily liberate a person from the wretchedness there without his ever leaving. Both desirous of drugs and powerless to protect himself against his suppliers, he is the ideal customer for organised crime.[28]

It is profoundly true that any successful attack on crime in the modern world must devote the most serious attention to the amelioration of social ills.

2. *The governmental dimension.* Michel Bergès correctly identifies as a fundamental error the notion that "L'Etat bureaucratique organisé échappe par définition (par nature, par essence?) à la corruption," such that "la corruption ne concerne que des personnes ou des groupes 'pré-étatiques' de la Société civile."[29] The state itself can indeed become a source of crime and corruption.

Why is this so? Not only because government is part of social reality but also because, as Cambridge historian Lord Acton so trenchantly put it, "Power tends to corrupt; absolute power corrupts absolutely." Those in power have a natural tendency to consider themselves above the law and to use their powerful positions to the advantage of themselves, their friends, and their families. No species of government is exempt: crime and corruption can be found in the corridors of power in the West as well as in the East, in democratic governments as well as in more authoritarian states.

The particularly sad aspect of government corruption derives from the fact that government is so visible and all pervading a factor in modern societal life. Government, good or bad, thus serves as an immediate and natural model for private life. Corrupt government will inevitably encourage, by powerful analogy, crime and corruption in the private sphere. "If state officials can justify and get away with it," the average citizen rationalises to himself, "why can't I?"

[28.] Clark, *op. cit.*, p. 53.
[29.] Michel Bergès, "Peut-on sortir de la corruption?," 31 *Pouvoirs* 75 (1984).

Once one is willing to admit that government enters into the crime equation, there is the realistic possibility of limiting state corruption. How? By moving away from a monolithic, totalitarian, paternalistic style of government to the greater separation of governmental powers. Where state powers are separated—where there is less concentration of power in the hands of the few—corruption, when it does occur, will not be possible on as massive a scale, and there will be reciprocal accountability, making it less possible to conceal criminal activity.

Essential also is the rule of law: the placing of *everyone*, including the highest government officials—even the head of state—under the restraints and punishments of the law. If *anyone* can flaunt the law, why cannot *everyone* do the same?

Finally, the government must respect the human rights of all its citizens. Where there is repression of free speech, free association, a free press, and arbitrary punishment without public trial, the citizenry will inevitably lose respect for the law and for those who enforce it and will see no reason not to engage in illegal and corrupt activity if they can get away with it.

3. *The individual dimension.* Even when socio-economic conditions are ideal and government is functioning most commendably, crime and corruption still occur. The well-to-do (not just the poor) cheat on their income taxes and murder their wives. Clearly, crime and corruption must be faced on the individual level, not just as social or governmental phenomena.

Indeed, it can be argued that the problem of counteracting crime and corruption in all spheres ultimately focuses on individual human motivation. The supremely important question then becomes: How can people be brought to a personal value system such that they will choose not to act illegally?

Human motivation can be influenced by education and by meaningful punitive measures, and these should of course be employed appropriately and intelligently; but even at best they are no guarantee of success. Education can simply produce cleverer criminals, and even draconian punishments do not eliminate recidivism. It is sobering, for example, to recall that when pickpocketing was a capital offence in England, cutpurses plied their trade during the public hangings at Tyburn! Indeed, increasing punishments can actually exacerbate the problem through the creation of a police state which is so hated that even the average citizen is moved to crime in retaliation.

As we have noted, the amelioration of social evils can reduce the necessity of crime. However, manipulation of the external conditions of life does not necessarily touch the internal founts of human motivation. Jesus' teaching that it is not what goes into a man that corrupts him but what comes out of his heart[30] is confirmed by commonsense and by rational analysis. Evil socio-economic conditions were after all created by human beings themselves (not imposed on the human race by Martians!), so correcting those conditions is no absolute guarantee that people will not fall back into bad habits and criminality. No political or economic philosophy has ever produced "new men," in the sense of people free from criminal or corrupt potentialities.[31]

What is evidently needed is personality change so radical that it would constitute "conversion." Such change can and does in fact occur, and where it is genuine, it invariably has a transcendent, religious source. An archetypal contemporary example is Charles Colson, the late President Nixon's hatchetman, who was jailed for his participation in the Watergate illegalities; while in prison, Colson experienced a Christian conversion, and has since that time devoted his life not to crime but to ministering to prisoners.[32]

[30.] Mark 7:14-23: "And he called the people to him again, and said to them, 'Hear me, all of you, and understand: there is nothing outside a man which by going into him can defile him; but the things which come out of a man are what defile him.' And when he had entered the house, and left the people, his disciples asked him about the parable. And he said to them, 'Then are you also without understanding? Do you not see that whatever goes into a man from outside cannot defile him, since it enters, not his heart but his stomach, and so passes on?' (Thus he declared all foods clean.) And he said, 'What comes out of a man is what defiles a man. For from within, out of the heart of man, come evil thoughts, fornication, theft, murder, adultery, coveting, wickedness, deceit, licentiousness, envy, slander, pride, foolishness. All these evil things come from within, and they defile a man.'" (Cf. Matthew 15:16-20.)

[31.] John Warwick Montgomery, "The Marxist Approach to Human Rights," 3 *Simon Greenleaf Law Review* 96-99, 167-83 (1983-1984).

The Alleged Myth of the Mafia   235

To be sure, not all religions are capable of producing such results. Peter Harris, professor emeritus of political science at the University of Hong Kong, has noted recently that "Confucianism, with its highly deferential code, was a largely ceremonial system, with no possibility for change."[33] I have argued elsewhere that "Chinese religion either considers man basically good and not requiring redemption (folk religion, Taoism, Confucianism) or sees him capable of saving himself through a consciously chosen renunciation of both the world in which he lives and the people with whom he has contact (Buddhism)."[34]

Effective inner change—the transformation of individual motivation—appears to constitute a unique by-product of Christian religious experience. When combined, as it is in that context, with a high moral code of transcendent dimensions and the assurance of a Last Judgement such that no crimes ultimately go unpunished, the result is a powerful counteractive to crime and corruption on every level.

However advantageous such a religious instrument might be in the fight against rampant criminality, we should be loathe to

---

[32.] See Colson's published wrintings (*Born Again*, etc.).

[33.] *The Times Higher*, 14 April 1995, p. 14.

[34.] John Warwick Montgomery, *Giant in Chains* (Milton Keynes, England: Nelson Word Ltd., 1994), pp. 135-36. German edition: *Wohin marschiert China?* (Kehl: Editions Trobisch; Stuttgart: Haenssler Verlag, 1991), p. 118. Chang and Chang provide fascinating literary confirmation of the point we are making: "Before 1949, the education of wealthy boys and girls [in China] began around the age of seven. Most likely, the first book they encountered was *Sàn zi jing*, the *Three Character Classic*. They used it as generations of [American] colonial children used their *New England Primer*, to learn elementary reading skills along with the philosophy fundamental to their culture. While Chinese children of the Ch'ing dynasty (1644-1912 A.D.) were poring over the first words of the *Three Character Classic*,

rèn　zì　chū　xìng　bèn　shàn
(man) (since) (beginning) (nature) (origin) (good)

'Men at their birth are naturally good,' English-speaking children were reading rhymed couplets for each letter of the alphabet, beginning with 'A/In Adam's fall/We sinned all,' a poem that appeared in countless primers published in England and America during the eighteenth century" (Raymond Chang and M.S. Chang, *Speaking of Chinese* [rev. ed.; London: André Deutsch, 1980], pp. 28-29).

employ it if its truth-claims were in fact incorrect, or, even worse, analytically meaningless. Fortunately, as we have pointed out earlier, this is not the case. The Hawkins thesis fails on two counts, not just one. The Verification Principle leaves untouched both God and the Mafia.

CHAPTER 13

GREEK OPPOSITION TO EVANGELISM

Greece is generally viewed through the eyes of classical education (Pericles' Oration on the Athenian Dead) or by way of Byronic 19th-century romanticism: the cradle of freedom cum laissez-faire sensuality ... Socrates and Zorba the Greek. Thus the popularity of the Greek islands for the perfect holiday.

In point of fact, one had better be very careful, at least religiously, while on that holiday. Since Byron's day, when Anglican missionaries first brought their wares to Greece, an antiproselytising law has made the country anything but an open shop for religions other than the established Orthodox Church.

On holiday, therefore, one must be especially careful not to give a Bible (constituting a "material inducement" to convert) to someone not a member of one's own church, or to criticise any of his religious ideas (one successful prosecution was for comparing a relic of St. Gerassimos to a "body stuffed with cotton") or to invite children to a daily vacation church school. The law criminalises religious evangelism which takes "advantage of a person's inexperience, trust, need, low intellect or naivety"; but, last we heard, everyone experiences religious "need" from time to time, and it is difficult to determine ahead of time (by an IQ test and psychological examination?) the intellectual and naivety level of the other person before getting into an evangelical discussion with him or her.

I. BACKGROUND

The present-day attitude of the Greek populace and the Greek Orthodox Church toward issues of religious freedom is remarkably negative. In the early months of the new millennium, an effort by the socialist government to drop church affiliation from Greek national identity cards caused a nationwide row, with the Church claiming that its very existence would be imperilled by such a move. Even though the government noted that it was the Nazis who first introduced faith-designation on identity cards, and that the new regulation was doing little more than to streamline the cards (fingerprints, profession, and spouse's name are also to be removed), the Church saw the move as a blow to national belief. Church spokesman Metropolitan Theoklitos asserted that "Orthodoxy ... is an indivisible part of our identity and we want it written on the identity cards."[1]

To understand such a reaction to what would generally be regarded as a tempest in a teapot, one needs to recall the modern religious history of Greece. Some 97% of the contemporary Greek populace are identified with Eastern Orthodox faith, in spite of low actual church attendance. Historically, the Orthodox Church in Greece held its own and indeed triumphed in bitter conflict with the Muslim-Ottoman empire, and the Greek-Turkish animosity today has a powerful religious component. Anglican missionaries in the 19th century were regarded as no less than heretics on the Greek scene; indeed, the first appearance of the modern Greek antiproselytism statutes (1844) was in large part due to the Greek Orthodox Church's passion to restrain such organisations as the Society for the Propagation of the Gospel.

When liberal or socialist governments have been in power in Greece, church-state conflict has characterised the Greek scene. In November 1901, fighting between police and demonstrators resulted in eleven deaths and eighty persons being injured—owing to a dispute over the introduction of a demotic Greek translation of the Gospels! In 1907, the Holy Synod claimed (and won) the sole right to appoint and dismiss cantors and sextons, over against government demands for a say in Church councils and Church management. When Yiannis Kordatos' book, *The Social Significance of the*

---

[1] Patrick Quinn, Associated Press dispatch, 15 May 2000. Cf. "Greek Church Fights Change in ID Cards," *New York Times*, 1 June 2000.

1821 Revolution, was published in 1924, containing negative criticism of the Greek patriarchate and higher clergy, the Church reacted fiercely.

> Another row broke out in 1925, when Christian associations and advocates of purist Greek complained of anti-national teaching methods at the Teachers' College and the Marasleio. In 1926, "long-haired communist" teachers were dismissed and the Teachers' College abolished, and in 1930 Nikos Kazantzakis and Dimitris Glinos went on trial for "mocking religion" in an article in a literary journal.
>
> In 1952, the Plastiras government threatened to expropriate Church land and stop clerical pay if the Church did not hand over some of its real estate for the use of 200,000 landless people. Eventually the Church handed over 750,000 stremmas. There was vigorous opposition in 1954, when the Holy Synod excommunicated Nikos Kazantzakis for his books, *Captain Michalis* and *The Last Temptation,* urging the patriarchate to do likewise and calling for the public prosecutor to lay charges. Both refused.
>
> In April 1959, Church and State were at loggerheads again over the transfers of metropolitan bishops. The government abolished the right of transfer in most cases, and empowered the education minister to halt the Holy Synod's proceedings. In May 1960, the crisis peaked with unprecedented episodes in eight bishoprics. In November 1965, when the government refused to recognise elections of bishops that were held despite their postponement by the Council of State, supporters of the Hierarchy clashed with members of religious organizations.
>
> Since the 1967-74 dictatorship, talk of separating Church and State comes up whenever there is a dispute. In the 1980s, large demonstrations protested against legislation to regulate the matter of Church property.[2]

But church-state conflicts in Greece have not persuaded the legislature to get rid of the Greek antiproselytism law, much less to disestablish the Orthodox Church. In most of the small towns and villages, the most influential person is still the local parish priest. Legislators are well aware of this fact, particularly at election time. They realise that to oppose Church influence on a grand scale would be political suicide.

[2.] *Kathimerini News,* 14 June 2000.

In the last quarter century, the Greek antiproselytism law has been used again and again to suppress religious views other than those of the established Church. The first substantial international opposition to such repression of religious freedom came by way of the *Kokkinakis* case, in which an elderly Jehovah's Witness, who had been arrested more than sixty times and convicted more than eight times for door-to-door proselytism, was criminally prosecuted for making the mistake of trying to convert the wife of an Orthodox priest while the priest hid behind a door and took notes! The Strasbourg Court completely exonerated the applicant on the facts but refused to declare the Greek law incompatible with the European Convention on Human Rights.[3]

The "Trial of the Athens 3" in 1986 constituted the first of the significant Christian evangelism cases in Greece to come before the courts. This case was resolved within the Greek court system itself and thus, unlike *Larissis et al.* (which we shall discuss later), it did not reach the European Court of Human Rights in Strasbourg. However, the arguments set forth—particularly those opposing the Greek antiproselytising law—laid the basis for subsequent litigation in Strasbourg.

II. THE "ATHENS 3" CASE

The Facts of the Case. In 1979, the M/V Anastasis arrived in the Bay of Eleusis, near Athens, for major refurbishing. The Anastasis is part of Mercy Ships International, a ministry of Youth With A Mission (YWAM)—a non-denominational, Trinitarian Christian missionary organisation of charismatic persuasion. The vessel is a nine-storey tall ship, built in 1953, with a gross tonnage of 11,695. The Christians who run the ship have a twofold mission: the first is to bring food, clothing and medical aid to needy people around the world. With living quarters for 600 crew members and a cargo capacity of 3,000 tons for food, clothing, medical supplies and other basic necessities, the M/V Anastasis is potentially suited to assist in

---

[3]. Case No. 3/1992/348/421.

any port city of the world. Secondly, they all share the common goal of presenting the Gospel to whoever will listen.

The leaders of the Anastasis were Don Stephens, an American missionary and the head of Mercy Ships International, and Alan Williams, a British missionary born in New Zealand.

Whilst the ship was in the middle of a three-year refurbishing project, a major earthquake hit the Athens area on February 24, 1981. The Anastasis crew responded to the disaster by distributing clothing and food to the many homeless victims, as well as providing spiritual counsel and relief.

It was at this time that Costas Kotopoulos, a sixteen-year-old Greek whose parents were divorced, made contact with crew members of M/V Anastasis. As Williams would later testify in court, "Young Costas approached us. He looked a bit sad, so we befriended him and accepted him like we would anyone anywhere."

He was given a Bible, at his request, and began reading it diligently. In addition, through his interaction with the Christians from the Anastasis, his life began to change.

Costas, who lived with his father, visited the Anastasis on a number of different occasions, each time either dropped off by or accompanied by his father. A Greek court banned the visits after Costas' mother, Catherine Dougas, accused the members of the Anastasis of violating the Greek antiproselytism law.

In 1982, before the Anastasis left Greece, Don Stephens gave Costas the name and address of Costas Macris, a distinguished Greek evangelical leader and former missionary to New Guinea, who now runs the Hellenic Missionary Center in Athens. In this way, they hoped that Costas would be able to have fellowship with other young Christians.

Almost two-and-one-half years later, Don Stephens and Alan Williams were notified, by an interested third party, that they were being tried for proselytism in Greece. They had not received any official notification or court summons. Costas' mother had filed suit against both them and Costas Macris on charges of "proselytism" and "support of the voluntary escape of a minor." The suit also demanded that the defendants be ordered to pay her 50,000 dracmas as pecuniary satisfaction for moral damage which she suffered.

Believing it was their duty as Christians to fight for the right of religious expression, Stephens and Williams returned to Greece for the trial in December of 1984.

At the trial, Costas' mother testified that the missionaries had ruined her son, that he no longer made the sign of the cross or believed in icons, that he now read his Bible daily and was a religious fanatic, that he no longer had ordinary sexual interests, and that the only time he stayed out late was when he attended meetings and Bible studies with other like-minded fanatics. Despite the fact that Costas was still a member of the Greek Orthodox Church and that the charge of having supported his "voluntary escape" was patently false, the judges found the defendants guilty. Their sentence, the harshest in over 150 years for this type of "offense" was three-and-one-half years imprisonment!

The defendants were freed on bail, pending appeal of their verdict. The conviction of the "Athens Three" became a global story overnight.[4]

As an international groundswell of public opinion rose against the Greek government, Greek officials seemed to harden rather than soften in their stance. Over 400,000 Americans alone signed petitions to Greek Prime Minister Papendreou. A number of U.S. congressmen sent letters asking the Greek government to reevaluate their stand. California governor Deukmejian wrote Greek president Sartzetakis expressing his "deep concern." So did President Reagan. However, the politically powerful Orthodox Church insisted that the government enforce the antiproselytism law and send the missionaries to prison.

The appeal was scheduled for May 21, 1986. If the defendants lost, they would go to prison immediately. During the interim, YWAM's house counsel in Hawaii, Max Crittenden, contacted this writer. He asked if I could help by submitting a legal brief detailing

---

[4.] See Don Stephens' book on the trial at first instance: *Trial by Trial* (Eugene, Oregon: Harvest House, 1985).

the reasons the original decision should be overturned. In addition he requested me as former Director of Studies at the International Institute of Human Rights in Strasbourg, France, to come to the appellate trial and testify as an expert on human rights.

The trial lasted for four days—with extensive international press and television coverage (e.g., Reuters News Agency, London, and the European edition of *Time* magazine). The International Commission of Jurists sent an observer to ensure that the human rights of the defendants were upheld. I was on the stand for almost an hour, and my theological and legal arguments were surprisingly echoed by the Greek public prosecutor, who told the judges that, in his opinion, the state had made a mistake in prosecuting the case. Finally, the three-judge panel adjourned to deliberate. After conferring for 2 1/2 hours, they found the defendants innocent of all charges.[5]

The Government's Argument. The prosecution in the "Athens 3" case relied upon arguments both of law and of fact to persuade the Athens Court of Appeal to uphold the convictions imposed by the court of first instance.

In law, the prosecution observed that the Greek antiproselytism statute was good law in Greece, and simply fleshed out the undefined but explicit prohibition against proselytism enshrined in the Greek Constitution. To question its validity would be to question the Constitution itself. The statute in its present form is not discriminatory (though prior to the Colonels' regime its application was limited to convincing or attempting to convince Greek Orthodox to leave their church, the existing version *totally* bans improper proselytism, regardless of the religion involved). Moreover, the law is explicit in its definition of proselytism: "By 'proselytism' is meant, in particular, any direct or indirect attempt to intrude on the religious beliefs of a person of a different religious persuasion, with the aim of undermining those beliefs, either by any kind of inducement

---

[5.] Material in the preceding paragraphs has been adapted from Montgomery, "The Christian Civil Liberties Union Wins Its First Case," *The Greenbag* [Simon Greenleaf School of Law—now the Law School of Trinity International University, Anaheim, California], No. 14 (July/August 1986).

or promise of an inducement or moral support or material assistance, or by fraudulent means or by taking advantage of his inexperience, trust, need, low intellect or naivety" (Law 1363/1938, as amended by Law 1672/39).

On the factual plane, the prosecution pointed to the age of the alleged victim: sixteen at the time. Clearly, they argued, this was a case of unduly influencing and corrupting a minor, to his personal and social detriment, and undermining his relationship with his family.

The Successful Defence. Against the prosecution's legal position, we argued along two lines. First, the Greek antiproselytism statute as interpreted by the lower court was inconsistent with Greece's commitment to the European Convention on Human Rights. Greece had signed and ratified the European Convention, containing the following two articles on freedom of religion and freedom of speech:

> Article 9 (1). Everyone has the right to freedom of thought, conscience and religion; this includes the freedom to change one's religion or belief and freedom, either alone or in community with others and in public or private, to manifest one's religion or belief, in worship, teaching, practice and observance.

> Article 10 (1). Everyone has the right to freedom of expression. This right shall include freedom to hold opinions and to receive and impart information and ideas without interference by public authority and regardless of frontiers.

Both of these articles are subject to certain restrictions (the second paragraph of each article sets these forth), but our brief contended that none of these restrictions applied to the facts of this case. Since Greece had accepted the compulsory jurisdiction of the European Court of Human Rights and had also just recently signed an article of the Convention allowing an individual to bring a petition before the Commission and Court in Strasbourg, this case could indeed properly be brought before the human rights legal machinery in Strasbourg, where the judgment of the national court would likely be overturned and perhaps the proselytism law itself struck down. To avoid this embarrassment, the Greek Court of Appeals should declare the defendants innocent.

Our second legal argument reminded the Court that the Greek Constitution of 1975 had incorporated the European Convention on Human Rights into Greek domestic law, giving the Convention priority over any contrary domestic law. This required the Appeals Court, at minimum, to interpret the antiproselytism statute in such a way that it did not contradict Articles 9 and 10 of the European Convention. Such an interpretation would result in an innocent verdict for the defendants.

Were the Appeals Court not to construe the antiproselytism law in a manner consonant with the European Convention (i.e., were it to argue that the law faithfully represented the true intention of the bare prohibition against proselytism in the Greek Constitution), this would put the Constitution and the European Convention on a collision course—resulting in no less than a constitutional crisis in Greek jurisprudence! Thus, the reasonable course of action for the Court of Appeals was to say, in effect, that whatever the undefined prohibition against proselytism means in the Greek Constitution, it *cannot* mean something contradicting Articles 9 and 10 of the European Convention on Human Rights (as would be the case if Law 1363/1938, as amended by Law 1672/39, were held to apply literally against the defendants).

Furthermore, we raised the question as to whether the antiproselytism law, taken on its face, had any genuine application to the present scenario. The law criminalises attempts to change another's religion. But the crew of the Anastasis never suggested that Costas Kotopoulos cease his connection with the Orthodox Church. His subsequent joining of Pastor Macris' local, independent, evangelical, Protestant church was his own decision. What the defendants sought was that Costas enter into a personal, saving experience with the living Christ—not that he change his denominational affiliation or join any particular church.

On discovering that the chief judge of the Athens Appeals Court had studied in Germany, I made this point clear by using the distinction between the German verbs *wissen* and *kennen*: "to know formally" (as in scientific knowledge, *Wissenschaft*) versus "to know personally/be personally acquainted with." The object of the evangelism by the crew of the Anastasis was not to alter Costas' formal, doctrinal subscription but to bring about a personal acquaintanceship with the Saviour common to all branches of Christianity, including the Eastern Orthodox Church.

On the factual issue of whether the evangelism had involved the "corrupting of a minor," the public prosecutor himself, in his closing statement to the Court, conceded our point. He observed that Syntagma ("Constitution") Square, the central square of Athens, was often populated at night by teenagers looking for thrills and drugs, and he reflected whether perhaps what Costas had received through his contact with the Mercy Ship Anastasis (Greek, not so incidentally, for "Resurrection") might not be an answer to this. At least there was one sixteen-year-old not engaged in those activities ...

And there was no way to demonstrate that the evangelism had had a negative effect on Costas' family. That family had been dysfunctional well before the encounter with the Anastasis: the parents had divorced and it was painfully evident that the mother had used the alleged proselytism of her son as a means of getting at her ex-husband.

In sum, neither legally nor factually could the convictions of the "Athens 3" be upheld—and they were not.

III. LARISSIS ET AL.

We now turn to Greek convictions of evangelical Christians for proselytism which, not being overturned within the Greek court system (i.e., after "all domestic remedies had been exhausted," as required for a case to be admitted in Strasbourg), were ultimately consolidated and judged by the European Commission and Court of Human Rights.

The Facts. In May of 1992, three Greek Air Force officers, D. Larissis, S. Mandalaridis, and I. Sarandis, all of Protestant Pentecostal persuasion, were cashiered by the Permanent Air Force Court of Athens for violating the antiproselytism statute and thereby not conducting themselves as officers and gentlemen. They were convicted of evangelising fellow Air Force personnel as well as civilians. Subsequent appeals in military and civilian courts did little more than to affirm their convictions, though sentences were reduced. Ultimately, their cases were taken to Strasbourg by the present writer, where the (now defunct) Commission, and later the Court of Human Rights, decided that their Convention rights had been violated relative to the evangelisation of civilians, but did not vindicate their evangelisation of military personnel.[6]

The Government's Position. The Greek government argued as to the Greek antiproselytism law (1) that it was not inconsistent with the religious freedom guaranteed by Article 9(1) of the European Convention on Human Rights; (2) that it in fact supported the Convention by protecting the religious rights of the weak and of those who were satisfied with their religious position and did not want to be importuned by other religionists; and (3) that Article 9(2) of the Convention properly allows governments to restrict religious activity for the sake of public order and the rights of others.

On the facts in the case at hand, the Greek government maintained that the civilian proselytism engaged in by the applicants involved undue influence, based in part on the weakness of the subjects of the evangelism and also on the superior societal role a professional military officer represents. As to the applicants' evangelistic efforts within the military, the government argued that such activity *per se* weakened military discipline and therefore went against the interests of the state, must never be engaged in on military bases, and, where an officer evangelised someone of lower rank, undue influence and the consequent violation of the statute were inevitable.

[6.] Case No. 140/1996/759/958-60.

The Applicants' Arguments. We strove mightily (and, ultimately, unsuccessfully) to convince the Commission and the Court that the Greek antiproselytism statute is in its very nature inconsistent with Article 9 of the European Convention on Human Rights. Our reasoning was—and continues to be—that the Greek statute is hopelessly ill-defined and overbroad, violating the principle of *nulla poena sine lege* as enshrined in Article 7(1) of the Convention: one cannot, on the basis of the vague language of the statute, predict whether or not one's expression of religious views will or will not transgress the Greek law and therefore trigger criminal sanctions. We repeatedly cited the Greek government's own, bizarre list of past prosecutions under the statute:

> Greek Courts have held that certain individuals were guilty of proselytism when they compared the Saints to "figures decorating walls," Saint Gerassimos to a "body stuffed with cotton" and the Church to "a theatre, a market, a cinema," when they delivered a sermon by demonstrating a picture showing a multitude of unhappy people dressed in rags and when they said that "this is how they all are who do not accept my faith" (Court of Cassation, Decision No. 271/1932, Themis XVII, page 19), when they promised to Orthodox refugees to give them shelter under particularly favourable terms if they adopted the faith of Uniates (Court of Appeal of the Aegean, Decision No. 2950/1930, Themis B, page 103), when they offered a scholarship for studies abroad (Court of Cassation, Decision No. 2276/1953), when they sent to Orthodox priests pamphlets with the recommendation to read them and to apply their contents (Court of Cassation, Decision No. 59/1956, Law Tribune 1956, No. 4, page 736), when they distributed "so-called religious" books and prospectuses free to "uneducated peasants" or to "young pupils" (Court of Cassation, Decision No. 201/1961, Penal Chronicles XI, page 472) or when they promised to a young seamstress to improve her position if she abandoned the Orthodox Church whereof the priests were accused of exploiting society (Court of Cassation, Decision No. 498/1961, Penal Chronicles XII, page 212). More recently certain courts convicted some Jehovah's Witnesses on the grounds that they proclaimed the doctrine of their sect "with importunity" and because they accused the Orthodox Church that it constituted "the source of troubles for the people" (Court of Appeal of Thessaloniki, Decision No. 2567/1988), that they entered other houses under the guise of being Christians who desire to propagate the New Testament (Misdemeanour Court of Florina, Decision No. 128/1989) and that they tried to dis-

tribute books and booklets to an Orthodox priest inside his car after having told him to stop (Misdemeanour Court of Lassithio, Decision No. 357/1990).

Not so incidentally, our same objections have been properly raised to the French Assemblée Nationale's sect criminalisation law of 22 June 2000. That law introduces for the first time into French jurisprudence, in defiance of the historic protections of freedom of speech and of religious expression, the *"délit de manipulation mentale."* What responsible commentators such as Jean-Claude Kiefer have observed concerning such legislation applies equally to the Greek antiproselytism statute:

> Firstly, who is to give the definition—obviously subjective—of such "manipulation"? Where does one start, and where will it end?
>
> The concept is too dangerous. Freedom is not monolithic and cannot be reduced to "mental correctness"—which has already been preceded by "political correctness" in our modern society.
>
> Let us use, to begin with and indeed as our sole recourse, the existing legal statutes. Let us apply the law as it exists now to prosecute the religious cheats, the charlatans, and the sectarian kidnappers. There is no sense in trying to go beyond this.[7]

As to the government's claim that the antiproselytism statute actually furthers religion by protecting the populace from unwanted interference with existing religious commitments, we pointed out the obvious: that the intent of Articles 9 and 10 of the Convention is to open the doors to freedom of expression both in general and in religious areas, not to offer protectionist possibilities to established or majority viewpoints. Indeed, it is precisely the minority and unpopular positions that require the guarantees contained in these Convention articles. We emphasised that in a pluralistic, democratic Europe, no government should treat its populace like children or the mentally defective who need to be protected from new or even offensive ideas. The Greek people should be considered mature enough to make their own religious decisions, accept-

---

[7]. *Dernières Nouvelles d'Alsace* [Strasbourg], 23 June 2000, p. 1. The French law as amended by the Senate for final vote in the House omits the expression "manipulation mentale," but commentators in general agree that the substance of the law remains unchanged by this semantic change.

ing or rejecting the ideological wares offered to them in an open marketplace of ideas.

The government appealed, as we have noted, to the second paragraph of Article 9, which allows limited state interference in religious matters when such interference is "necessary in a democratic society in the interests of public safety, for the protection of public order, health or morals, or for the protection of the rights and freedoms of others." We countered that the antiproselytism law certainly was *not* "necessary" for such purposes, since existing general civil and criminal law was sufficient to prosecute cases of duress, undue influence, false advertising, obtaining property by deception, and similar perversions of legitimate religious evangelism. The public weal in no sense requires overbroad legislation that in effect kills fleas with atomic weaponry—and which patently has a chilling effect upon legitimate religious expression.

The logic should be clear: Article 9 guarantees not merely the freedom of religious belief, but also the freedom to "manifest one's religion," and such manifestation expressly includes, according to the Article, "freedom to change one's religion or belief." But to have the meaningful opportunity to change one's religion, one must be able freely to encounter other belief-systems. *Ergo*, the Convention must be seen to guarantee the right to responsible evangelism without governmental obstruction.

On the facts of the instant case, the defence had to meet the government's condemnation of both civilian and military evangelisation on the part of the applicants. In presenting their gospel to civilians, the three Air Force officers were engaged in an activity which had previously been upheld by the European Court of Human Rights in the *Kokkinakis* case. We were successful in arguing that our case could not in this respect be distinguished from *Kokkinakis* on the facts: the objects of the civilian evangelism here, as there, were not so deficient in I.Q., understanding, or maturity as to have been improperly importuned religiously by the applicants.

As for applicants' evangelism within the military, we had a much harder, and ultimately unsuccessful, row to hoe. Even civil libertarian Judge de Meyer, who in his concurring opinion strongly agreed with us that "the [Greek] law in the present case is contrary to the Convention in its very principle, since it directly encroaches on the very essence of the freedom everyone must have to manifest his religion"—even Judge de Meyer went along with the majority of his colleagues in holding that, given the existing Greek law, the applicants' evangelistic efforts within the military "abused their position and rank."

We still contend, however, that our counter-arguments should have prevailed, vindicating even applicants' attempts to present Christ to fellow military personnel: (1) Christian work within the armed services has been an international, indeed European, tradition at least since the founding of the Officers' Christian Union in the British armed services in 1923; the OCU by its Articles justifies and encourages evangelism without restriction within and between the military ranks. It follows that evangelism in the military is not foreign to the general European lifestyle which the Strasbourg Court takes into account as background for its rulings. (2) One must not be forced to give up his or her human rights or civil liberties on joining the military. Indeed, for the Christian, evangelism is a universal duty and privilege, as enshrined in Jesus' so-called "Great Commission" (Mark 16:15 and parallel passages): "Go into all the world and preach the gospel to every creature." (3) We agree that if the particular beliefs of the individual engaging in evangelism in the military could be shown to have a potentially deleterious effect upon military discipline, they could legitimately be restrained (e.g., Quaker pacifism, New Age anarchism); but the beliefs of our applicants, standing in the tradition of historic, evangelical, Trinitarian Christian faith, should in no wise have been construed as imperiling military efficiency or state interests, or as undermining the security of the state. (4) The objects of applicants' evangelism (Air Force personnel) were old enough to die for their country, so they were presumably old enough to make mature religious decisions, accepting or rejecting applicants' beliefs—and the facts of the instant case make clear that this was precisely what they did.

IV. THE CURRENT LEGAL POSITION: THE GREEK CASES AND THE EUROPEAN COURT'S CONSERVATISM

Commentators have quite generally remarked that the European Court of Human Rights hesitates to upset the legal systems of the Member States, even when this would hardly result in a state's departing from the well-established and highly respected human rights club represented by the ECHR.[8] In the Greek proselytism cases, this has meant that, whilst the Court has clearly tried to uphold freedom of evangelism in general by vindicating the applicants, it has (1) refused to declare the Greek antiproselytism statute incompatible with the Convention, in spite of its patent ambiguities and provable chilling effect upon freedom of religious expression, and (2) narrowed permissible evangelism to the minimum, restricting it in effect to "transactions among equals," even though it should be obvious that hierarchical and superior-inferior relationships are part of the very fabric of all societies and that to remove legal protection for evangelism in such contexts is to open a Pandora's box for religious repression and the discriminatory treatment of minority religious positions.

Supporters of the adversarial system have often noted that truth is best defended in the context of opposition. The European Court operates more in the inquisitorial than in the adversarial mode, but we contend that in the cases discussed in this chapter the strongest reasons so far developed have been offered to encourage the Court to move in a more radical, principled, and dynamic direction vis-à-vis issues of religious freedom. Should such argumentation be

---

[8.] E.g., Malcolm D. Evans, *Religious Liberty and International Law in Europe* (Cambridge: Cambridge University Press, 1997), especially p. 365; and Montgomery, "When Is Evangelism Illegal?," *New Law Journal*, 10 April 1998, pp. 524-25. The Strasbourg Court clearly believes that "too great an interference in the domestic policies of Contracting States would damage its legitimacy" (Jessica Simor, "Human Rights: Strasbourg vs Luxembourg; the Human Rights Act and EC Law," Paper presented at the Bar European Group Annual Conference, Trier, Germany, 6-8 May 1999, p. [12]).

accepted in future cases, Europe could well become in practice what it is in theory: a level playing field for all belief-systems.[9]

---

[9] Cf. Montgomery, *Human Rights and Human Dignity* (2d ed.; Edmonton, Alberta: Canadian Institute for Law, Theology & Public Policy, 1995). For a book-length treatment of the Greek evangelism situation, with the full texts of the legal documents and pleadings in the cases discussed in this essay, see Montgomery, *The Repression of Evangelism in Greece: European Litigation vis-à-vis a Closed Religious Establishment* (Lanham, Maryland: University Press of America, 2000).

CHAPTER 14

PROPHECY, ESCHATOLOGY AND APOLOGETICS

Summary: *Many claim to have been drawn to Christian faith by charismatic prophecy or by the prophetic-eschatological themes in such popular works as* The Last Days of the Late, Great Planet Earth. *Millennium fever is currently driving some evangelicals to exaggerated claims as to the evidential value of end-time prophecy. We shall endeavour in this essay to determine in what sense and to what degree Scriptural prophecies have legitimate apologetic value and how they can be used properly in the contemporary defence of the faith.*

I. INTRODUCTION

The early Christian church employed two major styles of apologetic: miracle and prophecy, the first directed especially to the Gentiles, the second particularly to the Jewish community.[1] A remarkable feature of the Christian apologetic was the inherent interconnection of the two approaches, owing to the fact that miracles central to the faith (such as the Virgin Birth of Our Lord) had often been the object of specific Old Testament prophecies.[2]

Today, three forms of prophetic attestation are offered to support the truth of Christian faith: *charismatic* (experiential) prophecy, *end-time* (futuristic) prophecy, and *fulfilled* (historical)

[1.] Montgomery, *Faith Founded on Fact* (Nashville: Thomas Nelson, 1978), pp. 43 ff., and the references there given. See also Mark Edwards, et al. (eds.), *Apologetics in the Roman Empire: Pagans, Jews, and Christians* (Oxford: Oxford University Press, 1999).

[2.] Is. 7:14 (where the LXX translation, well before Christ's First Advent, employs the word *parthenos*, which signifies "virgin," not merely "young woman." Contrast Islam, where alleged miracles, such as Mohammed's so-called "Night Journey," are nowhere prophesied in the *Qu'ran*. An interesting recent example is that of the "Holy Tomato" as reported in *The Independent* [London], 16 September 1999: a Muslim Pakistani woman living in Bradford found a tomato whose vein structure presented an Arabic inscription reading "There is no god but Allah."

prophecy. We shall look briefly at each, finding the first two varieties fundamentally deficient, and endeavouring to strengthen the third through probability considerations.

II. CHARISMATIC PROPHECY

It is frequently maintained in charismatic and Pentecostal circles that, in line with 1 Corinthians 14 and other related references in the New Testament, miraculous tongue-speaking occurs with fair regularity among believers today. Indeed, it is an article of faith with Pentecostals that a "Second Blessing" is properly to be sought by all Christians and that with this empowering will normally come the miraculous gift of tongues. When the Christian speaks in tongues and another, possessing the gift of interpretation, makes known the meaning in an ordinary language, the miraculous truth of the faith is allegedly demonstrated.

What is the problem with this kind of "prophetic" apologetic? The difficulty will not be uncovered by higher critical dehistoricising of the key New Testament texts, as practiced by radical theologians or misguided liberal evangelicals.[3] Nor will the difficulty go away by aprioristic attempts to relegate miraculous gifts to the age of the New Testament alone.[4] The central apologetic problems with miraculous tongues-speaking are (1) that which is spoken lacks the structural characteristics of a language, and (2), even if what were spoken *did* have genuine linguistic characteristics, the unbeliever has no way of knowing that the "interpretation" in fact represents the "prophecy"—so for the non-Christian the phenomenon offers no evidence of Christian truth at all.

William Samarin puts these point succinctly:

> We know more about language than the glossolalist does. We know enough to declare what is and what is not language. We know as much as a mathematician, who can tell the difference between a

---

[3]. In the former camp: Krister Stendahl, "Glossolalia and the Charismatic Movement," in *God's Christ and His People: Studies in Honor of Nils Alstrup Dahl*, ed. Jacob Jervell and Wayne A. Meeks (Oslo: Universitetsforlaget, 1977), pp. 122-31.
[4]. Cf. B. B. Warfield's influential work, *Counterfeit Miracles*.

real formula and a pseudo-formula—one that *looks* like mathematical language but does not *say* anything....

A charismatist's religious experience can be real, revolutionary, reconstitutive. A glossolalist accepts this transformation as supernatural, that is, *caused* by God. If it is a dramatic change—taking place where one did not expect it or more quickly than one expected—it takes on all the more appearance of the supernatural. But none of this proves that glossolalia is supernatural. No number of "miraculous" transformations will make of glossolalia what it is not.[5]

At best, glossolalia can do no more than persuade the unbeliever on the basis of the drawing power of the believing assembly in which it is practiced or by virtue of the sincerity and genuineness of the practitioners themselves. But this is no more than an experiential argument—indistinguishable from the experiential persuasiveness of non-Christian religions and of the plethora of sects vying for converts today. Is is still true that inner faith *per se* "cannot validate God-talk."[6]

III. END-TIME PROPHECY

One can hardly avoid—even if one refuses to watch the televangelists—the vast number of current attempts to relate current events to the Second Coming and the end of the age. Not to be outdone by new editions of Nostradamus from the secular press, evangelical writers and publishers have been quick off the mark with their own millennial publications.[7]

---

[5] William J. Samarin, *Tongues of Men and Angels: The Religious Language of Pentecostalism* (New York: Macmillan, 1972), pp. 233-35. See also J. P. Kildahl, *The Psychology of Speaking in Tongues* (New York: Harper, 1972).

[6] Kai Nielsen, "Can Faith Validate God-Talk?," in *New Theology No. 1*, ed. Martin E. Marty and Dean G. Peerman (New York: Macmillan Paperbacks, 1964). Cf. Montgomery, *The Suicide of Christian Theology* (reprint ed.; Newburgh, Ind.: Trinity Press, 1998), pp. 99, 149, 260.

[7] This author has nothing against responsible millennial scholarship; he himself contributed the article, "Millennium," to the revised *International Standard Bible Encyclopedia*, ed. Bromiley—an article which appears in slightly different form in Armerding and Gasque's *Dreams, Visions and Oracles* (Grand Rapids, Mich.: Baker, 1977), revised and augmented as *A Guide to Biblical Prophecy* (Peabody, Mass.: Hendrickson, 1989).

Here is a very recent and sobering example from the lips of the Revd Ian Paisley of Northern Ireland fame (notoriety?):

> In his personal report from Strasbourg on the recent opening of Europe's fifth elected Parliament he described the new "crystal palace" which houses the MEPs as "space age" with a modern design of Star Trek crew seats. Of the 679 seats allocated to its members one seat remains empty at present; seat number 666. Dr Paisley believes it will eventually be occupied in accordance with Revelation 13:18 which states: "Here is wisdom. Let him that hath understanding count the number of the beast: for it is the number of a man; and his number is Six hundred threescore and six." With conviction he stated, "Today that scripture is being fulfilled before our very eyes. The Antichrist's seat will be occupied. The world awaits his full and final development." As a Bible-believing Protestant he took pleasure in quoting the prophetic words of 2 Thess. 2:8: "And then shall that Wicked One be revealed, whom the Lord shall consume by the spirit of His mouth (the Word of God), and shall destroy with the brightness of His coming."
>
> The leader of the Democratic Unionist Party is convinced that the "prophetic significance" of the European Union is steadily unfolding as it continues to develop. It has chosen as its symbol "the woman riding the beast" which features on its new currency, the Euro. He also disclosed that the "Tower of Babel" is being used on posters emanating from Europe and views this "as a truly suggestive prophetic sign."[8]

This reminds one of Hal Lindsey's earlier claim that the former European Economic Community (predecessor of the European Union) represented the ten toes of the great image in the Book of Daniel and thus was a vehicle of the antichristic end times.[9]

One could, of course, point out the factual difficulties with these "prophecies": the EEC has never had precisely ten members, and the "Tower of Babel" posters in Strasbourg—which I saw this last summer—were actually advertisements for rock concerts, not publications of the European Union at all!

---

[8]. News item, *Protestant Truth* [U.K.], September-October 1999, p. 80.

[9]. Hal Lindsey, *The 1980's: Countdown to Armageddon* (New York: Bantam, 1982), pp. 103-105. See Montgomery, *Human Rights and Human Dignity* (2d ed.; Edmonton, Alberta, Canada: Canadian Institute for Law, Theology and Public Policy, 1995), pp. 43-44, 277-78.

But the problem of futuristic prophecy as apologetic cuts much deeper. In essence, the intractable objection is that we simply do not have the perspective on our own time sufficient to be able to predict the future accurately or confidently relate biblical prophecy to what is happening at the moment.[10] A few illustrative examples may be helpful—taken from books in the author's personal collection.

In 1866, the Revd M. Baxter, "late missionary of the Episcopal Church," published his 355-page tome, with the lengthy and highly specific title, *Louis Napoleon the Destined Monarch of the World, and Personal Antichrist, foreshown in Prophecy to confirm a seven years' Covenant with the Jews about, or soon after 1864-5, and (after the Resurrection and the translation of the Wise Virgins has taken place two years and from four to six weeks after the Covenant,) subsequently to become completely supreme over England and most of America, and all Christendom, and fiercely to persecute Christians during the latter half of the seven years, until he finally perishes at the descent of Christ at the Battle of Armageddon, about or soon after 1872-3*.[11]

The end not having come as the Revd Baxter predicted, one S. D. Baldwin, A.M., President of Soule Female College, produced a second edition of his 480-page masterpiece, *Armageddon: or The Overthrow of Romanism and Monarchy; the Existence of the United States Foretold in the Bible, its future greatness; invasion by allied Europe; annihilation of monarchy; expansion into the millennial republic, and its dominion over the whole world*. The fortunate publisher of this work was the Southern Methodist Publishing House.[12]

Coming now to the 20th century, we have People's Church (Toronto) pastor-evangelist Oswald J. Smith's *Is the Antichrist at Hand? - What of Mussolini*, which went through at least seven editions, ac-

---

[10] This is, conceptually, exactly the same problem faced by secular philosophers of history, such as Hegel, Marx, Spengler, and Toynbee, when they endeavour to chart the future history of mankind; see Montgomery, *Where Is History Going?* (reprint ed.; Minneapolis: Bethany, 1972). It is also the problem of the so-called "theologians of hope" such as Moltmann.

[11] M. Baxter, *Louis Napoleon the Destined Monarch of the World* ... (Philadelphia: James S. Claxton, 1866).

[12] S. D. Baldwin, *Armageddon* ... (Nashville: Southern Methodist Publishing House, 1878).

counting for some 22,000 copies.[13] Mussolini's candidature for Antichrist is supported by such obvious considerations as his self-styled attempt to revive accoutrements of the ancient Roman Empire and the unarguable fact that he was a "hoar upon the seven hills" of Rome. My copy of this paperback is quite rare, deriving from my maternal great-grandfather's book collection. I understand that after the fall of Mussolini, Oswald himself tried to buy up all remaining copies of the book to destroy them.

The point does not need to be belaboured. We are not saying that such (rather pitiful) efforts at end-time prophecy reach the level of the false prophets condemned in the Old Testament: those who "speak a vision out of their own heart, and not out of the mouth of the Lord" (Jer. 23:16). But we *are* saying that end-time prophecy lacks the necessary factual grounding to make it an effective apologetic to the unbeliever—and that it can be and often is in reality counterproductive, lowering rather than raising the credibility of Christianity in the eyes of the outsider. The reason for this was well stated by Augustine in the 5th century; though he was speaking of cosmological theories propounded by Christians, his judgment applies *mutatis mutandis* to the evangelical purveyors of futuristic prophecy:

> Now it is an unseemly and mischievious thing, and greatly to be avoided, that a Christian man speaking on such matters, as if according to the authority of Christian Scripture, should talk so foolishly that the unbeliever on hearing him, and observing the extravagance of his error, should hardly be able to refrain from laughing. And the great mischief is, not so much that the man himself is laughed at for his errors, but that our authors are believed, by people without the Church, to have taught such things, and are so condemned as unlearned, and cast aside, to the great loss of those for whose salvation we are so much concerned.
>
> For when they find one belonging to the Christian body, falling into error on a subject with which they themselves are thoroughly conversant, and when they see him moreover enforcing his groundless opinion by the authority of our Sacred Books, how are they likely to put trust in these Books about the resurrection of the

---

[13.] Oswald J. Smith, *Is the Antichrist at Hand? - What of Mussolini* (Toronto: Tabernacle Publishers, 1927).

dead, and the hope of eternal life, and the kingdom of heaven, having already come to regard them as fallacious about those things they had themselves learned from observation, or from unquestionable evidence?[14]

IV. HISTORICALLY FULFILLED PROPHECY

The third, and, in our judgment, the truly useful variety of prophecy for the apologetic task consists of an appeal to the prophecies of the Old Testament which have already been fulfilled—principally the prophecies of Christ's First Coming. Though there are significant Old Testament prophecies of which secular history demonstrates the fulfilment (the destruction of Tyre and Sidon, etc.),[15] the most valuable for apologetic purposes are those concerning the First Advent of our Lord. This is because the centre of the apologetic task is the demonstration of the truth of the gospel itself, its acceptance being the *sine qua non* for personal salvation. We of course want to bring the non-Christian to accept the revelational character of Scripture as a whole, but first must come his or her answer to the question, "What think ye of Christ?" And it is worth emphasising that concentration on the New Testament fulfilments of Old Testament prophecies concerning our Lord will, in any case, add weight to our claim that the entire Bible is the product of divine revelation, since the fulfilled Old Testament prophecies come from a wide variety of Old Testament books, written at widely different times.

Fascinatingly enough, the value of such fulfilled prophecy can be specified mathematically. One can, by using the statistician's well-known "product rule," calculate the probabilities against mere chance accounting for a given number of such prophecies. The product rule states that the probability of the common occurrence of several mutually independent events is equal to the product of the probabilities that each of those given events will happen. Exam-

---

[14.] Augustine, *De Genesi ad litteram*, I. xix. 39.
[15.] See, *inter alia,* John Urquhart, *The Wonders of Prophecy* (Camp Hill, Pa.: Christian Publications, n.d.), and J. Barton Payne, *Encyclopedia of Biblical Prophecy* (New York: Harper & Row, 1973).

ple: since the chances of coming up with a "2" when rolling one die is 1 in 6 or 1/6, the probability of rolling two "2's" is 1/6 x 1/6, or 1/36; the chances of rolling three "2's" is 1/6 x 1/6 x 1/6, or 1/216; etc. Generalising, we have the formulation: *If the probability of one event's occurring is 1/x, the probability of a number of similar but mutually independent events will be $1/x^n$, where n = the number of events.*[16]

If one arbitrarily sets the probability of the occurrence of a single valid Old Testament prophecy of Christ at 50-50 (1/2), then the probabilities against 25 of them[17] happening by chance is $1/2^{25}$, or 1 in 33 million. But since the likelihood of any one of these prophecies succeeding is considerably less than 50-50 ("Behold a virgin shall conceive and bear a son", etc.),[18] we can legitimately lower the probability of one occurrence to 25% (1/4). The probability of 25 similar events transpiring would then be $1/4^{25}$, or 1 in a thousand trillion! After presenting this argument a generation ago, the then Chairman of Wheaton College's Department of Mathematics, Physics, and Astronomy wrote:

> Since there are many more than 25 prophecies of events surrounding the birth and life of Christ, and a compromise chance of success is undoubtedly less than 1 to 4, then the chance of success, if these predictions were all mere guesses, would be so infinitesimal that no one could maintain that these prophecies were mere guesses! The alternative must be true—these prophecies were all foreseen events, in which *"holy men of God spake as they were moved by the Holy Ghost."* The prophecies were given by revelation—divinely inspired.[19]

---

[16] See any standard statistics text, e.g., Paul Gerhard Hoel, *Introduction to Mathematical Statistics* (5th ed.; New York: John Wiley, 1984).

[17] In point of fact, far more than 25 prophecies of Christ's First Advent and earthly life occur in the Old Testament. For lists, see study editions of the Bible such as the *Thompson Chain-Reference Bible* and standard reference sources such as Halley's *Bible Handbook*.

[18] Consider, for example, the highly specific numerical prophecy in Daniel concerning the first coming of Christ, as worked out by Sir Robert Anderson in his classic, *The Coming Prince;* the essence of his argument is presented in Irwin H. Linton's *A Lawyer Examines the Bible* (Boston: W. A. Wilde, 1943), pp. 220-23, and in Montgomery (ed.), *Jurisprudence: A Book of Readings* (4th printing with corrections; Strasbourg, France: International Scholarly Publishers, 1992), pp. 494-97. See also Montgomery, *The Transcendent Holmes* (Ashcroft, BC, Canada: Calabash Press, 2000), pp. 129-39.

[19] Hawley O. Taylor, "Mathematics and Prophecy," in *Modern Science and Christian Faith*, ed. American Scientific Affiliation (Wheaton, Ill.: Van Kampen Press, 1948), p. 178. This essay is unfortunately not included in later editions of the book.

What objections can be raised to this mathematical treatment of fulfilled biblical prophecy? Two counter-arguments require answers.

First, a statistical complaint. One may object that this is just a piece of statistical prestidigitation—the sort of thing treated in Darrell Huff's little gem, *How To Lie with Statistics*.[20] Or, more darkly, that the argument suggests 17th-18th century Scottish mathematician and cleric John Craig's claim (a remarkable attempt at eschatological statistics) that by application of probability theory to the weakening of the force of testimony, one must conclude that the historical proofs of our Lord's ministry will decay entirely by the year 3150, such that Christianity would entirely disappear "unless the second coming of Christ prevent its extinction."[21]

More specifically, one might argue that our application of mathematical statistics to event-occurrences parallels that refuted by the California Supreme Court, the great Chief Justice Traynor concurring, in *The People v Malcolm Ricardo Collins*.[22] In that case, at trial court level, the prosecutor brought in as an expert witness a state college mathematics instructor to establish the probabilities against the defendants having committed the crime. The instructor arbitrarily set the probabilities for the individual elements of the crime, committed, as it was, by a Caucasian woman with a blond ponytail, accompanied by a Black man with a beard and mustache, the two driving a partly yellow automobile. On applying the "product rule," the instructor concluded that there was but one chance in

---

[20] Darrell Huff, *How To Lie with Statistics*, newly illustrated by Irving Geis (New York: W. W. Norton, 1993).

[21] John Craig (d. 1731), *Craig's Rules of Historical Evidence. From Joannis Craig Theologiae Christianae principia mathematica* ("History and Theory," Beiheft 4; The Hague, Netherlands: Mouton, 1964). Craig, to be sure, hopelessly misunderstood the application of statistics to historical testimony, and was roundly refuted by, *inter alia*, Ditton, Houtteville, and his later editor Johann Daniel Titius. One Petersen upstaged Craig in 1701 by increasing the rate of the deterioration of testimony such that the events of the beginning of the Christian era would, according to him, become unbelievable by 1789—which turned out to be the very date of the French Revolution! See the brief biographical articles on Craig in Hoefer's *Nouvelle Biographie Générale*, the *Dictionary of National Biography*, and the *New Schaff-Herzog Encyclopedia of Religious Knowledge*.

[22] 438 P.2d 33 (1968).

twelve million that anyone but the defendants could have committed the crime with which they had been charged.

The California Supreme Court, to put it mildly, reversed the lower court decision, pointing up "two basic and pervasive defects—an inadequate evidentiary foundation and an inadequate proof of statistical independence." The probabilities assigned by the instructor to the individual factors were in no way demonstrable (e.g., girl with ponytail: 1/10; interracial couple in car: 1/1000). And "to the extent that the traits or characteristics were not mutually independent (e.g. Negroes with beards and men with mustaches obviously represent overlapping categories), the 'product rule' would inevitably yield a wholly erroneous and exaggerated result even if all of the individual components had been determined with precision."

But our use of the "product rule" does not suffer from these defects. The prophecies of the Old Testament are indeed "mutually independent," in that they were set out by diverse authors at diverse times, and the fulfilments were recorded by more than one Gospel writer.[23] And though we do set arbitrary values for the probability of any one prophecy's occurrence, our values are exceedingly conservative: we are simply maintaining the *a fortiori* position that even if the likelihood of the success of a single prophecy were but 50% or 25%, the conclusion would be inescapable that the totality of fulfilments could hardly be attributed to chance.

A second objection to our argumentation involves a question of logic: even if we have shown the extreme improbability of chance fulfilments of Old Testament prophecies of Christ, we have (the objector argues) hardly established the nature of the non-chance explanatory factor. Probability reasoning does not automatically lead to conclusions as to specific causation! Logically, the "success" of these "predictions" could be due, not to divine inspiration, but

---

[23.] A trait is "independent of a second trait when the occurrence or non-occurrence of one does not affect the probability of the occurrence of the other trait" ("Evidence: Admission of Mathematical Probability Statistics Held Erroneous for Want of Demonstration of Validity," *Duke Law Journal* [1967], pp. 669-70; cf. David V. Huntsberger, *Elements of Statistical Inference* [London: Prentice-Hall International, 1962], p. 77).

simply to (1) Jesus having conformed his life to the prophecies, to "make" them come true, and/or (2) the New Testament writers having "fudged" the life of Christ to fit the Old Testament prophecies.

But neither of these alternative causal explanations will wash (if you can believe *them*, you should have no trouble believing in genuine fulfilled prophecy!). (1) Jesus might have been responsible personally for the fulfilment of a Messianic prophecy when he said on the Cross, "My God, my God, why hast thou forsaken me?," but he could hardly have set up the time, place, and manner of his own birth, the number of pieces of silver for which he would be sold, etc. (2) Had the Gospel writers altered the facts of Jesus' life to fit the Old Testament prophecies, they would never have gotten away with it. The preaching of the facts of Christ's life, death, and resurrection, as well as the circulation of the Gospel narratives of these events, took place whilst hostile witnesses of Jesus' career were still alive (the very Jewish religious leaders who had brought about his demise); it is unthinkable that they would not have easily refuted such claims to fulfilled prophecy when (a) they knew the Old Testament and (b) they knew the actual facts of Jesus' life.[24]

It follows that the "product rule" argument we have presented is sound, and, more important, so is the use of historically fulfilled prophecy in the defence of central Christian claims.[25] We encourage fellow believers to tie their prophetic waggon to this star rather than to the squibs of experientialism and futurism, which burn out almost before they are ignited.

[24.] I have developed these points of historical and legal apologetics at considerable length in several of my books. See, for example, *Where Is History Going?* and *Human Rights and Human Dignity* (op. cit.).

[25.] As exemplified, for example, by the old classics such as Alexander Keith, *Evidence of the Truth of the Christian Religion Derived from the Literal Fulfilment of Prophecy* (16th ed.; Edinburgh: William Whyte, 1837) and E. A. Edghill, *An Enquiry into the Evidential Value of Prophecy*, with Preface by H.E. Ryle (London: Macmillan, 1906). For more recent material, see the essays by John A. Bloom and Robert C. Newman in Montgomery (ed.), *Evidence for Faith: Deciding the God Question* (Dallas, Tx: Probe, 1991), pp. 173-214.

CHAPTER 15

ADVOCACY, CLASSICAL RHETORIC, AND LEGAL ETHICS: MUST THE GOOD ADVOCATE ALSO BE A GOOD PERSON?*

Summary: We shall examine the requirement set forth by the classical rhetoricians that success in advocacy depends in large part on the moral character of the advocate himself or herself. Such a requirement is conspicuous by its absence in modern theories of advocacy and forms virtually no part of contemporary advocacy training. Is this requirement chimerical and indeed of no consequence to the modern lawyer? Or is there something to it? If so, what, precisely? The purpose of this essay is not to resolve such questions finally, but to encourage maximum thought and discussion on a vital and neglected aspect of advocacy theory.

I. ADVOCACY ISOLATED FROM ETHICS: THE MODERN VIEW

None of us is unfamiliar with the longstanding stereotype of the immoral (or amoral) legal advocate: the unprincipled hired gun. Passages such as the following, from John Grisham's *The Runaway Jury*, could be duplicated *ad nauseam*:

> Krigler was telling the truth, but the truth needed to be blurred at this point. This was a cross-examination, a crucial one, so to hell with the truth. The witness had to be discredited![1]

To be sure, such a philosophy produces disquiet not only outside but even within the legal profession. In another contempo-

---

* The present essay was delivered by invitation at the Worldwide Advocacy Conference 1998, held under the auspices of the Inns of Court School of Law, London, England, 29 June - 3 July 1998.

[1] John Grisham, *The Runaway Jury* (New York: Dell Publishing Island Books, 1997), p. 238.

rary work of legal fiction, a young lawyer reflects on the purpose of trial advocacy:

> His father's vision of the trial process made Warren uncomfortable. A battle, a joust between opposing counsel, where each victory is sweet and each defeat adds zest to the next challenge. In law school Warren had understood that most trial lawyers yearned to win—and so did he. Cross-examination was the ultimate confrontation, the gunfight that left either lawyer or witness bleeding in the dust. The great trial lawyer Racehorse Haynes had once said, "I continue to dream of the day when I am examining a witness and my questions are so probing and so brilliant that the fellow blurts out that he, not my defendant, committed the foul murder. Then he will pitch forward into my arms, dead of a heart attack."
>
> But there had to be more, Warren thought. More than adversaries and great actors, lawyers should be the standard-bearers of what was decent and fair. Should be, but rarely were: for they were born and shaped as human before they could be turned into lawyers.[2]

One might expect law school, bar school, or pupillage training in advocacy and trial technique to impart the ideals of "decency and fairness" to the novice barrister or trial lawyer. This, however, does not appear to reflect pedagogical reality as we find it. As far as law school instruction in general is concerned, Kronman has argued that the prevalent "case method" in American law schools, developed at Harvard in the late 19th century by Dean Christopher Columbus Langdell, in opposition to deductivistic, "black-letter" instruction, has produced generations of lawyers who find great difficulty in relating the treatment of cases to larger principle, ethical or otherwise.[3] And both in America and in England (where the case method is less prevalent), the deleterious effect of Karl Llewellyn's reduction of jurisprudence to the pragmatic concept of "law jobs," coupled with Legal Positivism's denial of any eternal

---

[2.] Clifford Irving, *Trial* (New York: Dell Publishing, 1991), p. 64.
[3.] Anthony T. Kronman, *The Lost Lawyer: Failing Ideals of the Legal Profession* (Cambridge, Mass.: Belknap/Harvard University Press, 1995), pp. 109 ff.

reference points for the law, has driven the sharpest of wedges between legal training and ethical values.[4]

As for the teaching of advocacy *per se*, instruction focuses on technique rather than on character or ethics. A few examples will more than suffice.

John H. Munkman's classic textbook, *The Technique of Advocacy*, upon which two generations cut their teeth at the English bar, devotes its first chapter to "Advocacy: Its Nature, Aims and Background." There are listed six "qualities needed by an advocate": a good voice, command of words, confidence, persistence, practical judgment, and experience of handling cases. The only mention of ethics is provided by a two-sentence reference to professional conduct rules in a separate discussion of desirable "background knowledge."[5]

J.A.C. Brown's *Technique of Persuasion* carefully analyses "attitude formation" psychologically and sociologically, attempting to understand how persuasion succeeds or fails in such diverse areas as propaganda, advertising, religious conversion, and brainwashing. Fledgling advocates have certainly picked up useful ideas from this magisterial work, but nowhere in it does the character of the advocate enter into the equation.[6]

Butterworth's "legal listening" audiocassette *Successful Advocacy* describes "the good advocate" in terms of "manner – dress –public speaking – nerves" and discusses "outstanding advocates" and "irritating habits"; but the distinguished panel of contributors (irritatingly) leaves entirely aside the question of whether the advocate's value-system could have any bearing on the success or failure of one's professional objectives.

[4.] *Ibid.*, pp. 121 ff. Cf. John Warwick Montgomery, "The American Law Teaching Experience," *Law & Justice*, No. 126/127 (Trinity/Michaelmas 1995), 120-37; also, John Warwick Montgomery, *Law and Morality: Friends or Foes? An Inaugural Lecture* (Luton: University of Luton, 1994).

[5.] John H. Munkman, *The Technique of Advocacy* (London: Stevens, 1951), pp. 4-7.

[6.] J.A.C. Brown, *Techniques of Persuasion: From Propaganda to Brainwashing* (Harmondsworth, Middlesex: Penguin Books, 1963).

Keith Evans, formerly a head of chambers in London, now practising and teaching law in the United States, is much more explicit. His widely-read *Golden Rules of Advocacy* begins with the following "first dimension" of the advocate's world: "In the common-law countries a trial is *not* an exercise to discover the truth." Evans stresses that this doesn't mean that the advocate can get away with anything and everything, for "the Bar Council can be quite Draconian in dealing with members who stray." In practice it means, says Evans, that "by the time you get to trial ... you should no longer be conducting an inquiry. Rather, *you should be putting on a presentation designed to persuade.*"[7]

To be sure, in the trial setting one constantly aims to persuade, but is this endeavour in no sense "an exercise designed to discover the truth"? Are we simply engaged in an amoral game, equivalent to Schopenhauer's "stratagems," or ways to win arguments?—including such gems as "carry your opponent's proposition beyond its natural limits; exaggerate it"; "attack something different than that which was asserted"; "confuse the issue by changing your opponent's words or what he or she seeks to prove"; "make your opponent angry"; "try to bluff your opponent"; "if you find that you are being beaten, you can create a diversion—that is, you can suddenly begin to talk of something else"; "a quick way of getting rid of an opponent's assertion, or of throwing suspicion on it, is by putting it into some odious category" (suggestions: Idealism, Atheism, Spiritualism); "should your opponent be in the right but luckily for you, choose a faulty proof, you can easily refute it and then claim that you have refuted the whole position"; and "you may also puzzle and bewilder your opponent by mere bombast."[8]

[7.] Keith Evans, *The Golden Rules of Advocacy* (London: Blackstone, 1993), pp. 7-8 (italics Evans'). Other examples of textbooks stressing technique to the exclusion of the advocate's character are: O.C. Mazengarb, *Advocacy in Our Time* (London: Sweet & Maxwell, 1964); R.K. Soonavala, *Advocacy: Its Principles and Practice* (2d ed.; Bombay: Tripathi, 1960); Paul Bergman, *Trial Advocacy* ("Nutshell Series"; St. Paul, Minn.: West, 1979); Michael Hyam, *Advocacy Skills* (London: Blackstone, 1990); Andy Boon, *Advocacy* ("Essential Legal Skills Series"; London: Cavendish, 1993).

[8.] Arthur Schopenhauer, *The Art of Controversy, and Other Posthumous Papers*, ed. and trans. T. Bailey Saunders (London: Swan Sonnenschein, 1896), pp. 15-48.

II. ADVOCACY UNITED WITH ETHICS: THE CLASSICAL VIEW

The modern approach to advocacy, as just described and illustrated, has ancient roots, for example, the Sophists of Plato's day, who "made the worse argument appear the better" and who in legal practice brought down upon themselves Plato's condemnation as having "small and unrighteous" souls.[9] But, in general, the divorce between advocacy and ethics is characteristic of post-Enlightenment modernity. One of the earliest examples is the European-educated African scholar A. Amo's *Tractatus de arte sobrie et accurate philosophandi* (1738), where the "common duties of disputants" are discussed in almost total isolation from ethical considerations: advocacy is a matter of "alacrity and ingenuousness of mind," "serenity," and "perspicuity and brevity of words and phrases." But at the end of his discussion, Amo feels compelled to add: "*Scopus esto veritas eiusque stabilimentum*" ("Let the goal be truth and its strengthening").[10]

Prior to the 18th century, the tradition of classical rhetoric insisted absolutely on the intimate relationship between advocacy and ethics.[11] The three greatest ancient authorities on the matter were Aristotle, Quintilian, and Longinus; from antiquity through the Renaissance and Reformation (15th - 17th centuries) their views were accepted and enlarged upon in the training of public speakers and professional advocates. Indeed, since from medieval times rhetoric comprised one of the three fundamental educational disci-

---

[9] Plato, *Theaetetus*, 172-173, in his *Dialogues*, ed. and trans. B. Jowett (3d ed., 5 vols.; Oxford: Clarendon Press, 1892), IV, 231. Here Plato's Socrates distinguishes "the inpracticality, leisurely discourse, and freedom of the philosopher from the time constraints and servitude of the lawyer"—A.A. Long, "Plato's Apologies and Socrates in the *Theaetetus*," in Jyl Gentzler (ed.), *Method in Ancient Philosophy* (Oxford: Clarendon Press, 1998), p. 127.

[10] Anthony William Amo, *Tractatus de arte sobrie et accurate philosophandi* (Halle-Magdeburg: Kitler, 1738), pp. 200-202.

[11] The importance of the character of the advocate in classical rhetoric and its unimportance in modern rhetorical theory is far more significant than the generally emphasised "rational/emotional," "persuasion/communication" distinctions between the two; see A.A. Lunsford and L.S. Ede, "On Distinctions between Classical and Modern Rhetoric," in Robert J. Connors, *et al.* (eds.), *Essays on Classical Rhetoric and Modern Discourse* (Carbondale: Southern Illinois University Press, 1984), pp. 37-49.

plines (the so-called "Trivium," consisting of grammar, rhetoric, and logic), its principles were part of the mental furniture of every educated person before the onset of modern secularism. This was particularly so for lawyers, for "only with Irnerius in the early twelfth century did law cease to be a subdivision of rhetoric."[12]

Aristotle states the classical position clearly and succinctly. After defining rhetorical skill as "the faculty [power] of discovering in the particular case what are the available means of persuasion," he writes:

> Of the means of persuasion supplied by the speech itself there are three kinds. The first kind reside in the character [*ethos*] of the speaker; the second consist in producing a certain [the right] attitude in the hearer; the third appertain to the argument proper, in so far as it actually or seemingly demonstrates.
>
> The character [*ethos*] of the speaker is a cause of persuasion when the speech is so uttered as to make him worthy of belief; for as a rule we trust men of probity more, and more quickly, about things in general, while on points outside the realm of exact knowledge, where opinion is divided, we trust them absolutely. This trust, however, should be created by the speech itself, and not left to depend upon an antecedent impression that the speaker is this or that kind of man. It is not true, as some writers on the art maintain, that the probity of the speaker contributes nothing to his persuasiveness; on the contrary, we might almost affirm that his character [*ethos*] is the most potent of all the means to persuasion.[13]

This may seem the strongest possible argument for the place of character in the advocate's armoury. But it has been maintained that the greatest of the literary critics of Rome's silver age, Quintilian, following in Cicero's footsteps, took the matter even further. Whereas Aristotle, when dealing with *ethos*, is concerned primarily with establishing believability in the context of the given speech situation or argument, Quintilian insists on the actual, inherent pos-

---

[12.] Richard J. Schoeck, "Lawyers and Rhetoric in Sixteenth-Century England," in James J. Murphy (ed.), *Renaissance Eloquence* (Berkeley: University of California Press, 1983), p. 274 (and the literature there cited).

[13.] Aristotle, *Rhetoric*, ed. and trans. Lane Cooper (New York: Appleton-Century-Crofts, 1932), pp. 7-9 (1355b-1356a).

session of good character by the advocate prior to and apart from the act of advocacy.

> The *Institutio Oratoria* is one long protest against the tastes of the age. Starting with the maxim of Cato the Censor that the orator is "the good man who is skilled in speaking," Quintilian takes his future orator at birth and shows how this goodness of character and skill in speaking may be best produced. No detail of training in infancy, boyhood or youth is too petty for his attention. The parts of the work which relate to general education are of great interest and importance. Quintilian postulates the widest culture; there is no form of knowledge from which something may not be extracted for his purpose; and he is fully alive to the importance of method in education. He ridicules the fashion of the day, which hurried over preliminary cultivation, and allowed men to grow grey while declaiming in the schools, where nature and reality were forgotten.[14]

Longinus, an Alexandrian writer influenced by Philo, was apparently a 1st-century contemporary of Quintilian. His impact on rhetoric continued even into the days of John Dryden and Edmund Burke.[15] Longinus' great work, *On the Sublime*, maintains that rhetorical success depends in the last analysis on "sublimity," that is to say, on the elevated character or (in Rudolf Otto's language) the numinosity of the argument, which in turn is a direct product of the elevation of spirit—the character—of the advocate.

> There are, it may be said, five principal sources of elevated language. Beneath these five varieties there lies, as though it were a common foundation, the gift of discourse, which is indispensable. First and most important is the power of forming great conceptions, as we have elsewhere explained in our remarks on Xenophon. Secondly, there is vehement and inspired passion. These two components of the sublime are for the most part innate....
>
> Now the first of the conditions mentioned, namely elevation of mind, holds the foremost rank among them all. We must, therefore, in this case also, although we have to do rather with an endowment than with an acquirement, nurture our souls (as far as that is possi-

---

[14.] James Smith Reid, "Quintilian," *Encyclopaedia Britannica*, 11th ed., XXII, 761. Cf. Edward Meredith Cope and John Edwin Sandys (eds.), *The Rhetoric of Aristotle, with a Commentary*, I (Cambridge: Cambridge University Press, 1877), 29-30.

[15.] See Sir Arthur Quiller-Couch, "A Note on Longinus," in his *Studies in Literature: Third Series* (Cambridge: Cambridge University Press, 1929), pp. 141-60.

ble) to thoughts sublime, and make them always pregnant, so to say, with noble inspiration.

In what way, you may ask, is this to be done? Elsewhere I have written as follows: "Sublimity is the echo of a great soul." Hence also a bare idea, by itself and without a spoken word, sometimes excites admiration just because of the greatness of soul implied. Thus the silence of Ajax in the Underworld is great and more sublime than words. First, then, it is absolutely necessary to indicate the source of this elevation, namely, that the truly eloquent must be free from low and ignoble thoughts. For it is not possible that men with mean and servile ideas and aims prevailing throughout their lives should produce anything that is admirable and worthy of immortality. Great accents we expect to fall from the lips of those whose thoughts are deep and grave....

Similarly, the legislator of the Jews, no ordinary man, having formed and expressed a worthy conception of the might of the Godhead, writes at the very beginning of his Laws, "God said" — what? "Let there be light, and there was light; let there be land, and there was land."[16]

The author of *On the Sublime* was not a Christian, but was acquainted with and deeply moved by the Old Testament. The classical rhetoricians' focus on the character of the advocate resonated fully with the central message of primitive Christianity, that one can only be saved by an inner transformation of character (being "born again"), produced by personal faith in the Christ who died for one's sins and rose again for one's justification.[17] Doubtless this explains in large part why the views of the classical rhetoricians were accepted and promulgated in the medieval Christian world and continued to have profound influence until the secular replacement of what C.S. Lewis called "Old Western Man."

[16.] Longinus, *On the Sublime*, ed. and trans. W. Rhys Roberts (2d ed.; Cambridge: Cambridge University Press, 1907), pp. 57-61, 64-65.

[17.] John 3: 1-21; Matt. 15: 16-20; Mk. 7: 14-23; Rom. 3: 21-26; 1 Cor. 15: 1-4; 2 Cor. 5: 17-21. Cf. Vasile Florescu, "Les théologiens chrétiens et la rhétorique," in his *La rhétorique et la néorhétorique*, trans. M. Munteanu (Paris: Société d'Edition "Les Belles Lettres," 1982), pp. 71-98; George A. Kennedy, "Rhetoric," in Richard Jenkyns (ed.), *The Legacy of Rome: A New Appraisal* (Oxford: Oxford University Press, 1992), pp. 269-94; and George A. Kennedy, *Comparative Rhetoric: An Historical and Cross-Cultural Introduction* (New York: Oxford University Press, 1998), p. 211.

The impact of the classical view is particularly evident during the Renaissance period, that era felicitously described by Jakob Burckhardt as the "rediscovery of the world and of man." In a letter to Lorenzo Lippi, a professional teacher of rhetoric, the Florentine neo-Platonic philosopher Marsilio Ficino offers the following advice:

> Since you have studied the Greek and Latin orators, I take it that you teach your pupils always to remember that their audience must be swayed not by what is pleasing, but by what is right. For he who urges what is just will win the case most easily, for of course he has Justice as his patron. Let them be mindful of their own integrity, because if a man's life is a lie, his speech will give him the lie. Facts carry greater weight than words, and the speaker who is most deeply moved himself will move others most deeply, whereas the man who sings one tune and plucks another from his lyre totally offends the ear. Divine music is the true harmony of thought, word and deed....
>
> Let them study to be good rather than learned, for learning begets envy which goodness destroys. Goodness is both more useful to men and more pleasing to God than learning. It is also more enduring. We forget more quickly some fact which was quickly learned than we lose principles of conduct which we have attained by arduous daily practice. Learning in itself brings little of value, and that for only a short time, while goodness is eternal and leads to the realisation of God. Therefore, following the example of Socrates, advise your pupils to use human learning to dispel the clouds of the senses, and to bring serenity to the soul. Then will the ray of truth from the divine sun illumine the mind, and never in any other way. That is the only useful study. A man who acts otherwise labours vainly and miserably.[18]

During the English Renaissance, Thomas Wilson (d. 1581) produced his *Arte of Rhetorique*, which is generally regarded as the earliest systematic treatise on literary criticism in the English language. Of its aim and underlying philosophy, Schoeck writes:

> I would suggest that for a large part of his intended audience Wilson had in mind the young noblemen and gentlemen who were students at the Inns of Court; this is supported by the legal content and the frequent resorting to legal experience for illustration, and

---

[18.] Marsilio Ficino, *Letters*, intro. Paul Oskar Kristeller, I (London: Shepheard-Walwyn, 1978), pp. 162-63 (letter 109).

by the dedication. Though Wilson, again, is writing to make rhetoric serve contemporary needs and is addressing those professions which especially spoke, and wrote: preachers and statesmen-diplomats—one should remember, however, that a large part of the diplomatic and political ranks were filled from the Inns of Court.

We may find it surprising that a humanist like Wilson should be so much the lawyer in a rhetorical treatise, and perhaps even more surprising that Wilson, a civilian, should make so much use of the common law and think so highly of it. But he was of Elyot's metal, and bore the same stamp of the older humanism of men like More: in the words of Mair, "he was one of a band of grave and dignified scholars, men preoccupied with morality and citizenship as well as with the lighter problems of learning and style," and in Tawney's view, "Wilson for all his scholarship, belonged to the older tradition, the tradition which held that 'this is the true ordering of the state of a well-fashioned commonwealth, that every part do obey one head, one governor, one law, as all parts of the body obey the head, agree among themselves, and one not to eat up another through greediness, and that we see that order, moderation, and reason bridle the affections'"—a tradition of men whose social philosophy (and theories of communication) was based ultimately on religion, therefore on an order of law and justice.[19]

III. COMMUNICATIONS THEORY TODAY AND THE QUESTION OF THE RELEVANCE OF THE ADVOCATE'S CHARACTER

In the most general sense, modern communications theory has shifted attention from the communicator and his message (the subject and subject-matter of the communication) to the recipient of the message (the object of the communication). In terms of Schramm's well-known electronic model of communication

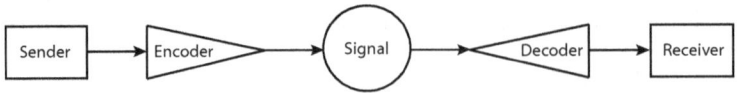

[19.] Schoeck, *op. cit.*, pp. 286-87. See also Schoeck, "Rhetoric and Law in 16th Century England," 50 *Studies in Philology* 120-21 (1953).

the focus is now predominantly on the "receiver" and his decoding of the signal sent to him or her.[20] Thus the emphasis in the advocacy texts on "techniques" and "skills" by which the audience (judge, jury) can be persuaded or even manipulated to arrive at the advocate's viewpoint.[21]

Nonetheless, specialists in the communication field are coming to recognise that the character of the communicator cannot be ignored if one is going to provide a full account of the advocacy process. In discussing the impact of "source credibility" on successful argumentation, Rieke and Sillars cite an impressive experimental literature going to prove that

> Persons who are perceived by receivers to be *trustworthy* ... have high credibility. In the literature since classical times, other words have been used that may help to define the meaning of trustworthiness: "probity," "character," "evaluative," "reliable," and "safety." Again, common sense would tell us that we tend to accept ideas more readily from persons whom we regard as being trustworthy.[22]

Gronbeck and his co-authors make the same point:

> In every speaking situation, the speaker's success in winning agreement, inspiring confidence, or promoting ideas is significantly affected by the listeners' estimate of his or her credibility. The term *credibility*—and its relative, image, or *ethos* (Greek for "character")— refers to the degree to which an audience finds you trustworthy, competent, sincere, attractive, and dynamic. Research has repeatedly demonstrated that a speaker who can raise an audience's esti-

---

[20] Wilbur Schramm, "Procedures and Effects of Mass Communication," in *Mass Media and Education: The 53rd Yearbook of the National Society for the Study of Education, Part II*, ed. Nelson B. Henry (Chicago: University of Chicago Press, 1954), pp. 114-15. Cf. John Warwick Montgomery, "Mass Communication and Scriptural Proclamation," 49/1 *Evangelical Quarterly* (January-March, 1977).

[21] Out of scope for this paper is a discussion of the variety of contemporary schools of rhetorical thought, such as Perelman's "Nouvelle rhétorique," General Semantics Theory, etc. Readers are referred, *inter alia*, to Daniel Fogarty, *Roots for a New Rhetoric* (New York: Columbia University Teachers College, 1959); I.A. Richards, *The Philosophy of Rhetoric* (New York: Oxford University Press, 1936); and Ch. Perelman and L. Olbrechts-Tyteca, *La nouvelle rhétorique: traité de l'argumentation* (Paris: Presses Universitaires de France, 1958).

[22] Richard D. Rieke and Malcolm O. Sillars, *Argumentation and the Decision Making Process* (New York: John Wiley, 1975), p. 145.

> mate of these qualities will significantly heighten the impact of the speech....
>
> Your ability to project yourself as a competent, trustworthy, sincere, attractive, fair, and dynamic speaker may well determine the fate of your message. The message and the messenger are usually inseparable in people's minds.[23]

Granting the necessary interconnection of "the message and the messenger": does this *per se* justify the classical view that (to use Australian judge John Phillips' book title) true advocacy must be "advocacy with honour"[24] and that the genuinely successful advocate must operate with what André Toulemon called the right *"parole intérieure"*?[25] Does it follow, over against the views of Keith Evans quoted earlier, that, in the words of Argentinian lawyer Mario Martinez Crespo, "el campo proprio de la abogacía es la justicia; en todo su accionar el abogado debe procurar hacer justicia"?[26] Is it now established that the "lamp of honesty" is in fact the first of "the seven lamps of advocacy" and that Cockburn's philosophy rather than Brougham's was correct?

> When Lord Brougham, at a dinner to M. Berryer, claimed in his speech that the advocate should reckon everything as subordinate to the interests of his client, Lord Chief Justice Cockburn, "feeling that our guest might leave us with a false impression of our ideals," set forth his views of an advocate's duty, concluding with these memorable words: "The arms which an advocate wields he ought to use as a warrior, not as an assassin. He ought to uphold the interests of his client *per fas*, and not *per nefas*. He ought to know how to reconcile the interests of his clients with the eternal interests of truth and justice."[27]

The sceptic might well respond that, even though messenger and message may well be interlocked, (1) the object of the advo-

---

[23] Bruce E. Gronbeck, et al., *Principles and Types of Speech Communication* (11th ed.; New York: HarperCollins, 1990), p.12.

[24] John Phillips, *Advocacy with Honour* (Sydney, Australia: Law Book Company, 1985).

[25] André Toulemon, *La parole intérieure: essai de psychologie oratoire* (Paris: Dalloz, 1974).

[26] Mario Martinez Crespo, *Nosotros los abogados: Reflexiones acerca de una profesión controvertida* (Buenos Aires: Editorial Hammurabi, 1995), p. 63.

[27] Edward Abbott Parry, *The Seven Lamps of Advocacy* (London: T. Fisher Unwin, 1923), pp. 18-19.

cate's activity is persuasion, and that means conforming one's arguments and values to those of the trier of fact and the judge, who will ultimately decide the case, and (2) such conformity entails personal agnosticism, not a fixed standard of "character" or "integrity."

Such arguments are not difficult to answer. Kronman speaks to the first:

> To be sure, the known identities of jurors may suggest ways in which an advocate can tailor his appeal to their biases and beliefs. But despite the exaggerated claims that are sometimes made on behalf of the "science" of jury selection, such knowledge remains severely limited, and there is, in addition, the pressure of opposing counsel to constrain its use where it exists. This means that in arguing to juries, an advocate must often proceed on the same counterfactual assumption as when arguing to a judge, by treating his audience as if it were composed of anonymous officials clothed with certain powers and responsibilities but lacking known attributes of a more personal kind. Both sorts of advocacy are similarly constrained, and both therefore depend, in the end, on the advocate's own devotion to the law's internal good to achieve their intended effect.[28]

To the second, related sceptical argument (that advocacy requires value agnosticism coupled with moral relativism), Professor Rhode responds:

> Appeals to agnosticism are problematic in one final respect. Those who refuse to pass judgment on a client generally seem to assume that such neutrality is value-free. But individuals cannot market their loyalty, avert their eyes to the consequences, and pretend they have not made a normative decision. To decline to take a moral stance is in itself a moral stance and requires justification as such. Thus the critical question is not by what right do lawyers impose their views, but by what right do they evade the responsibility of all individuals to evaluate the normative implications of their acts?[29]

Highly satisfactory formal, rational answers of this sort can certainly be given in support of the classical view that the good advo-

---

[28] Kronman, *op. cit.*, p. 151.

[29] Deborah L. Rhode, "Ethical Perspectives on Legal Practice," 37 *Stanford L. Rev.* 589, 623 (January 1985). Cf. also Osvaldo R. Agatiello, *La ética del abogado* (Buenos Aires: Abeledo-Perrot, 1995), pp. 51-54.

cate must, first and foremost, be a good person. But fascinating empirical issues remain uninvestigated. *Are* triers of fact better convinced when the advocate is a person of integrity? What *is* the actual effect on the trier of fact when faced with an immoral or hypocritical advocate who consciously argues for what he or she does not believe to be true? And what about the psychopathic communicator, who convinces himself or herself of what he knows to be untrue? Might it not be possible to test the classical philosophy of advocacy in controlled experiments such as:

- A convinced non-smoker and a chain-smoker (of equal skill in the techniques of advocacy) endeavour to persuade mock juries as to the merits of legally proscribing all manufacture, distribution, and recreational use of tobacco products. Would the result be different in the two instances?

- A believer in absolute moral values (for example, a "born-again" Christian) and an atheistic relativist equally skilled and competent in the courtroom argue the identical case to two different mock juries. Same or different results?

- An advocate intentionally deceives a mock judge on the law, either by misstating it or by concealing controlling authority in the given jurisdiction. Another equally-skilled advocate offers parallel arguments which do in fact represent the true state of the law. Would the judge sense or be able to identify the difference?

It is of course possible that the classical view of the moral advocate cannot be justified experimentally: perhaps it represents a non-empirical ideal, or has to do not with particular moral decisions but with the total character, the general ethical *Gestalt* of the advocate as a person. But even so, would the position hold? Advocates are frequently compared with actors[30]—actors who, in the courtroom, write their own scripts. Surely a great actor does not have to hold the moral values or dysvalues of the individual he portrays, so why should the advocate need to believe in his client's case or take any particular ethical position while representing him or her?

[30.] See the selections included in John Warwick Montgomery (ed.), *Practical Exercises, 1996-1997* (London: BPP Law School, 1996), Units 5-6, "Techniques in Advocacy, I-II," pp. 207 ff.

The answer, of course, is that the courtroom is far more than a theatre. When the lights come up and the audience go home from a West End production, no-one loses his liberty or his property as a consequence of the production. Legal activity impacts individual and societal life on the deepest level and lack of character and solid values here can have the worst possible consequences. Perhaps a better analogy for the advocate than that of the actor is that of the historian, as understood by Benedetto Croce or by R.G. Collingwood. For them, the great historian "gets inside" the mind of the past by empathic identification with it and thus conveys its deepest meaning. Writes Collingwood:

> When a scientist asks "Why did that piece of litmus paper turn pink?" he means "On what kinds of occasions do pieces of litmus paper turn pink?" When an historian asks "Why did Brutus stab Caesar?" he means "What did Brutus think, which made him decide to stab Caesar?" The cause of the event, for him, means the thought in the mind of the person by whose agency the event came about: and this is not something other than the event, it is inside of the event itself.... All history is the history of thought. But how does the historian discern the thoughts which he is trying to discover? There is only one way in which it can be done: by re-thinking them in his own mind.... This re-enactment ... is not a passive surrender to the spell of another's mind; it is a labour of active and therefore critical thinking. The historian not only re-enacts past thought, he re-enacts it in the context of his own knowledge and therefore, in re-enacting it, criticizes it, forms his own judgement of its value, corrects whatever errors he can discern in it.[31]

Possibly the classical connection between advocacy and ethics is another way of saying that the best advocates are persuasive because, on a personal foundation of integrity and solid values, they do not merely act a part: they "get inside" their client's case, re-thinking and re-enacting it, helping the trier of fact to understand and appreciate it on the very deepest level. When that occurs, successful—and just—verdicts should come as no surprise.

[31.] R.G. Collingwood, *The Idea of History* (New York: Oxford University Press' Galaxy Books, 1956), pp. 214-16. Cf. John Warwick Montgomery, *The Shape of the Past* (2d ed.; Minneapolis: Bethany, 1975), pp. 90-92.

APPENDIX

FOUR REVIEWS —
AND A DEFENCE OF THE TRIAL OF CHRIST

Duncan Forrester's *Christian Justice and Public Policy**

This volume, which raises vitally important questions concerning the relationship of Christianity to contemporary political theory, law, and social policy, is the tenth in an academic series which has included such titles as *A Theology of Reconstruction: Nation-Building and Human Rights* (Charles Villa-Vicencio), *Protestantism in Contemporary China* (Alan Hunter), *Religion and the Making of Society: Essays in Social Theology* (Charles Davis), *Pastoral Care and Liberation Theology* (Stephen Pattison), *Power, Gender and Christian Mysticism* (Grace Jantzen), and *God's Just Vengeance: Crime, Violence and the Rhetoric of Salvation* (Timothy Gorringe). The book has a distinguished pedigree: its author is Professor of Christian Ethics and Practical Theology at New College, University of Edinburgh, and did much of the writing at the Center of Theological Inquiry at Princeton. Some of the included material was previously given in the F.D. Maurice Lectures in King's College, London (1995) and as a Bishop Butler Lecture in the University of Bristol (1996).

In line with the general purpose of the series to go beyond "studies by social-scientists who often adopt a functionalist and reductionist view of the faith and beliefs which motivate those directly involved" in Christian social action, the author contends that even though "religion no longer occupies the place it did in western societies as an institution, ... that does not mean it must be restricted to the private, domestic or leisure spheres of life" (pp. xi-xii). Forrester wants the Christian believer to impact today's secular, global, and pluralistic society in an intelligent, principled, and effective way. His object is to answer the question: "What kind of Christian voice is appropriate in the public realm in relation to debates about public policy, and how might it be most appropriately articulated today?" (p. 9). He focuses on "the central issue of justice" (p. 36), going from the theoretical to the practical by way of such

---

* Cambridge, England: Cambridge University Press, 1997 ("Cambridge Studies in Ideology and Religion," ed. Duncan Forrester and Alistair Kee); xiv + 274 pp.

moral issues as poverty and punishment/imprisonment. A significant part of the book (pp. 111-92) is devoted to a theological examination and critique of influential contemporary secular theories of justice (Rawls, Hayek, Habermas). Finally, the author offers his personal suggestions and insights under the general rubic "Theological Fragments" (pp. 193 ff.).

In evaluating the degree of success to be attributed to Forrester's laudable endeavour, we shall first look at his treatment of those secular political philosophers with whom he disagrees, and then go on to examine the theological approach which he himself espouses. To be sure: effective or ineffective criticism of other viewpoints in no way proves or disproves one's own worldview; but the quality of one's handling of opponents is important to the credibility of one's general position.

Forrester, who favours "a far more equitable distribution of material things" (p. 110), is deeply troubled by Hayek's notion of the spontaneous order of the market, and unhappy with Margaret Thatcher's confidence in it. The moral indifference of the open market—its status "simply as the aptest device for the orderly and efficient running of a morally fragmented society" points up "the tension between the Hayekian moral universe and the Judeo-Christian tradition" (pp.150-54). He analogises Hayek's spontaneous order of the market to the Protestant Reformers' doctrine of the "Orders of Creation," uncritically accepting Karl Barth's view that to believe in divinely-created structures of society is tantamount to accepting the status quo no matter how morally inadequate it is, and thus to divinise the market.

Here Forrester shows little understanding of the classic doctrine of the *Schöpfungsordnungen* and no apparent acquaintance with Emil Brunner's modern exposition of it in his *The Divine Imperative*, Bk. III. Over against Barth, Brunner rightly sees that the creative "orders" (marriage and the family, the state, the cultural orders, religious institutions, economics) are in themselves purely *formal*: they are the sine quibus non of human existence in society, without any necessary built-in *content*. It is through the natural law written on the human heart, and more particularly the pronouncements of special revelation in Holy Scripture, that we learn the proper content of the orders. Thus, every society will have a marital/family order, but conscience and Scripture set forth the monogamous ideal. (Cf. Montgomery, *The Shape of the Past*, pp. 358-74.)

In the economic realm, therefore, the issue is not a spurious parallel between Hayek's market philosophy and the *Schöpfungsordnungen*, but a determination of proper biblical standards for economics—i.e., *should* the free market be regulated, and, if so, on what principles? By way of Brian Griffiths, Forrester rightly notes that Christianity will put "certain limits on the market place" and will insist that government display a genuine "concern for the poor" (p.156), but he does not work out the biblical principles which would draw a proper line between individual freedom on the one hand and state regulation and the public redistribution of wealth on the other.

Thus the author never faces the question of the negative consequences of economic levelling. Without concentrations of wealth, would great eleemosynary endeavours be possible? (It is passing strange that Forrester, teaching in Scotland, never thinks of Andrew Carnegie.) Is this possibly one reason why our Lord did not—in contrast with much of today's Liberation Theology—condemn the rich *per se*? And where government regulation of the economy is seen as a moral solution to social problems, one must always ask: who now makes the moral decisions? The answer is, often and sadly, unprincipled bureaucrats who are seeking career advantages rather than the public good. Since, as the Apostle says, "*all* have sinned and come short of God's glory," it is a fatal mistake in effect to exempt centralised officialdom from the operations of original sin whilst emphasising its presence among capitalists.

The author's inevitable illustration of the theological inadequacy of a free-market philosophy lies in the realm of health care: he points up the shortcomings in America versus the caring national-health systems in Britain and Continental Europe. Now, there is little doubt that America needs a comprehensive national health-care plan, but, as one who has lived both there and here, I can only marvel that the backwardness, incompetence, and waste of much of the bureaucratic British system did not more impress the author. The Bible not only instructs us to care for the weak, poor, and downtrodden; it also supports freedom of decision and opposes totalitarian control. The Israelite monarchy was God's grudging concession to a sinful people, not an endorsement of government regulation.

John Rawls' theory of justice is seen in a much more positive light. The author holds that in at least four respects it is compatible with the Christian position: it "gives priority to justice"; it "affirms and assumes human equality"; Rawls' concern for the least-advantaged is "at least a partial expression of a Preferential Option for the Poor"; and, though justice is not synonymous with fairness, as Rawls apparently holds, his philosophy properly illustrates that fairness must be "a central component of any adequate account of justice" (pp.133-34).

The analysis of Rawls' system which underlines these judgments is, however, exceedingly superficial. Rawls' Original Position with its Veil of Ignorance is adequately described and its difference from the Garden of Eden noted. ("Behind their very different Veil of Ignorance, Eve and Adam make a false choice ... and in a broken world the justice of the Original Position is present primarily as a memory and as a hope"—p. 122.) But then the author jumps to Rawls' post-*Theory of Justice* concept of "overlapping consensus" and claims that his "notion of justice" is based on that consensus (p. 127). In point of fact, Rawls' Principles of Justice derive, not from the overlapping consensus but from what Rawls has called "reflective equilibrium" (involving the conditions of the Original Position, fitting as they do our considered moral judgments, and our intuitions as to the meaning of justice) combined with Kantian "philosophical reflection" (i.e., the rational perception that these Principles of Justice must apply to everyone, not just to the agent).

Moreover, Forrester neglects the keystone of Rawls' entire system, his "thin theory of the good" on which Rawls' notion of the Primary Social Goods is based. This theory, in turn, is grounded in "a basic principle of motivation which I [Rawls] shall refer to as the

Aristotelian Principle," defined as "a preference for ascending the chain or chains which offer the better prospects of exercising the higher abilities with the least strain." In consequence, for Rawls, the most important of the Primary Social Goods is self-respect or self-esteem—a person's sense of his own value and confidence in his own ability. Finally, Forrester does not touch Rawls' critically important 1993 Oxford Amnesty Lecture, in which he applied his general theory internationally, in an effort to justify the creation and maintenance of regional and worldwide mechanisms for the protection of human rights.

Why is all this important? Because the fallacies in Rawls' theory are not simply the product of a naïveté in thinking that fairness will automatically come about by consensus in a pluralistic society. Rawls' fundamental problem is his underlying rationalistic, Enlightenment belief that man is essentially good and will, through self-respect, ascend to higher moral goals, choose proper societal principles, and be able to put them into practice nationally and internationally. Had Forrester also looked at the parallel neo-Kantian theories of Alan Gewirth, he would have seen the common thread: the belief that man will act rationally once the truth is presented and that he will allow that truth to be universalised so as to be applied even to his own disadvantage (Kant's Categorical Imperative, Gewirth's Principle of Generic Consistency). Of course, this has little to do with actual human life, which, as Hobbes well described it, is "nasty, poor, brutish and short." Theories of man that do not adequately take original sin into account have always failed, and will always fail.

Forrester's critique of Habermas is stronger than his treatments of Rawls and Hayek. He recognises that Habermas has more affinity with Hegel and Marx than with 18th-century Enlightenment thought. He realises that Habermas' "discourse ethic" is utopian: it "holds up the utopian hope of a broad community in which people attend to one another's feelings and listen to what they are saying and what they are afraid to say" (p. 186). And, almost as a throwaway line, he makes the crucial point: "A theologian might echo Anselm in suggesting that he [Habermas] has not yet considered the gravity of sin and its pervasive distortion of human judgements" (p. 173). Remarkably, however, though Forrester employs Kierkegaard later in another connection (pp. 202-203), he does not apply the Danish lay theologian's devastating critique of Hegelian secular-rationalistic, synoptic worldviews to point up the key failing in Habermas. Apart from a transcendent, divine revelation, no-one of us is capable of grandiose solutions to the problems of justice. Habermas (like Rawls, though on a different theoretical basis) is vainly trying to pull himself up by his own ideological bootstraps.

Granted the limited value of Forrester's critiques of secular theorists of justice: what positive Christian answers does he give us? Early in his book he quotes social scientist Barbara Wooton's assertion that "nobody knows what justice is" (p. 38). Does *Forrester* know? Though his book contains many insightful anecdotes and pregnant thoughts, no distinctively Christian theory of justice emerges. The tone is set in the author's Introduction: "The Christian position from which I write assumes that both knowing what justice is and doing justice are inherently and deeply problematic." Problematic, yes, but since Christian faith is founded on revelation—not obscurity—one would expect the Christian to be capable of shedding far more light than the secularist offers.

The source of the difficulty seems to lie in the author's lack of theological rigour. Thus, in his section on "Justification" (the *articulus stantis et cadentis ecclesiae*, or so the Reformers thought!), there is a hopeless confusion of *justification* with *justice*. From the ambiguous assertion that "in the experience of being justified is revealed the true justice of God, which is justice itself" one passes to Gustavo Gutierrez's statement that "justice and right cannot be emptied of the content bestowed on them by the Bible" (p. 207). But (1) justification is not an "experience": it is God's forensic declaration that in spite of our sin we are declared righteous because of what Christ did for us on the Cross, and (2) the issue is not whether the Bible can bestow content (of course it can!) but what that content in fact *is* relative to the problems of human justice in a fallen world.

A further illustration. The author uncritically repeats the old saw (deriving essentially from Ernst Troeltsch) that Luther's doctrine of the Two Kingdoms produced a quietism and acceptance of the political status quo, such that proper social reform was neglected, unjust rulers allowed to remain on the throne, and the world in essence permitted to go to hell. Particularly obnoxious is Forrester's utterly unhistorical claim that "under Hitler such an interpretation of the Two-Kingdoms theory was used to justify a church policy of non-interference in the political realm which in fact became collusion with Nazism" (p. 212).

This defamatory allegation, first set out by Peter Wiener in 1945 (*Martin Luther: Hitler's Spiritual Ancestor*), thoroughly refuted by Gordon Rupp (*Martin Luther – Hitler's Cause – or Cure?*), and revived and popularised in William L. Shirer's *Rise and Fall of the Third Reich*, cannot be seriously maintained today (see, e.g., Montgomery, "Shirer's Re-Hitlerizing of Luther," *Christian Century*, 12 December 1962). Moreover, the ideological collaborationists of Nazism were not the theologians and pastors faithful to the Lutheran theology of the Reformation (e.g., Martin Niemöller) but secular philosophers (Martin Heidegger) and neo-orthodox to liberal theologians (Gerhard Kittel).

As for the Two Kingdoms doctrine, it does not at all deny God's action or the believer's responsibility in the secular realm. Luther's view of social ethics centres on the individual Christian as the point of contact—the connecting link—between the two kingdoms: it is he or she who has the responsibility (and privilege) of remedying social injustice by becoming a "little Christ" to the neighbour. This is anything but quietism; it is faith active in love, based upon a "theology of the Cross." What Lutheran theology does not tolerate is a "theology of glory"—a utopian, millennial triumphalism in which God's participation in secular life offers believers the possibility of creating a perfect society. A sinless society must wait for Christ's personal return, when "the kingdoms of this world will become the kingdoms of our Lord and of his Christ." (Cf. Montgomery, *Human Rights and Human Dignity*, pp. 198-202.)

Finally, Forrester's sources—those he relies on and those he ignores—assist us in understanding why his book offers so little systematic guidance. He is acquainted with and cites the mainline, critical theologians (Barth, Bultmann, Bonhoeffer, Carl Braaten, George Lindbeck, Jürgen Moltmann, the Niebuhrs, Albert Schweitzer, Paul Tillich, *et al.*) but never refers to the vast and far more helpful literature of Christian social ethics produced by classical Reformation and evangelical scholars, particularly, but not limited to, those on the other side of the Atlantic: Carl F.H. Henry, Robert Mounce, David O. Moberg, Timothy L. Smith, Richard V. Pierard, Ronald Sider, Vernon C. Grounds, Tom Skinner, Werner Elert (*The Christian Ethos*), George W. Forell (*Faith Active in Love: An Investigation of the Principles Underlying Luther's Social Ethics*), C.E.B. Cranfield, David Kilgour, J.W. Montgomery (*Christians in the Public Square*). Forrester refers often to pronouncements and ecumenical declarations of the World Council of Churches and of mainline church bodies without observing that such organisations have often, in the absence of any clear revelational moorings, uncritically supported or at least aided and abetted liberal, quasi-revolutionary, and totalitarian activities which have produced immense injustice worldwide in the long term.

Like so much contemporary theological writing, this book is far better at pointing up needs than in treating them. One is reminded of the old adage: the philosophers don't know the solutions but they certainly know the problems. One expects more of Christian theologians, however, since they presumably endeavour to apply to human problems a revealed faith, once delivered to the saints, and still eternally relevant.

ALISTER MCGRATH'S *IUSTITIA DEI: A HISTORY OF THE CHRISTIAN DOCTRINE OF JUSTIFICATION**

The author, a prominent Anglican evangelical known on both sides of the Atlantic, serves as Principal of Wycliffe Hall, Oxford. In his Preface to this one-volume revision of the original two-volume edition, he rather immodestly informs us of its purpose and scope: "The history of the development of the Christian doctrine of justification has never been written. It is this deficiency which the present volume seeks to remedy.... The first edition of this work appeared in two volumes in 1986, and quickly established itself as the definitive work on the subject." The British price of the new edition is £55, the equivalent of $90 U.S., so the author's claims need to be (we hesitate to use the word) *justified*—if only on economic grounds—to warrant purchase.

McGrath treats the doctrine of justification in a strictly chronological fashion, beginning with the Patristic period and St Augustine. (McGrath does not deal with Paul's views in the New Testament as such; we shall return to his reasons for this at the end of this review.) The medieval period is discussed in considerable detail, with helpful distinctions made as to the different approaches to justification characteristic of major monastic orders and ideological schools (Dominicans, Franciscans, Augustinians). The Reformation period is, needless to say, central to the book, with a description of Luther's theological development followed by a comparison of the Lutheran and Reformed approaches to the doctrine and a brief discussion of justification in Protestant Orthodoxy. Then follows Trent; the English "Reformation legacy" (including not just Tyndale, Hooker, and the Puritans, but also, oddly enough, John Henry Newman—owing to his critique of Luther in his *Lectures on Justification*); and the period from the Enlightenment through the Protestant liberalism of Schleiermacher and Ritschl to

---

* 2d ed.; Cambridge, England: Cambridge University Press, 1998; xiii + 532 pp.

Barth, Tillich, Bultmann, the post-Bultmannian new hermeneutic (Ebeling), and the 1983 U.S. Lutheran-Roman Catholic dialogue group's *Justification by Faith* document.

Before going into details, we may legitimately ask a preliminary question or two: How revised is the revised edition? and, Is the work indeed unique? As to the degree of revision, it is very slight: aside from minor updating of references and a few stylistic improvements, the only new material is the addition of two final sections (a grand total of 19 pages—the equivalent of a short journal article) updating the book with references to recent Pauline scholarship and ecumenical endeavours to bridge the Protestant-Catholic gap. No new sections are intercalated; all section numbers of the first edition remain the same in the 1998 edition (which at least has the advantage of allowing us to give section references equally applicable to both editions). Much as this reviewer—a genetic bibliomaniac—favours book buying, he must advise owners of the two-volume paperback first edition that they would in consequence surely be wasting their money to purchase this "revision."

What about the author's claim to have produced the only extant "history of the development of the Christian doctrine of justification"? If this means a single volume devoted to the subject and published in our time, he may be strictly correct. But the great histories of Christian thought have hardly been able to avoid a doctrine so central to Christian faith. One thinks not just of the likes of Harnack but of 20th century treatments such as J. L. Neve and O.W. Heick's *A History of Christian Thought* (2 vols.; Philadelphia: Muhlenberg Press, 1946) and J.L. González's work of the same title (3 vols.; Nashville: Abingdon, 1970-1975). Looking at random at Neve and Heick, one finds, for example, an entire chapter devoted to "Positions on Justification" in their discussion of the New England theology of Jonathan Edwards (Edwards receives only a page and a half in McGrath). Neither Neve and Heick nor González is anywhere referred to by McGrath, and one gets the distinct impression that he did not benefit greatly from the synoptic histories of doctrine in doing his own work. Often these histories provide more careful and more detailed discussions of justification than he himself gives.

To be sure, a single work focusing on a cardinal doctrine is always useful. McGrath admits in his Preface that "in effect, the present study is a bibliographical essay." As such, it will often provide insights hard to find elsewhere. Thus, there is a fine critique of John Henry Newman's gross misunderstandings of Luther and the drawing of a fairly uncomfortable parallel between Newman and Calvin (sec. 33): "Newman's critique of Luther in the *Lectures* appears to rest upon the quite fallacious assumption that the Reformer regards faith as a human work.... In his discussion of the relation between faith and works, Newman takes the remarkable step of citing Luther in support of his own opinion that justification is to be ascribed to 'believing deeds' (that is, both faith and works, as taught by Bull and Taylor).... A similar critique could be made of his totally inadequate references to Calvin. Had Newman studied Calvin seriously, he could hardly have failed to notice the remarkable similarities between them on the nature of justification. Thus Calvin regards both justification and sanctification as notionally distinct yet inseparable aspects of the believer's incorporation into Christ through the Holy Spirit in a mystical union."

But sweeping treatments of historical topics must in the final analysis be judged by their adequacy on the level of the particular. Toynbee was unsuccessful in defending himself against the critics of his *A Study of History* when he declared that "a committee may be able to run a country but a book must be the product of a single mind." The fact is that no one person can be the master of gigantic amounts of detail, so the specialist treatments are often much more useful than one person's attempt to cover the whole field. (Cf. the discussion of Toynbee in Montgomery, *The Shape of the Past*.) How does McGrath's book stand up to detailed analysis?

Not very well. Here are but a few examples. He properly recognises that the chief influence on the nascent Anglican theology of the Reformation period was Lutheran ("Despite this clear alignment with the Lutheran Reformation, rather than the Swiss Reformations of Zurich or Geneva, the Elizabethan period witnessed a general decline in the fortunes of Lutheranism in England"—sec. 30), but he shows no acquaintance with the best of the detailed treatments of the matter: H.E. Jacobs, *The Lutheran Movement in England During the Reigns of Henry VIII and Edward VI* (Philadelphia: G.W. Frederick, 1890) and N.S. Tjernagel, *Henry VIII and the Lutherans* (Saint Louis, Missouri: Concordia, 1965). Indeed, one of the most remarkable features of the McGrath volume is its obliviousness to American scholarly literature in general, much of which reaches a greater level of theological depth than the British material.

The author's handling of the Lutheran theologians of the period of 17th century Protestant Orthodoxy is truly lamentable. This does not apparently arise from dependence on A.C. McGiffert's *Protestant Thought Before Kant* or on Jaroslav Pelikan's stereotyped treatment in his *From Luther to Kierkegaard* (they are nowhere referred to), but his underlying point is the same as theirs: these theologians departed from Luther, hardened their categories, and contributed to the rise of Pietism and ultimately to Enlightenment rationalism. McGrath shows no contact whatsoever with the groundbreaking work on the theologians of Lutheran Orthodoxy by the brothers J. A.O. Preus and Robert D. Preus (cf. the latter's two-volume, *Theology of Post-Reformation Lutheranism* [Saint Louis, Missouri: Concordia, 1970-1972]).

Particularly irritating is the impact of the author's own Calvinism on his interpretations. Thus the Lutheran dogmaticians of the late 16th and the 17th centuries invariably come out less attractively than their Calvinist counterparts: "Significantly, the Reformed school is considerably closer to Luther (especially the 1525 Luther) than Lutheranism. Given that both confessions adopted a strongly forensic concept of justification, which set them apart from Luther on this point, the strongly predestinarian cast of Reformed theology approximates to that of Luther to a far greater extent than Lutheran Orthodoxy. Similarly, the strongly Christological conception of justification to be found in Luther's writings is carried over into Reformed theology, particularly in the image of Christ as *caput et sponsor electorum*, where it is so evidently lacking in Lutheran Orthodoxy. Both in terms of its substance and emphasis, the teaching of later Lutheran Orthodoxy bears little relation to that of Luther" (sec. 24). These calumnies derive not from careful analysis of the corpus of dogmatic writings in question, but from a tacit acceptance of such Reformed attempts to assimilate Luther to Calvinist double-predestination as that of James Packer in his edition of Luther's *Bondage of the Will*. It is also not easy to see a one-to-one relationship between Luther's very definitely Christological centre and the Calvinist dogmaticians' emphasis on our Lord as "head and sponsor of the elect"! (Cf. David Chytraeus, *On Sacrifice*, ed. and trans. Montgomery [2d. ed.; Malone, Texas: Repristination Press, 1999].)

McGrath holds that the Lutheran dogmaticians based their doctrine of election upon God's foreknowledge of the faith of the one to be justified. "In effect, Lutheran Orthodoxy interpreted the concept of election as God's affirmation of that which he foreknows will occur within the sphere of his ordained will—in other words, election takes place on the basis of *fides praevisa*" (sec. 24). He is evidently totally ignorant of the controversies over the question of the actual teaching of Luther and of the dogmaticians of Orthodoxy on this issue that led to the formulation of the theology of the Lutheran Church-Missouri Synod (see, *inter alia*, A.R. Wentz, *A Basic History of Lutheranism in America* [Philadelphia: Muhlenberg Press, 1955], pp. 212-16). The literature of that 19th century controversy, involving also the old Buffalo, Iowa, and Ohio Synods, leads to the inevitable conclusion that the Lutheran view was not at all as McGrath formulates it. Neither the Calvinists *nor* the classic Lutherans focused on foreknowledge of freewill; they *both* saw God's election and the work of the Holy Spirit as the sole source of the believer's status. They differed in attempting to account for the lost, the Calvinist theologians attributing this to a divine decree, either supralapsarian or infralapsarian, the Lutherans to man's own fallen condition and perverse misuse of his freewill (F. Pieper, *Christian Dogmatics* [4 vols.; Saint Louis, Missouri: Concordia, 1950-1957], II, 419-22, III, 471-503). In the (now omitted) Preface to the original second volume of *Iustitia Dei*, McGrath does make the following admission, and for this, I suppose, Lutherans can be somewhat grateful: "Although the reformed churches never attached quite the same importance to the doctrine [of justification], they accorded it a place of honour, partly in recognition of its foundational importance for Luther." But it would be nice if McGrath better understood the theologians whose views he is treating.

Karl Barth's position on justification comes under criticism, but not, it would seem, for the best reasons. McGrath notes that "Barth cannot share Luther's high estimation for the *articulus iustificationis*" (sec. 37). He explains this as stemming from Barth's theological method: for Barth, "soteriology is necessarily secondary to the fact of revelation, *Deus dixit.*" Now Barth's lack of appreciation for the centrality of justification certainly relates to his theological method, but that does not concern his attitude toward revelation at all as much as it does (1) his overarching stress on the sovereignty of God and (2) his appallingly weak doctrine of sin (sin as an absence of something—see Gustaf Wingren's criticism of Barth in Wingren's classic, *Theology in Conflict;* and my *Where Is History Going*). Moreover, it does not seem entirely responsible for McGrath to stress Barth's doctrine of revelation and not inform his readers that, as a matter of fact, Barth's view of revelation was evacuated of any and all empirical grounding by his absorption of Kähler's distinction between revelatory *Geschichte* and the ordinary facts of history (*Historie*). But that is doubtless due to the fact that McGrath, like many English evangelicals, refuses himself to acknowledge the inerrancy of Scriptural revelation.

The treatment of Tillich is even more inadequate. Here is the *whole* of it: "In an important essay of 1924, Tillich noted that the doctrine of justification applied not merely to the religious aspects of moral life, but also to the intellectual life of religion, in that it is not merely the *sinner*, but also the *doubter*, who is justified by faith. Tillich thus extends the scope of the doctrine to the universal human situation of despair and doubt concerning the meaning of existence. Tillich thus argues that the doctrine of justification, when rightly understood, lies at the heart of the Christian faith. While nineteenth-century man was characterised by his idealism, his twentieth-century counterpart is characterised by existential despair and anxiety—and it is to this latter man that the Christian message must be made relevant. Tillich attempts this task by the 'method of correlation,' by which the Christian proclamation is 'correlated' with the existential questions arising from human existence. For Tillich, the doctrine of justification addresses a genuine human need: man must learn to accept that he is accepted, despite being unacceptable" (sec. 38).

It is truly amazing that McGrath can set forth such a viewpoint without pointing out its utter incompatibility with anything historic Christian faith or Holy Writ has said concerning justification. (The only semblance of an evaluation is the single sentence in a footnote: "Despite the verbal parallels with the concept of *acceptatio Dei,* it is difficult to see quite how Tillich understands man to be accepted *by God.*") Moreover, no attempt at all is made to relate Tillich's metaphorical recasting of justification to (1) his presentation of God as Being Itself (the ontological dimension of his thought), (2) Christ as the New Being (his soteriology), or (3) his so-called "Protestant principle," on the basis of which every religious assertion stands under criticism—thus, ironically, making doubt endemic! Altizer, according to Hannah Tillich, hastened Tillich's demise by pointing out that if *no* religious claims are indefeasible that would of course include Tillich's Being Itself, the foundation of his entire system—and Altizer's point would, of course, equally apply, *mutantis mutandis,* to any "doctrine" of justification he espouses. For the hopelessly short treatment of Tillich just quoted, McGrath cites only Tillich's *Protestant Era* and *The Shaking of the Foundations*—and gives but a single secondary reference, and that to a relatively unimportant treatment of Tillich's correlation principle. Surely a theologian of Tillich's influence deserves a more thorough analysis and critique than this.

It is also difficult to understand how a history of the doctrine of justification by grace through faith could be written with no mention of such overarching ideas in the history of doctrine as Anders Nygren's magisterial analysis of the interplay of *agape* (God's self-giving love) and *eros* (man's self-centred love)—a thesis unsuccessfully refuted by M.C. D'Arcy. (McGrath cites a minor journal article by Nygren, but not his *Agape and Eros,* and the concept is nowhere treated.) If justification is understood forensically as God's unmerited act of love in eternity toward a fallen race, as the Reformers believed, whilst Roman theology sees the infusion of grace as requiring human acceptance by way of adherence to the Church's teachings, then it should be quite evident why Augustine's uneasy *caritas*-synthesis of *agape* and *eros* fractured at the time of the Reformation, and why Trent unqualifiedly condemned justification by grace through faith alone. Appreciation of the Nygren thesis would also have helped McGrath to see more clearly the weaknesses in contemporary ecumenical attempts to blend the Protestant and Roman Catholic positions on justification. (See Montgomery, "Eros and Agape in Pico of Mirandola," in his *The Suicide of Christian Theology* .)

Unquestionably, the most troubling aspect of this book comes in a paragraph of the Preface, before one even encounters problems such as those we have just described. The author writes: "Some readers of the first edition expressed puzzlement that there was to be found no specific treatment of Paul's view on justification. It may be helpful to such readers to recall that every generation believed that it had understood Paul correctly, and was duly puzzled when its own settled convictions were called into question by a later generation. What one generation takes to be an accurate analysis of Paul is seen by later scholarship as that generation's analysis of Paul, reflecting its own values, presuppositions, goals and prejudices. The present volume can thus be seen, at one level, as a continuous analysis of the church's interpretation of Paul on justification, which takes no fixed view on what the correct interpretation of Paul should be."

One understands not wanting to be criticised for one's theological views by those who disagree, but the kind of relativism which this passage conveys goes beyond mere scholarly reticence. It is, in effect, the refusal to assert that Scripture has any objective, absolute meaning: its teachings, even those as central as justification, are defined only in the continuing history of its interpretation. Of course, this is in fact to espouse precisely Newman's "organic" model of doctrinal development which is basic to Roman Catholic ecclesiology. Contrast Luther to Erasmus (who was arguing essentially the same thing): "If you are referring to essential truths—why, what more irreligious assertion could a man possibly make than that he wants to be free to assert precisely *nothing* about such things? ... I certainly grant that many passages in the Scriptures are obscure and hard to elucidate, but that is due, not to the exalted nature of their subject, but to our own linguistic and grammatical ignorance.... Who will maintain that the town fountain does not stand in the light because the people down some alley cannot see it, while everyone in the square can see it?" (*De servo arbitrio*, WA, 18, 604-605; cf. Montgomery, *In Defense of Martin Luther* and *Crisis in Lutheran Theology*).

This is the same McGrath who wrote in a Foreword to a recent evangelical interpretation of Richard Hooker: "The vision which Hooker encourages for modern evangelicalism is that of a movement which is deeply grounded in and nourished by Scripture, yet strengthened and sustained by a sense of solidarity within Christian orthodoxy down the ages" (in Nigel Atkinson, *Richard Hooker: Reformed Theologian of the Church of England?* [Carlisle, Cumbria: Paternoster, 1997]). But how can the church be "grounded in and nourished by Scripture" if the meaning of the major doctrines of Scripture—to say nothing of the rest of its content—is at the mercy of the "values, presuppositions, goals, and prejudices" of each generation of Christian believers? Here, one holds *either*, in Anglo-Catholic fashion, that the Holy Spirit continuously preserves the church from error through control of its traditions, *or*, in the unshakeable conviction of the Reformers, that an objective, perspicuous Scripture must forever judge the church: *Ecclesia semper reformanda est*. A firm doctrine of inspiration *and* a rock-solid hermeneutic are essential for the latter viewpoint. Neither is needed for the former.

Is it accidental that McGrath is becoming a hero to mediating American evangelicalism, with its desire to accommodate to all theologies that have a "warm heart," a non-rigorous bibliology, and a temperamental dislike for antitheses alongside theses? The aura of Oxford (though McGrath does not have a professorship) is probably enough for American evangelicals who worship at the shrines of Wesley and Oxbridge (or, at home, in the presence of Christian football heroes, former Presidential aides, and media personalities). As for us, we shall not forget the words of the *Formula of Concord* (Sol. Dec., Summary Formulation, 9): "Luther explicitly made this distinction between divine and human writings: God's Word alone is and should remain the only standard and norm of all teachings, and no human being's writings dare be put on a par with it, but everything must be subjected to it."

BRIAN TIERNEY'S *RIGHTS, LAWS AND INFALLIBILITY IN MEDIEVAL THOUGHT**

Variorum (Ashgate Publishing Ltd) has provided the scholarly community with a number of volumes (the "Collected Studies Series") which bring together previously published journal articles by distinguished scholars of the medieval history of ideas, jurisprudence, music, and canon law, generally of Roman Catholic persuasion. Stephan Kuttner's *Studies in the History of Medieval Canon Law* is a prime example of the quality productions in this series, and Brian Tierney has been previously represented *(Church Law and Constitutional Thought in the Middle Ages)*. These volumes merely photoreproduce original journal articles with no continuous pagination, but, whilst a genuine irritant, this does not constitute an absolute bar to their utility, given the fact that the publishers provide a general subject index to all included materials.

Brian Tierney's *Rights, Laws and Infallibility in Medieval Thought* reprints in one volume eighteen essays by a Roman Catholic graduate of Cambridge University (B.A., Ph.D.) who presently holds the Goldwin Smith chair of Medieval History at my alma mater, Cornell University. Space limitations prevent a discussion of more than a few of these articles; we shall focus on those of greatest potential interest.

One of Tierney's special foci is the origin of the modern language of human rights. Typically, human rights are seen as deriving from 18th-century deistic thinkers (Thomas Paine, the French Encyclopedists) and as first concretely embodied in the French Declaration of the Rights of Man and the American Declaration of Independence. Concession is grudgingly made to traditional Christian influences, especially by way of John Locke, but human rights are seen essentially as the product of modern Enlightenment thinking. Tierney demonstrates the superficiality of such interpre-

---

* Aldershot, Hants, England, and Brookfield, Vermont, U.S.A..: Variorum, 1997; x + 340 pp.

tations: "In the twelfth century a concern for the moral integrity of human personality led to the first stirrings of natural rights theories" (I, 174). "But [those canonists] did not, like some modern critics of rights theories, expect such language to justify a moral universe in which each individual would ruthlessly pursue his own advantage" (II, 646).

Human rights in general suggest the constitutional and theological issue of religious freedom: to what extent ought one to be able to choose his or her religious commitment in an open marketplace of ideas? Tierney opts for openness, but, consistent with post-Vatican II conciliation toward non-Christian faiths, argues for it ecumenically. "The West had to learn—or relearn—the practice of nonviolence from India, through Mahatma Ghandi" (IV, 43). "Among all the founders of the great world religions we can find an attitude of respect and compassion for the human person that is the best argument—the only ultimately compelling one—for religious liberty" (IV, 44). In point of fact, Ghandi himself admitted that his revulsion toward the caste system derived from early Christian influence on him, not at all from Hinduism; and the "great world religions" have not maintained, doctrinally or historically, a consistent position favouring religious freedom: Islam, to take only one egregious example, converted by the sword, currently persecutes Christians where it can get away with it (Pakistan, etc.), and does not to any degree regard the female of the species as a "human person" deserving equal treatment.* Tierney would have done far better to ground religious freedom in Christian special revelation rather than in vague, natural-law, *consensus gentium* ecumenism.

Papal infallibility is a particular historical interest of the author. He holds that "the historical evidence shows that the doctrine was not part of *depositum fidei*. It would seem that the papacy in adopting the doctrine for purely pragmatic reasons has done itself and the church more harm than good" (XVI, 841). Tierney does not arrive at this conclusion, as did Hans Küng, through a specious

---

* Cf. Montgomery, *Human Rights and Human Dignity* (2d ed.; Edmonton, Alberta, Canada: Canadian Institute for Law, Theology & Public Policy, 1995), pp. 114-19.

philosophical commitment to the rationalistic principle *finitum non capax infiniti:* his position is the historian's who sees that even Thomas Aquinas was cognisant of the canonical and theological arguments "that a general council possessed a greater authority than a pope alone, that some popes had erred in faith, that Christ gave authority to all the apostles and not to Peter alone, that Paul rebuked Peter" (XVIII, 319).

Unlike Küng, Tierney does not go to the point of denying infallible judgments *per se.* But they make him uncomfortable: "It may be that the Church cannot define a moral doctrine in such a way as to guarantee in advance that the content of the doctrine will remain irreformable through the whole course of future time" (XVII, 517). True, *ecclesia semper reformanda est.* But were we to shift attention from the necessarily fallible church to the Scriptures, which, according to our Lord, "cannot be broken," we could certainly arrive at apodictic moral principles which remain true under any and all historical or sociological conditions: the principle of non-discrimination, for example.* Tierney is correct, historically and doctrinally, when he rejects ecclesiastical infallibility; but theology, like physics or any other discipline, cannot survive epistemologically in a state of unqualified relativism. One needs the Word of God which alone "stands for ever."

---

* Acts 10:34, Gal. 3:28; cf. Montgomery, *op. cit.,* pp. 168-69.

NORMAN GEISLER'S *BAKER ENCYCLOPEDIA OF CHRISTIAN APOLOGETICS*

This hefty tome, published by Baker Book House, Grand Rapids, Michigan, in 1999, is vastly superior in its coverage and detail to predecessors such as Kreeft and Tacelli's *Handbook of Christian Apologetics*. The problem is that its title would suggest a neutral reference work, the collaborative product of a number of scholars in the field. However, the work is the lengthened shadow of its single compiler, and reflects at every point his particular philosophy of apologetics, that which he terms "classical apologetics" (i.e., the traditional Thomist approach of first arguing by "natural reason" to God's existence and then adding arguments in behalf of a special revelation from the God whose existence has been so proven). The result is less than a balanced reference work, though it contains much helpful material.

Here are just a few evidences of prevailing imbalance:

1) There is overwhelming use of citations to the author's previous books and even minor periodical articles (his material is by far the most extensive in the general Bibliography—well exceeding the citations to Pascal, Butler, Paley, Newman, Carnell, C.S. Lewis). I am, I suppose, fortunate, with 8 citations (Butler has only 3), but this doesn't cover a fraction of my publications in the area. The author, on the other hand, is represented by no less than 44 entries.

2) "Classical apologetics" gets its own lengthy article. There is no article on "Evidentialism."

3) In line with the author's evangelical neo-Thomism, there are long articles on "Thomas Aquinas," "God, Nature of," "Analogy, Principle of," etc. However, Luther receives only sketchy treatment, and the standard works on his understanding of reason (e.g., that by B.A. Gerrish) are not mentioned.

4) When the author has maintained a controversial position on a disputed issue, e.g., hierarchical ethics vs the lesser-of-evils, lo! an article appears on the subject, arguing for the author's viewpoint

(here: "Lying in Scripture"). Where the author's interests are not involved, no article appears, even when the apologetics area is very important. Thus literary apologetics (the work of Dorothy Sayers, Charles Williams, J.R.R. Tolkien, et al.) is neglected; and the vast amount of legal/juridical apologetics (the defence of the faith using legal reasoning and legal categories) finds no place, save for an article on Simon Greenleaf, who is well known to evangelicals anyway.

5) There is a strange reticence to cite other contemporary apologists who do not agree fully with the author's approach, even when objectivity would seem to require it. Thus (if I may be permitted personal examples): my historic debate with Thomas J.J. Altizer at the University of Chicago's Rockefeller Memorial Chapel is considered by many to have marked the death (not of God, but) of the death-of-God phenomenon, at least as represented by the more radical side of the movement. The debate is still available on audiotape, has been published in transcription again and again, and my article on the movement was included in Bernard Murchland's standard collection, *The Meaning of the Death of God* (Random House). In the article on Altizer, none of this is mentioned. Likewise, my refutation (in *Faith Founded on Fact*) of Antony Flew's argument that psychological miracles (disciples stealing the body of Christ and yet proclaiming his resurrection) are preferable to biological miracles (the resurrection itself) is nowhere discussed, though that refutation has had widespread impact. Likewise, there is no mention of my London debate with G.A. Wells or the international discussion resulting from it (*New Oxford Review*, May, 1993; *Christian News*, 17 May and 13 September 1993).

6) Omissions of significance to the history of apologetics occur when (evidently) they do not relate to or advance the author's concerns. For example, we hear nothing of Theodore Abu Qurra, the Syrian theologian and bishop of Harran (9th century), whose apologetic parable in his treatise on God and the true religion is of great continuing value. To be sure, the work of Theodore appears only in German among Western languages, but an encyclopedia is supposed to be, well, an encyclopedia. In general, the author limits

himself to easily accessible English-language materials and does little with apologetic treatments, however important, that require one to read Latin, French, or German.

7) Evaluations are often idiosyncratic. Wittgenstein is characterised as a fideist, and no effort whatever is made to see the compatibility of the *Tractatus* with the later *Philosophical Investigations*, even though Wittgenstein himself wanted the *Philosophical Investigations* to be published together with the *Tractatus*. Wittgenstein's positive value for Christian apologetics is nowhere suggested—neither the epistemological possibilities of his approach to verification nor the value of his "language games" for biblical hermeneutics. We are told that Wittgenstein was "the archenemy of the Platonic"; yet there is a remarkable similarity between Plato's statement in the *Phaedo* (85d) that he longed for "a raft" of revelation—"some word of God," and Wittgenstein's cry, "Oh, my God!" as if "imploring a divine intervention in human events" (to use the words of my late Cornell philosophy professor and friend of Wittgenstein, Norman Malcolm).

8) The author is a Baptist. Thus, he cannot resist including an article—of somewhat questionable apologetic character—on "Infants, Salvation of." There he assimilates the views of Roman Catholics, Lutherans, and Anglicans (!) and implies that in their view unbaptised infants are necessarily unsaved. No attempt at all is made to understand the actual positions of these three different theologies, nor is there any citation of the Biblical passages relied upon by these viewpoints. It is passing strange that the author did not do more, in such instances, to control the content of his work.

With all of the above difficulties, the *Encyclopedia* is certainly useful. Out-of-the-ordinary, helpful articles abound, such as: "Muhammad, Alleged Miracles of," "Kabir (Kabirpanthis)," "Dooyeweerd, Herman." When I studied Reference Materials for a graduate library-science degree at the University of California, Berkeley, my professor said: "A good encyclopedia is the one where you find the answer to the question you are looking for." In that sense, the present work will certainly satisfy many readers—as long as they are looking for what is in it, and do not mind the all-pervasiveness of the author's presence.

THE TRIAL OF CHRIST DEFENDED: JEAN IMBERT'S *LE PROCÈS DE JÈSUS*

The legal proceedings that resulted in the crucifixion of our Lord have been the source of numberless commentaries and homilies throughout Christian history. Most evangelical pastors are acquainted with the standard older works on the subject—such as Chandler's *Trial of Jesus* (1909) and Linton's *Sanhedrin Verdict* (1943). These accept the Gospel narratives as historical fact and endeavour to determine on the basis of them the relative legality or illegality of what occurred.

Today, however, the trial accounts in the New Testament are viewed with a jaundiced eye by many influential interpreters of them. Liberal biblical scholarship has directed its form-critical weaponry against the reliability of the narratives (e.g., Paul Winter's *On the Trial of Jesus*, Berlin, 1961, and his 1963 German article on the subject in *Das Altertum*). Jewish sensitivity to the anti-Semitic claim that "the Jews murdered Jesus" has led not only to journalistic outcrys against the Passion Play at Oberammergau but also to serious objections to the historicity of the Gospel accounts of Jesus' trial.

No less an eminent jurist than Haim Cohn, an Israeli Supreme Court Justice who has represented Israel on the UN Human Rights Commission, thus expanded his 1967 *Israel Law Review* article on the subject into a book-length onslaught, *The Trial and Death of Jesus* (English translation from the Hebrew, published by KTAV in 1977). And in 1974, Hans Küng, perhaps the most widely read liberal Catholic theologian alive today, flatly declared in *Christ sein* ("On Being a Christian") that it is "no longer possible to reconstruct the events of Jesus' trial, for we possess neither the original documents nor the actual testimony."

The appearance, then, in 1980 of a powerful defense of the reliability of the trial accounts is of more than routine interest. The work, titled *Le Procès de Jésus* ("The Trial of Jesus") and published by Presses Universitaires de France, is written not by a theologian but by a distinguished and prolific legal scholar, Jean Imbert, professor at the University of Paris. Though disagreeing at some important points with the finest previous defense of the trial narratives, Blinzler's *Der Prozess Jesu* (3rd ed. 1960), Imbert updates and generally confirms that author's work. He leaves little doubt that the Gospels are indeed a truthful source of information on the judicial condemnation of Jesus.

We offer here—particularly for readers who lack access to Imbert's work—a brief catalogue of the standard objections to the reliability of the Gospel accounts of the trial and Imbert's decisive refutations of these arguments.

1. The examination of Jesus before the Sanhedrin court involves "such wholesale violation of all the rules of law and procedure" (Cohn) that it is "inconceivable" that the legalistic Pharisees would ever have permitted it.

But—even if one admits that there were substantive and procedural errors committed (and those claims, as I we shall see, are often exaggerated)—it hardly follows that the Jewish religious leaders were incapable of such acts! Indeed, several other trials are reported from Jesus' time in which the authorities played fast and loose with Mishnaic law and procedure (e.g., Rabbi Elazar ben Tsaddok saw an adulteress executed by fire, whereas the law insisted on strangulation [*Mishna Sanhedrin* 7:2, 11:1]; note also in John 8 that stoning and not strangulation of an adulteress was clearly accepted).

Blinzler had argued that the law of the trial was not traditional, Pharisaic, Mishnaic law at all, but a Sadducean law that later became obsolete—thus making the trial of Jesus indeed a true trial, but one that constituted "judicial murder." Imbert takes a less convoluted route to much the same conclusion: Pharisaic criminal law and procedure were in force in Jesus' time, but the disregard of them in this trial points to an occasion less judicial than political in nature—"a pseudo-judicial means employed essentially to reduce Jesus' prestige" among the Jews.

2. The Gospels put all the trial events in one night and the day following, thereby hopelessly violating Mishnaic proscriptions against trials at night or on the eve of a feast day.

But Imbert makes short work of this hoary criticism by noting that Jaubert's discovery among the Dead Sea Scrolls of a "Jubilees-Qumran" calendar allows for a three-day chronology of the events, obviating these difficulties. Imbert admits that Jaubert's dating has not been unanimously accepted, but rightly observes that "her theory has been elevated to quasi-certainty by the discovery of a new group of manuscripts, the *Mishmarot*, establishing that the Essene festival cycle began with Passover on Tuesday evening the 14th of Nisan," thus confirming a Tuesday date for the Last Supper and the "long chronology" of the trial.

3. The Gospel of John "displays not the least knowledge of a Jewish trial" (Cohn) and so offers "formidable support" to Cohn's thesis that there never was a Jewish trial of Jesus at all—that the Romans alone were responsible for Jesus' condemnation.

Imbert points out, however, that John surely is aware of the Sanhedrin episode (John 18:24, 28). Moreover, "if John doesn't give the details, this omission is intentional: John knew that the procedure before the Sanhedrin was amply described and commented upon by his predecessors, the Synoptic writers.

4. Pilate was only a procurator—essentially a financial administrator—so he doubtless could not have handed down a death penalty; and psychologically he could hardly have referred Jesus to Herod or been influenced by the crowd or suggested a choice between Jesus and Barabbas.

However: (1) The Pilate inscription discovered in 1961 designates the governor also as "prefect," so he was fully capable of rendering the death penalty; moreover, even procurators exercised the *jus gladii*. (2) Two fragments in the *Digest* declare that a Roman governor could refer an accused to the local magistrate having jurisdiction over the accused's place of residence, and in A.D. 67 Vespasian turned over to Herod Agrippa II the Galilean rebels he had captured. (3) Instead of the release of Barabbas being "a product of the Evangelists' imagination" (Paul Winter), there is plentiful contemporary evidence that both Roman and Jewish procedure allowed for such judicial discretion (see, e.g., Steinwenter in *The Journal of Juristic Papyrology*, 1965, pp. 9-10, and Chavel in *The Journal of Biblical Literature*, LX [1941], 272-78). (4) An entire volume—J. Colin's *Les villes libres* ... (Brussels, 1965)—collects examples of Roman provincial governors' acceding in their sentences to crowd pressure.

We could go on with additional examples, but Imbert's conclusion has already been sufficiently illustrated: "Nothing in the story of Jesus' trial as presented by the Gospel writers transgresses historical reality. To the contrary, everything given there allows us to maintain that the Gospels were written by men of great intellectual honesty.... Far from contradicting themselves, the Evangelists each add certain new elements, and it is only by viewing them all together that one can obtain a comprehensive picture of the different stages of Jesus' trial."

INDEX OF NAMES

Index numbers in italics refer to names appearing only in notes.

A

Acton, Lord 232
Adam, Karl 40
Adonis 72
Agatiello, Osvaldo R. *279*
Albrecht, of Brandenburg *68*
Alexander II., Pope 118
Althaus, Paul *123*
Altizer, Thomas J.J. 298, 306
Amo, A.W. 271
Anderson, Robert *262*
Antony, Marc 178
Aquinas, Thomas 16, 46, 305
Archer, Gleason L. *38*
Aristotle 16, 271–272
Astruc, Jean 14
Atiyah, P.S. *173*
Atkinson, David 126
Atkinson, Nigel 300
Augustine 16, 46, 119, 260–261, 292
Austin, John 22
Ayer, A.J. *222–223*

B

Baas, Jan 135
Bach, J.S 113
Bahnsen, Greg L. 146
Bainton, Roland 61
Baldwin, S.D. 259
Barry, F.R. *69*
Barth, Karl 15, 25–26, 285, 291, 293, 297
Baum, L. Frank 9
Bauman, Michael 25, 107

Baxter, M. 259
Beaumont 75
Bell John 33
Bell, Daniel *221*
Bellah, Robert 151
Bentham 162
Bentham, Jeremy 22
Berges, Michel 232
Bergman, Paul *270*
Berman, H.J. *180*
Berryer, M. 278
Bertrams 72
Betjeman, John 114–115
Beyleveld, Deryck *31*
Blackstone, William 17–18, 20, 22, 138, 156, *164*, 174
Blakey, Robert 224
Blinzler 310
Boehmer, H.J. 57
Boehmer, J.H. 35, *69*
Bonhoeffer, Dietrich 291
Bork, Robert 108
Bousingen, de Denis Durand *204*
Bowman, Michael *45*
Bowring, John 22
Braaten, Carl 291
Bradley, F.H. 223
Bradney, Anthony 133
Breeze, R.E. 207
Brooke, Christopher *118*
Brougham, Lord 278
Brown, J.A.C. 269
Brundage, James A. *118*
Brunner, Emil *67*, 285
Brutus 178
Buckley, William 221
Bugenhagen 68
Bull 294
Bultmann, Rudolf 25, 29, 36, 291, 293
Bunyan 113

Burckhardt, Jakob 275
Burke, Edmund 273
Butler 305
Butterworth 269

C

Calvin, John *67*, 294
Cameron 203
Caparros, E. 136
Capone, Al 230
Carles, Jules 203
Carnegie, Andrew 286
Carnell 305
Carty Anthony 32
Casini, Carlo 204
Cass 76
Cassin, René 191
Cassius 178
Catherine of Aragon 119
Celsus 21
Chandler 309
Charles, V. 59, 62, 119
Chytraeus, David 296
Cicero 16, 272
Clapp, Rodney *149*
Clark, Brain 169, 185
Clark, R. Scott *64*
Clark, Ramsey 225, 231
Clement VII. 119
Clifford, Ross *177*
Clough, Hugh 185
Cockburn. Lord 278
Cohn, Haim 309
Cohn, Norman 228
Colin, J. 312
Collingwood, R.G. 281
Collins, Francis 200
Colson, Charles 234
Compston, Chritopher *121*
Comte, Auguste 22
Connors, R.J. *271*

Index of Names

Cook, Walter Wheeler 92
Cooper, Yvette 199
Cope, E.M. 273
Cot, Pierre 28
Coward, Noël 188
Craig, John 263
Cranfield, C.E.B. 78, 291
Crespo, Marion Martinez 278
Crispin, Ken 121
Crittenden, Max 242
Croce, Benedetto 281
Crofton, John 230
Cross, F.L. 136
Cullmann, Oscar 41
Culver, Sharon 207

D

D'Arcy, M.C. 298
Danforth, John C. 111
Dante 113
Davidson, Alastair 32
Davis, Charles 284
DeMar, Gary 147
Denning, Alfred 135
Denning, John 135
Dennis, John 38
Derrida, Jacques 45
Descartes, René 158
Dewey, John 23
Dibelius, Martin 36
Dickens 161
Dillon, Sandra 207
Dimwoodie, Cameron 39
Doe, Norman 120
Donaldson, Thomas 164
Donne, John 164
Donohue, William A. 109
Dooyeweerd, Herman 307
Dryden, John 273
Dubroff, Jessica 184
Dulles, Avery 36, 43
Dumbauld, Edward 20
DuMouchel, William 207
Dworkin, Ronald 13, 16, 25, 27-28, 44, 47, 91, 173, 186

E

Eastwood, R.A. 22
Ebeling, E. 293
Eck, Johann 56, 58, 63
Eddy 44
Ede, L.S. 271
Edmund-Davies, Lord 141
Edwards, Jonathan 293
Edwards, Mark 255
Eekelaar, John 33
Eidelberg, David 207
Elert, Werner 291
Eliot, T.S. 114-115
Elliott, D.W. 144-145, 150
Emiliou 72
Emser 56
Erasmus 299
Evans, Keith 270, 278
Evans, M.D. 252

F

Fahn, Stanley 207
Feinberg, Joel 187
Ficino, Marsilio 275
Field, W.C. 157
Filson, Floyd V. 37
Finnis, John 34, 119
Fitzpatrick, Peter 32
Fletcher, Joseph 121, 165-166, 181, 205
Flew, Antony 178, 306
Fogarty, Daniel 277
Forell, George W. 291
Forrester, Duncan 55, 284-285, 289, 291
Fox 199
Fransen, Piet F. 43
Frederick, the Wise 62
Freed, Curt R. 207

G

Gairdner, J. 119
Geisler, Norman 305
Gerassimos, St. 237
Gerhard, Johann 124-125
Germain, Christopher St. 17
Gerrish, B.A. 305
Gewirth, Alan 25, 29, 31, 288
Ghandi, Mahatma 303
Gledhill, Ruth 120
Glinos, Dimitris 239
Goede, Henning 58
Goff, Lord 184
González, J.L. 293
Gormally, L. 190
Gorringe, Timothy 284
Graf 14, 36
Gramsci, Antonio 32
Gray, John Chipman 21
Greene, Paul E. 207
Greenleaf, Simon 306
Griesbach 98
Griffiths, Brian 286
Grigg-Spall, Ian 32
Grisez, Germain 119
Grisham, John 267
Gronbeck, Bruce E. 277-278
Grounds, Vernon C. 291
Gutierrez, Gustavo 289

H

Habermas, Jürgen 16, 285, 288
Hägerström 22
Hahn, H.F. 38
Hailsham, Lord 188-189
Hall, David 25, 45, 107
Hamer, Jean 77
Händel, G.F. 113
Harnack, A. 293
Harris, J.W. 33
Harris, Peter 235

Index of Names   315

Hart, H.L.A. 13, 16, 25-26, 70, 186
Hawkins, Gordon 219-221, 223-225, 228, 236
Hayek 285
Hegel, G.W.F. 21, 259, 288
Heick, O.W. 293
Heidegger, Martin 290
Hélie, F. 176
Helmholz, Richard H. 69
Helms, Jesse 111-112
Henry VIII. 57, 130, 295
Henry, Carl F.H. 291
Henry, Nelson B. 277
Herget, James E. 16
Herod Agrippa II. 311
Hewley, J. 94
Hewley, Sarah 82, 93-96, 101-103
Hillerbrand, Hans J. 123
Himmelfarb, Gertrude 162
Hitler, Adolf 290
Hobbes, Thomas 288
Hoel, P.G. 262
Holmes, Oliver Wendell 23, 149
Homer 38
Hook, Sidney 179
Hooker, Richard 300
Hooper, W. 130
Huff, Darell 263
Huizing, Peter 71, 73, 77
Hull, John M. 105-106
Hume, David 178
Hunnings 73-74, 76
Hunt, Alan 32
Hunter, Alan 284
Huntsberger, D.V. 264
Huxley, A. 158, 202
Hyam, Michael 270

I

Ibsen 224
Imbert, Jean 309

J

Jacobs, C.M. 130
Jacobs, H.E. 68-69, 295
James, William 23
Jantzen, Grace 284
Jefferson, Thomas 20
Jeremias, Joachim 41
Jervell, Jacob 256
John Paul, Pope 51-52
Johnson 114
Jukes, John 53

K

Kähler, M. 297
Kaiser 72
Kamisar 189
Kant, Immanuel 29-30, 288, 295
Kao, Richard 207
Kaptchuk, Ted J. 156
Kapteyn 71, 74-76
Kasel, J.J. 71
Kass, Leon 208
Kauper, Paul 88-89, 91
Kazantzakis, Nikos 239
Keeton, G.W. 22
Kefauver, E. 225
Keith, A. 265
Kelman, Mark 32
Kelsen, Hans 23, 26
Kennedy, Anthony 170
Kennedy, Duncan 32
Kennedy, G.A. 274
Kenrick 102
Keown, J. 177, 185, 187, 190
Kierkegaard, Sören 46, 295
Kilgour, David 78, 291
King-Hamilton, Alan 141
Kittel, Gerhard 290
Knight, Max 23
Kordatos, Yiannis 238
Kotopoulos, Costas 241
Kraft, Victor 222
Krause 21

Kreeft, Peter 305
Kronman, A.T. 268, 279
Kuenen 14, 36
Kuhse, Helga 157, 202
Küng, Hans 303, 309
Kuttner, Stephan 60-62, 302

L

Langdell, C.C. 268
Larissis, D. 247
LaVey, Anton 112
Lawler, M.G. 119
Lazareth, W.H. 122
Lehmann, Paul 121
Leiser, Clara 28
Lemon, Denis 134
Lenin 155
Leo, Pope 57, 68
Levy, Leonard W. 133
Lewis, C.S. 114, 130, 146, 274, 305
Lindbeck, George A. 36, 291
Lindsey, Hal 258
Linton, I.H. 262, 309
Lippi, Lorenzo 275
Llewellyn, Karl 23-24, 32, 172-173, 268
Locke, John 46, 99, 302
Longinus 271, 273-274
Luck, William F. 119
Lugt, Vander H. 126-127
Lunsford, A.A. 271
Luther, Martin 17, 29, 55-63, 66-70, 122-124, 130, 290, 292, 294-297, 299

M

MacArthur, John F. 122
Macgregor 39
Macris, Pastor 245
Maier, Gerhard 130
Malcolm, Norman 307
Marcel, Gabriel 46
Marcuse, Herbert 33

Index of Names

Martin, Walter R. 44
Marty, M.E. 257
Marx, Karl 259, 288
Mattes, John C. 126
May, William 119
Mayendorff, John 40
Mazengarb, O.C. 270
McDonald, John D. 153
McGiffert, A.C. 295
McGrath, Alister 292–293, 295–296, 298–300
McLuhan, Marshall 229
Meeks. W.A. 256
Melanchthon, Philip 56, 68
Mendelssohn 114
Metz 72
Meyendorff, John 41
Meyer, de 251
Mill, John Stuart 161
Milton 113
Minh, Ho Chi 155
Moberg, David O. 291
Moir 75
Moltmann, Jürgen 43, 291
Montesquieu 178
Moore, Edmund F. 89
Moore, G.E. 21
Moquin, W. 225
Moriarty, M.G. 122
Morion 39
Mortimer, John 134, 137
Mounce, Robert 291
Moyers, Bill 146
Muchall, William 18
Mulholland, L.A. 157–158
Munkman, John H. 269
Munteanu, M 274
Murray, John 126
Mussolini, Benito 260

N

Napoleon 221, 259
Nash, David 134
Nash, J.R. 226
Nash, Robert 226
Neve, J.L. 293
Newman, John Henry 292, 294, 305
Newman, R.C. 265
Niebuhr 291
Nielsen, Kai 257
Niemöller, Martin 290
Nixon 234
North, Gary 146–147
Nozick, Robert 31
Nygren, Anders 298

O

Oaks, Dallin H. 88
Olbrechts-Tyteca, L. 277
Olivecrona 22
Orwell, George 130
Otto, Rudolf 273

P

Packer, J.I. 296
Paine, Thomas 20, 139, 302
Paisley, Ian 258
Paley, William 46, 305
Palmer, Humphrey 103, 129
Parry, E.A. 278
Pascal, Blaise 114, 305
Patterson, Dennis 21
Pattison, Stephan 284
Paul, The Apostle 16, 39, 95, 99, 123–125, 299, 304
Payne, J.B. 261
Peerman, G. 257
Pelikan, Jaroslav 68, 295
Perelman, Ch. 24–25, 277
Peter, Carl. J. 42
Peter, The Apostle 42, 304
Phillips, John 278
Philo 273
Pico, of Mirandola 299
Pieper, F. 296
Pierard, Richard V. 291
Pike, James 14
Pius XI., Pope 72
Pius XII., Pope 71, 77
Plato 271, 307
Poll, van de Rijk 135
Preus, A.O. 295
Preus, Robert D. 295

Q

Quiller-Couch, Arthur 273
Quinn, Patrick 238
Quintilian 271–273
Qurra, Theodore Abu 306

R

Rahner, Karl 43
Rawls, John 25, 29, 31, 285, 287, 289
Reid, James Smith 273
Rembrandt 114
Rhode, Deborah L. 279
Richards, David A.J. 30
Richter, A.L. 68
Rieke, Richard D. 277
Ritschl, A. 292
Robertson, Geoffrey 134–135
Robertson, William O. 154
Rogers, Arthur 204
Roper, Edith 28
Rose, H.J. 38
Rosenbaum, Alan S. 25
Ross, Alf 22
Rothley, Willi 204
Routledge, Graham 151
Rumble, Wilfrid E. 22
Rupp, Gordon 70, 290
Rushdie, Salman 133, 142
Rushdoony, R.J. 136, 146–147
Russell, Bertrand 221–222
Ryle, H.E. 222, 265

Index of Names

Rymar 38

S

Safley, Max 123
Samarin, J. 257
Samarin, William 256
Sandys, J.E. 273
Sayers, Dorothy 306
Scarman, Lord 137, 141-142
Schelling, F.W.J. 15, 29
Schleiermacher, Friedrich 292
Schoeck, R.J. 272, 276
Schopenhauer, Arthur 178, 270
Schramm, W. 276-277
Schröder, Gerhard 218
Schweitzer, Albert 291
Schwiebert, E.G. 56-57, 61
Scott, Arthur P. 139
Selden, John 35
Seneca 16
Shannon, Peter 60
Shaw, George Bernard 106
Shirer, William L. 290
Short, M. 224
Sider, Ronald 291
Sillars, Malcon O. 277
Skinner, Tom 291
Smith, D.C. 221
Smith, Oswald J. 259-260
Smith, Peter M. 133-134
Smith, Timothy L. 291
Socrates 237
Sohm, Rudolf 67
Souter, David 170
Speaker, Acting 193, 195
Spengler, Oswald 259
St. John-Stevas, N. 181
Stendahl, Krister 256
Stephen, James Fitzjames 137, 174, 187
Stephens, Don 241-242
Stiller, Günther 114
Stokes, Simon 134
Stuart, Mackenzie 76
Stump, Joseph 66
Sugden, Edward 94, 96
Summers, R.S. 173
Sutton, T. 187
Swidler, Leonard J. 41

T

Tacelli 305
Tavard, George 40-41
Taylor 294
Taylor, Hudson 78
Teresa, St. 142
Thatcher, Margaret 285
Themaat, van VerLoren 71, 74-76
Tierney, Brian 302-304
Tillich, Hannah 298
Tillich, Paul 25, 29, 31, 150, 291, 293, 297
Tinbergen 79
Tjernagel, N.S. 68, 130, 295
Tolkien, J.R.R. 114, 306
Tooley, Michael 157, 201-202
Toulemon, André 278
Toynbee 259
Traynor 263
Troeltsch, Ernst 55, 290
Trojanowski, J.Q. 207
Troplong 71
Tsaddok, Rabbi Elazar ben 310
Tsai, Wei-Yann 207
Turow, Scott 228
Tyrie 72

U

Unger, Robert M. 32
Urmson, J.O. 222
Urquhart, John 261

V

Veatch, Robert 159
Vespasian 311
Villa-Vicencio, Charles 284
Voltaire 178

W

Walker, Samuel 145
Wallace 72
Walter, Nicolas 133
Walther, C.F.W. 65
Wamboldt, William J.S. 119
Warfield, B.B 256
Warnock, G.J. 222
Watson, Philip 62
Weatherill 75
Webster, Richard 142
Weiner, William 207
Wellhausen, Julius 14, 36
Wendel, François 125
Wengert, Timothy J. 66
Wernow, J.R. 190-191
Whitehead, A.N. 221-222
Whitehouse, Mary 141, 143
Whittaker, W.G. 114
Whyte. W. 265
Wiener, Peter 290
Wilke 72
Williams, Alan 241
Williams, Charles 306
Williams, Glanville 175-176, 188
Wilson, Claire 117
Wilson, Thomas 275
Winfield, Howard 207
Wingren, Gustaf 297
Wingrove, Nigel 142
Winter, Paul 309, 311
Wittgenstein, Ludwig 179, 221-222, 307
Woestman, W.H. 119
Wolff, Robert Paul 30
Wooton, Barbara 289

Wren, Christopher 114
Wright, G. Ernest 37

Y
Yamauchi, Edwin 38

Z
Zimring, F.E. *219*
Zollmann, Carl *90*
Zorba the Greek 237

www.ingramcontent.com/pod-product-compliance
Lightning Source LLC
Chambersburg PA
CBHW061429300426
44114CB00014B/1599